Here's w

"It is not invention, but re-invention that is the mark of a hero. Gratitude and abundance only find room where pain once lived. Dave Letterfly is indeed a hero to me. By daring to build a life on the road with his paint brush, he overcame his own demons. Against preposterous odds, he has succeeded. His passion and storytelling are good for your lonely soul. It surely has been good for mine."

Kevin Venardos

"In the days after he graduated from high school the author launched like a human cannonball into a life with the traveling circus. However, just as gravity always pulls the human cannonball back to earth - sometimes on target, sometimes not - life has challenged Letterfly to evolve over the years. In his memoire "The Galloping Snapper" he provides an introspective view into his evolution from circus drummer to showman to artist. When Winston Churchill said "Success is not final, failure is not fatal: It is the courage to continue that counts." he could have easily been describing Letterfly's approach to life. You will find this book to be entertaining, educational, and inspirational but above all else true to the author's belief that many people helped shape his growth and he aspires to do the same for many more."

Larry K. Blakely

"Once again this book is a page turner. Following his trials and tribulations opens one's eyes. The author takes you on another journey across this great country. It enlightens the reader to remember to always follow your dreams and live to your heart's content. Live life to the fullest and remember to always keep your eyes on your path and give God the glory for all things good and bad. Dave continues to bring us along on his exciting journeys. Look so forward to the next read."

Kathy Lewis

"What a wonderful slice of Americana! Love it! When's the movie?"

Neil S. Dickerson

"As predicted, I was completely engulfed in The Galloping Snapper! Letterfly truly has a way to paint a picture so vivid – the words dance off the page and flood your mind. As a fellow AA member - the imagery and inner dialogue really resonated on a deeper level. The Galloping Snapper made me stop and appreciate those who have played pivotal roles in my life. Give your mind a gift with this beautiful read. I am blessed to have met such an amazing artist, friend and author!"

Alex Harrison

"Excellent read! Colorful words are so well chosen that I can picture what is happening as I read. This moving memoire holds my attention. Now I want more."

Ellen Bower

"Wow! What an adventure! This book is a wonderful read. I found myself right there with you in the pages of this story of your life. My friend you paint more than pinstripes with this gripping memoire. I could smell those sausages in that little food vendors trailer! I was praying for you when you were at the bottom when though I already knew that you triumphantly prevailed your battles. This book truly shows the reader that every single event in your life is indeed taking you on your own adventure. Some things need to happen to teach you the lessons so that you can move to the next level. Truly blessed to have read this and the other books you have written! Keep them coming Dave!! I can hardly wait to see what's on the horizon!"

Paul Seal

"After picking this wonderful slice of Americana up, I found it hard to put down til I finished the full read.

George Weeks.

Tales of a Traveling Airbrush

THE GALLOPING SNAPPER

CONFESSES EVERYTHING

by

DAVE *Letterfly* KNODERER

The Galloping Snapper Confesses Everything

Series: Tales of a Traveling Airbrush
Cover by Cathy Helms Avalon Graphics

ISBN #9798878231015

This Book Is Dedicated To…

…my father - an adventurer, hero, and creative who provided the catalyst to live life others only dream about. "Why live a life surrounded by safety?" During one glorious summer traveling the circuit together, we healed everything that had previously separated us, entering into the union that a father and son are meant to enjoy. I will be forever grateful for his shift in perspective that allowed us to become best friends as we saw the value in one another's journey.

…all the folks of the outdoor amusement business who toil with relentless dedication to outdo yesterday's success, and especially to the men and women of the circus from all four corners of the earth who fascinate, entertain, and amaze children of all ages in this glittering, exciting, turbulent, and often unforgiving world.

…equine lovers everywhere. Not only the aficionados of classic horsemanship but all who know "there is something about the outside of a horse that is good for the inside of a man." (Winston Churchill).

…my brothers of the brush who stand with one foot in tradition, sharing a mutual passion for mastering the vast domain of creating beautiful art by hand.

…the members of Alcoholics Anonymous who introduced me to my true purpose—saving lives. While witnessing the dramatic turnarounds of my various mentees, I am blessed to gain further clarity on my own journey. By exposing my vulnerable experiences in the pages of this book, my desire is to establish a greater understanding of the work we do in this fellowship and encourage others to seek the poetic healing AA can bring about in more ways than you may even anticipate.

...all those who have touched my life by being an example and providing important life lessons - most notably, Betty the mule.

...those who had a dream interrupted by an event that appeared to sidetrack, derail, or even stop them in their tracks. May my rugged rise to stardom reveal how divinity, happenstance, and serendipity can intervene with an even greater plan for your life.

...and to you, my readers. If you find the surprise twists and turns within this mémoir entertaining with stories of grit, inspiration, and enlightenment, please consider submitting an honest review on Amazon, GoodReads, or the Online Book Club. Your words would be like gold to me.

My "why" for writing the book? To be a blessing to the world. I hope you find it so.

Thank you in advance for your interest in helping make this book a success!

DAVE Letterfly KNODERER

Acknowledgments

My life has been touched by an endless stream of people. A precious few established themselves indelibly in my soul and remain a foundational influence. Everyone contributed something. Some taught me what to avoid, and others what to embrace. Most provided a mix of these two vital life lessons. Among those who propelled me upward along my journey were those whose examples spoke volumes and those who taught me to appreciate what happens next. They each gave me a dedication to becoming and remaining ready for anything. And above all else, they showed me how to happily go wherever the road of life may take me.

Although too numerous to mention, the list of people who touched my hand and heart would read like the combined Who's Who in the spheres of the circus, animal training and performance, and show business production. They were the aerialists, performers, and artists of a fascinating life of entertainment and adventure who taught me invaluable lessons that blended into the rest of my life.

The unsung heroes of ingenuity, inventiveness, resourcefulness, and brass, the showmen of the fairgrounds demonstrated a spectrum of behaviors, introducing effective mindsets, covert ploys, and strategies to select from while forming my own grassroots campaign for success. Also leaving an indelible mark on my path were the gawkers, admirers, cynics, and members of the innumerable audiences who laughed, cheered, scoffed at, and applauded my efforts, letting me know there was value in what I did, yet always room for improvement and growth.

The combined society of circus horsemen, dressage instructors, and classical horsemanship aficionados provided examples of leadership, ethics, and benevolence. Each horse that I was ever blessed to call mine taught me a lesson in trustworthiness, patience, mutual respect, and learning when it was time to say goodbye.

I am thankful to my fellow Toastmasters who helped me grow and mature in countless ways. The academic professors of a litany of specialties, members of all aspects of the publishing industry, and the men and women from creative writing circles each taught me technique, aspects of story, information about style, and how to get at the essence of crafting the message.

The music makers, choreographers, and historians of the pictorial, custom paint, and sign lettering trades laid the foundation for my career, while the members of the pinstriping, gold-leaf gilding, and airbrush painting fellowships across the country inspired me to continue growing in my ability. Treasured are the endless customers who beat a path to my art pavilions across the various campgrounds and RV dealerships, extended an invitation for me to come into their home, or traveled long distances to commission artwork of their own. Cherished most are those who started as clients and quickly became friends.

Surprisingly, the challenges that came from the unscrupulous, dishonest, and greedy people who provided many life lessons proved to be especially valuable. They were the ones who demonstrated the futility of worthless prejudices, self-centered fear, and contempt for the unknown. These were the people who provided clarity about manageability, humility and self-worth, knowing when to walk away, and the importance of maintaining my priority to stay on the spiritual beam.

Also worthy of accolades are the personalities, friends, and lovers who rocketed my ambition to be the best in every possible way. Through their encouragement, leadership, and examples, they became my closest allies. Most valuable were the intellectual heroes, attitudinal idols, and spiritual mentors who gently introduced me to myself, encouraged me to grasp an upgrade to my trajectory, and inspired me to develop a practical relationship with my beliefs, thought processes, and emotions.

These many pillars of my life guided me with their subjective abilities, leadership qualities, and perceptional skills that provided a segue for me to find a life filled with purpose, joy, and union with all my surroundings. They stressed that the wisest thing to do is to remain expectant in the moment while standing on a foundation of gratitude. But if I must look at the past, they taught me to do so forgivingly, and if I must gaze into the future, to do so prayerfully.

To all these and many others, I simply want to say thank you from the bottom of my heart. You have enriched my life and taken part in making me the man I am today.

DAVE *Letterfly* KNODERER

Table of Contents

Introduction *1*
Frozen Remorse **1**
Career Shift **4**
Inevitable Changes **9**

Chapter 1 The Show Painter *17*
The Calliope Truck **17**
The Fun House **20**
Midway Marketing **23**
The Riding Stable **26**
Mechanical Marvels **30**
A Gifted Man **34**

Chapter 2 Finding My Place *39*
Fair Time **39**
Unusual Sights **41**
Nicknames **44**
The First Airbrush **45**
The Big One **50**
The Allegan Circus **54**
A Lesson in Fair History **56**
Farewell Fair Season **59**
Hillsdale **60**

Chapter 3 Relativity *65*
A Different Reception **65**
New Wardrobe **68**
Ozark Signs **72**
Holiday Lights **73**
Netterfield's **74**
Show Town **81**
Getting Ready **87**

Chapter 4 Switching Gears ... *89*
Visual Coup ... **89**
The Unforeseen ... **97**
Up Here from Zenith ... **104**
Speedball ... **107**

Chapter 5 The Entrepreneur & the Circus ... *117*
The First T-Shirt Stand ... **117**
Wearable Advertising ... **123**
The Tip Top ... **126**
Wake-Up Call ... **131**
Circus Equestrianism ... **135**
Class 'n' Sass ... **137**
Sensational ... **142**

Chapter 6 Bigger, Better, Brighter ... *147*
Behind the Scenes ... **147**
From the Wreckage ... **150**
Lake Winnepesaukah ... **155**
E.S. Webb Company ... **162**
Elliott Amusement Company ... **166**
Bird's-Eye View ... **174**

Chapter 7 The Golden Age ... *179*
The High School Rider ... **179**
Airbrushing T-Shirts ... **185**
Maryland ... **191**
Opportunity ... **196**
Lipizzan Horses ... **200**
Not-So-Special Guest ... **203**

Chapter 8 Society Horses ... *211*
The New Horizon ... **211**

Surprise in St. Louis 218
Calm Before the Storm 221
Dysfunction Junction 224
A Lesson in Integrity 233
Building Tensions 236

Chapter 9 Big D *241*
The Excursion 241
Friend or Foe 250
Expanding the Quest 254
The Big D 256
Equine Ballerina 259
Equestrian Enthusiasts 267
Eye-Opening 270

Chapter 10 The Turning Point *275*
The Big Change 275
The Obsession is Lifted 283
In the Fog 286
A Love Story 291
Change of Direction 293
A Light in the Darkness 298
A Miracle Cure 301
From the Depths 305
Exodus 311

Chapter 11 To Walk With Purpose *317*
The Sign Shop 317
Searching for Home 319
The Purge 323
A New Beginning 326
Unceasing Progression 333

Chapter 12 Finding My Rhythm 337
Evanescent Love 337
Letterfly Sign Works 339
Gail 342
Blossoming in Jackson 346
Soaring to New Heights 348
Lettering Race Cars 351
The Golden Age 354
Enlightenment 358
A Life of Abundance 365

Conclusion 367
Planting a Seed 367
No Small Miracles 368
Deuces Wild 370

About the Author 377

Get In Touch! 381

Other Books by Dave Letterfly Knoderer 383

Introduction

"You and I possess within ourselves, at
Every moment of our lives, under all circumstances,
the power to transform the quality of our lives."
—Werner Erhard

Frozen Remorse

My left hand gripped the steering wheel as my right hand went through the well-worn gear pattern. Shifting through all ten speeds, I bobtailed west while the painted lines of the highway blurred beneath me. I searched inwardly for my particular brand of zeal; I found none. A flat uncaring attitude prevailed.

Trees devoid of life grappled against the ominous gray sky—a stark, yet fitting, metaphor for the turmoil I felt within. A realm of grief enveloped me more the farther I got from Canada. This wasn't the first time I'd crossed the Queen's Highway in the aftermath of a life-changing event, but it certainly wasn't any easier this time around.

What have I done? I thought in disbelief, scanning the horizon for a hint of how to move forward. I was easily flagged on through as I crossed the bridge into Detroit, this time without my trailer full of liberty ponies or any idea what would come next for me.

A hundred years ago, showmen often used the same team of horses to perform an act in the show as those that pulled their wagon to the next town. During the off season, the horses were turned out on pasture with little overhead. Unfortunately, that wasn't always the case anymore.

My six-pony liberty act had seemed like the perfect small business for an aspiring circus man in his early twenties. Once over the start-up hurdle, an act like this could work for many years. Entering into the process of learning how to train and present my pony act had also introduced me to the mindset of having regard for other living beings. As the years went by, I learned how to elicit the desired response from the horses in the circus ring through patience, trust, and respect. Our act became more consistent as our connection deepened.

What I didn't realize at the time was that opportunities for horse acts in the circus were dwindling. When I was discarded by the circus at the last minute that summer, the disruption in my performance career had led to a continuation with the apprenticeship with a sign shop. In the off season of the winter months, I worked alongside journeymen sign painters to raise money for my passion of performing, but painting when I should be out touring and performing soon became an issue.

During that time, my father saw my palomino ponies on pasture as neglected and turned on the pressure to sell them. He didn't understand what the circus world meant to me. It provided me with a place to feel welcomed, a part of a community, and validated. But with performing opportunities diminishing and the ponies still needing to be fed and cared for, Dad's words slowly crept into my mind. Reluctantly, I prepared marketing information about the act and began broadcasting my offer to sell throughout the industry.

One man who owned a circus in Canada recognized a coup. My huge investment of time, energy, and love proved a benefit to Ian Garden—my seasoned act would help his son get into performing with far less training and prep required before they could actually enter the ring. But as I left my beloved ponies in Ontario in the winter of 1979, I felt only sadness as the distance between us grew larger and more permanent. I was losing my children and grieving the loss of my professional ambition at the same time.

The sale of my liberty act and the Fruehauf semitrailer to Garden Bros Circus interrupted a pattern of behavior I'd established over the last ten years in the rhythm of performing with the circus. The circus had been a big part of my life, and although I still had my quarter horse Bingo, I lacked the fundamentals to perform. I would need a new rig in order to get back into the circus world, but in the meantime, I was forced to change direction in my career.

Over the past year, I had begun developing my sign painting skills while serving as an apprentice at a sign shop. Since painting was another of my passions, an idea soon began to form out of the fog. Until I could figure out how to rejoin the circus, I would put my experience with the apprenticeship to good use. Maybe I'd even be able to merge the two somehow. The fairgrounds was the place where I was most reminded of the circus life, and it was there that I would also find a multitude of opportunities for my creative talents as a painter.

My decision was made. I would go to the headquarters of the W.G. Wade Shows where I had worked two summers ago, and there I would become the best carnival show painter on the planet.

Career Shift

Deadheading through Michigan, remnants of snow mixed with dirty gravel lay undisturbed along the road as a testimony to the long hibernation. In Mason, I pulled into the drive of the Wade Shows' winter quarters. A well-worn foot path meandered among the multitude of vehicles and around the mobile homes that acted as headquarters for the crew, leading to the office and the central building.

I climbed down from the cab and looked toward the middle of the vast yard filled with parked carnival equipment. Following the footprints to a Quonset hut the showmen called the barn, I found several men huddled inside as they worked on a big project. This was the skeleton crew that stayed during the after-season of the fair circuit.

A prevalent attitude radiated among the carnival men as a mixture of fear and defiance that culminated in a reluctance to accept outsiders. It was as if a cautionary stand-offishness and tough-guy persona would work to protect them from those who sought entry into their inner circle. But I wasn't looking to impose or cause harm, and soon they would recognize that and count me as one of their own.

I was looking for someone specific. Hayes, my mentor from Clarklake, Michigan, had introduced me to his longtime friend Jim Elliott two summers ago when I'd made a pattern for him. It just so happened that Jim was one of the owners of the Wade Shows, and all my hope now rested upon his shoulders. After an awkward moment with the carnies eyeing me and whispering, I finally caught sight of Jim smoking a pipe while overseeing the bustle of activity taking place. Taking a deep breath, I mustered all my confidence and approached.

"Hello, Davee," he said, perking right up. "Good to see you." Before I could tell him why I was there, he said, "Hey,

I've got someone I want you to meet."

Jim motioned for me to follow him over to a big man standing at the workbench with a freckled, wrinkled face whose relentless smile showed evidence of metal dental work.

"Hey, Red," Jim called. "Here's the guy who made that pattern for me a couple years back."

I discovered through conversation that F.G. "Red" Wood was the carnival co-owner. Red rose above the aura of worthless energy that seemed to permeate the air, turning on the charm and reassuring me that I'd come to the right place.

"Is that so? Glad to meet you," Red greeted me. "I have the perfect job for you."

Red was clearly at the helm of all the goings-on. He beamed as he escorted me through the men.

"Let me show you what we've been working on all winter."

He practically bubbled over with excitement, proud of the accomplishment on display in the center of the barn.

"The older farmers will remember using this sort of truck," he said as we drew closer to it. "This is a 1927 White Horse van. I found it in Pennsylvania in rugged condition. It's almost done, and then it'll be used as a parade feature and a centerpiece at our fairs."

What I saw was an old horse truck from the era of a central-louvered engine housing, flanked by large gaping front fenders, with twin stainless headlight housings that hovered on brackets. A gigantic rectangular cube with a windshield and a graceful shielding appendage above the glass rose behind this portion. The truck had been restored to mechanical and physical integrity and was almost complete. The men had painted it fire-engine red, and I began to get the notion that this van would require my painterly touch to really bring it to life.

"In the prime of its life, it would have been used to haul up to a half-dozen horses!" Red said.

"Wow!" I exclaimed. I always enjoyed learning about the old ways of showmen from long ago, especially when it involved horses.

Red showed me the antique calliope mounted inside and explained the plan was for this to become a showpiece that also produced nostalgic music. Remembering the circus décor I'd painted for Jack and Sid on their cotton candy booths two summers prior, Red finally revealed his request.

"I want you to cover the outsides of this old truck with a tremendous amount of old-time circus scrollwork to fit with the era of the truck."

A vision already began to fill my mind, easing the depression that had been shadowing me ever since I'd left Canada without my ponies. As I studied the exterior of this majestic old vehicle, I mentally reviewed the processes learned from an old sign painter who had introduced me to scrolling up a circus truck. A sense of familiarity filled my heart with comfort, and this old truck gave me hope for a brighter future.

"Yes," I blurted, gratefully accepting his challenge to transform this old truck into a work of art. But first, I had a few loose ends to tie up.

"I will return in the spring of the year to get started."

My mentor lived in Clarklake, only forty miles away. I had befriended Hayes ten years earlier when he provided encouragement for my aspirations as a circus man. Because this was not something I received from my father, I clung to Hayes to fill that void. I knew in my hour of need that his friendly ear would help ease the loss of my ponies, even more so since Hayes had been the one who'd helped me acquire them in the first place.

"Oh, Dave," his grinning face appeared after I knocked on

the door. "What a pleasant surprise. Come on in."

We settled into chairs in his living room and I took in a deep breath. I was safe here.

"How the heck are you?" Hayes asked genuinely.

I fought the emotions coming to the surface.

"I'm sad," I admitted.

He scratched Nipper behind the ears for just the right amount of time before prompting, "Pray tell."

"I sold the ponies."

My disclosure opened a floodgate of feelings accompanied by explanations of what had been taking place that led up to this kink in my trajectory. Hayes listened patiently, validating my feelings and supplying encouragement. Then he revealed something very special.

"The prettiest sight I ever had on my farm was your herd of yellow ponies grazing and playing out on the pasture when they were babies. It remains indelible in my mind to this day. While savoring that beautiful sight, I couldn't quite believe that I was actually looking at a future circus act, right here on my farm in Clarklake." Hayes looked me in the eye. "I want to thank you for giving an old farmer the opportunity to share in the creation of your circus act. Nothing could have made me prouder to witness all you have accomplished."

Through watery eyes, I listened with pure gratitude for this wonderful man who could find the goodness in my sorrow. His positivity helped me to focus on the time I'd had with my ponies, fondly remembering the experience and joy they had given to me, and apparently to others as well.

"Your performance career is not over, Dave." Hayes leaned forward in his seat, making sure he had my full focus. "I am certain the best is yet to come."

He was right. The ending of one chapter didn't have to mean the whole story was over. One event did not determine the outcome. There was hope in the unknown of the future.

"Thank you," I said, truly grateful for his friendship.

As I drove the semi-tractor across Illinois, I reviewed the life I had found with the circus. Among my fellow performers I'd found love, recognition, and approval on a regular basis, not to mention an interesting and thrilling way to live. The season I shared with King Bros. Circus two years ago was undoubtedly the best of my life. All my efforts to become a significant part of the circus had coalesced into a busy time of being a star.

The circus taught me the concept of a life on the road—constant travel with one-day stands. Each day, we'd set up, provide two shows, tear everything down, and drive to the next town at night. Although performing was my passion, this was a turbulent pace not without vicissitudes. In an effort to cope, it wasn't long before I developed the habit of sipping beer between shows and during the jump to the next town.

The parking locations for all the rigs on the show were arranged in a familiar pattern at every location. Most of the performers and working people parked quickly and went to sleep, but because I had six ponies and a horse I had work to do late into the night. I drove stakes with a sledgehammer prior to setting up the awning on the side of the semitrailer for the livestock. Then I unloaded, watered, and bedded them up to their bellies in hay before I went to sleep for a few hours. My early morning alarm clock was the sound of a driver pounding stakes into the ground for the big top. That was my cue to prepare for the shows.

Despite the fast pace of life on the road, soothing nostalgia washed over me as I reflected on all of this, reminding me why the circus had become my home for so many years. Now minus six ponies and an act, I still had a deep desire to perform with the circus again someday, but in the meantime, I would need another form of income to fill the void. I was grateful for my developing skills with a paintbrush and the crossover it provided with the carnival.

Inevitable Changes

While lost in the memory of those grand days gone by, a serious vibration began in my truck while going across the Mississippi River. I gritted my teeth and hoped it would stop, but it just seemed to get worse. My truck broke down past St. Louis, ceasing all forward movement and forcing me to acknowledge the problem. When I checked it out, I saw a bearing on the back of the transmission had gone dry and burnt up, but I was bewildered what to do about it.

I managed to find a mechanic willing to fix it, but I would have time on my hands until it was ready. I found an old truck stop, but the usual distractions of waitresses would only satisfy briefly. When the mechanic informed me he would need a few days for parts, I knew I would need somewhere to stay.

I begrudgingly thought about my older brother who lived nearby in his travel van. I hadn't planned to see John. I didn't want to, especially in such tight quarters. The idea of seeing him would reopen the hatred I had for his condition—a then-unnamed ailment that produced bizarre behavior and resulted in my parents' favoritism. Unable to make sense of it all had left me frustrated as a child and I despised the idea of stirring up such memories. Unfortunately, I had nowhere else to go.

Resigning myself to a fated visit, I called John. He was delighted to hear from me and happily agreed to share his time while I waited for repairs. Still guarded, I wasn't anticipating a pleasant experience, but John's positive tone gave me hope that maybe it wouldn't be as bad as I expected either.

"I want to show you something," John said when he picked me up, beaming from ear to ear.

I hopped into his van and he began driving to an unknown destination. I wondered what he might want to show me. Could it be an apartment? The additional space would certainly be welcomed during my unplanned visit.

"I wanted a place for customers to be able to come to me," he said, speaking of his work as a custom computer programmer for customers in Illinois and Missouri. Awkward though he was, I had to hand it to John—his fierce brilliance had him blazing through an intellectual echelon untrod by most.

When he parked in front of a storefront called The Software Center, I was confused. Did he get a job working for someone else? Was he done freelancing?

"Ta - da!" he said, proudly pointing at the business.

I scrunched up my forehead briefly before my jaw dropped open. Was this his brainchild for the newly emerging computer trend? Did he really open his own business?

"Is this yours?" I asked.

"Yep," John answered, puffing out his chest. "Come on! Let's go inside."

I followed John into his store, mystified with how he'd managed to get this far. After all, his peculiar condition invited ridicule from others our whole lives and he completely lacked the ability to produce what most people considered acceptable behavior. John didn't have the discipline to get up early, the savvy for retail exchanges, or the ethic that it took to run a business. I also suspected that the complete lack of common sense displayed in childhood likely remained on his roster. So how in the world did he manage to open a business?

"Who gets up to open the door each day?" I asked.

"Oh, I hired a guy to do that for me," John confessed nonchalantly.

I had to admit, I was impressed. As I looked over his retail space, new ideas began to replace the skepticism that previously permeated my perception of my older brother. Then he surprised me even further.

"I'm actually glad you're here, Dave," he said, smiling. "I have a request—I want signs that look like computer punch cards with one corner snipped off to hang above the different categories of products we sell. Do you think you could do that for me?"

Impressed by my brother's growth and honored that he would ask me to help dress it up, I answered, "Absolutely, John. Yeah, I can do that."

Perhaps old dogs really could learn new tricks after all.

Although I grew up in the Midwest, my parents had found a piece of property in a pretty corner of the Ozarks on which to build a house. I wound my way to Sulphur Springs, where my parents had been attracted by the lively charismatic commune housed there. The folks of Shiloh taught spiritual principles, baked sprouted grain bread, and promoted information about health and nutrition. In this enlightened place filled with like-minded people, my parents found a refuge in which to feed their spiritual hunger during retirement.

Even though I'd only been gone two weeks since dropping him off, Superdog wiggled and jumped with excitement when he saw me pull up. My parents always offered to take care of my companion of ten years whenever he couldn't travel with me.

"Hey, Superdog!" I greeted him with just as much excitement, rubbing behind his ears and scratching his neck.

Looking up at the progress of my parents' new home, I saw they now had an excavation site on a hill with forms in place waiting for concrete. With preparation for their new home underway I would help fence in their place during this visit, which would provide pasture for my livestock whenever I was in town.

"Dave!"

I looked toward the garage my folks had equipped for a temporary living space and saw my mom and dad exit to welcome me. I stood straight from petting Superdog, smiling as I greeted them. Although this didn't feel like home, it was always nice to catch up with my parents and all the Shiloh gossip. I would enjoy several nutritious meals here before the time came to return to my home in Florida.

My VW Microbus emblazoned with "Krazee Davee" on the side and outfitted to paint out of was here at my parents' new home, but in my absence my dad had found it useful to haul supplies for their construction project. I didn't need it just yet.

I had a sun-bleached red VW bus waiting with my roommate back in Florida.

I also had a job at Sign King, and after a wonderful visit the time had come to return home and resume the other part of my life. No longer needing my cab-over, I painted a "For Sale" sign on an old piece of plywood to place in the cab and parked it next to the sole gas station in town. Superdog and I would hitchhike back to the Sunshine State.

I stood with my thumb in the air and my happy dog at my side. While waiting for a friendly driver to offer us a ride, I found a thrill that accompanied the sense of freedom and adventure. The road was calling to me.

When I returned to the Sign King, my place of employment for the past eight months, the boss told me that my job no longer existed. I was blindsided. What now? I thought. I still had the project Red requested, but that wasn't until the spring. What would I do until then?

I considered my situation. The sudden loss of employment forced my hand to strike out on my own. I had been freelancing every weekend anyway. Why not become a full-time snapper? After all, that's what I was - a sign painter who had no shop.

With nothing left tying me to the Sunshine State, I gave notice to my roommate, and Superdog and I headed back to the Ozarks in our tomato soup-colored bus. My folks needed assistance with their home building project for a few weeks and I suddenly had the free time to help. While there, I could trade out my buses to take the Krazee Davee bus to the carnival and formulate a plan for the future.

Upon arrival, I was put straight to work. I wielded a wheelbarrow filled with concrete as the workmen filled the forms for the foundation. Among the dust and noise, my mind entertained thoughts about the upcoming summer. In addition to becoming a snapper, I also decided to live a life on the road. The thought had been percolating in the back of my mind for a long time now, and it seemed there was no time like the present to give it a try.

The lure of the road is a simple instinctive part of most men. Trusting and following what could be called an intuitive hunch had many times provided opportunities unrealizable without it. The highway as a home was a concept I had found when I packed up my drums and a few paintbrushes to join the circus right out of high school.

Following my heart, I was ready to fully dive into the nomadic life and enjoy the freedom and adventure that came with it. But first, I had one problem that needed solving. Though I still had a horse and a desire to perform, I didn't have a trailer. To be able to transport my gelding, I took the money from selling my circus pony act and ordered a new two-horse trailer from a manufacturer in Tulsa, Oklahoma. When it arrived, Bingo would be able to travel with me. As I would soon discover, the same environment that provided an interesting arena for my emerging talents with a brush would also provide a break to perform with a horse once again.

After a few weeks of helping as a construction worker, it was time to fulfill the commission from Red at the Wade Shows' winter quarters. I gathered my gear and sign-making supplies and loaded up the bus. I knew what to expect on the carnival due to my experience two summers prior. I was ready.

I headed for Michigan, where Bingo and my original riding instructor Clarence Hastings were waiting for me. I could resume taking riding lessons while painting for Wade Shows. My future was wide open, and the possibilities were endless.

Chapter 1
The Show Painter

"All our dreams can come true, if we have the courage to pursue them."
—Walt Disney

The Calliope Truck

Late April in Michigan was a time of renewal. Tender sprouts emerged, the tips of the tree branches budded, song birds returned, and dormant plants peeked through the soil. Despite the harsh winter, nature was resilient, and so was I. Thank goodness. After the bleak period of letting go of my six-pony liberty act and grieving the end of an era, I sought a new avenue of fulfillment by painting for the carnival.

Although Superdog and I arrived in the Krazee Davee bus, I had coined the new brush name, Letterfly, two winters prior while painting in South Florida. One day, I'd have to repaint the bus to reflect my rebranding, but for now there was paid work to be done.

We pulled into a shopping center parking lot where the W.G. Wade Shows was set up for the still dates—when customer traffic was at its least. As I headed to check in at the office, Superdog began his investigation. The stark contrast of this fill-in-the-gap setup from my experience during fair season two summers ago was appalling.

During the regular season, the manicured grass dotted with trees and rows of comfortable barns at the fairgrounds made for a people-friendly experience. The central area was scattered with rides, each with their protective loop of fencing. The backside had a wall made of attractions with one side like the funhouse, an avenue near kiddie land and the grand carousel was filled with games of chance, and the popcorn trailer was parked right in the middle. In the most strategic location, a large generator semitrailer sat with a web of heavy electric cables that ran on the ground in all directions. The dull roar of the generator provided relentless background noise as it pumped electricity to the large variety of lights, attractions, and mechanical rides.

In contrast, the off-season layout I was currently viewing sat in a large bland parking lot. During the still dates, the show played a series of these shopping center parking lots in order to rehearse the ride crews and train new members to efficiently move and operate the equipment during the busier season when the rides would need to be moved from spot to spot rapidly with expertise and familiarity.

On this overcast day during early spring, this impersonal location lacked any ounce of charm. It was as if the fairyland I had come to know and love had drifted from its primary purpose into a darkened theme. Fortunately, as the weeks went by, the still dates of the carnival would soon transform into more organized street and church festivals, and all my hard work would come to life on full display in front of hundreds of patrons.

My first project was to paint the calliope truck that Red had requested last winter, the old White Horse truck that had been restored to pristine condition with an antique calliope mounted inside the cargo area.

It only needed my specialized touch, and it would be ready to be placed in the carnival lineup. Red wanted a calliope painted on the side, along with plenty of circus scrollwork to cover the exterior, the way show wagons used to be decorated over a century ago. This project would be vastly different from sign painting, and I was eager to get my hands dirty. There was an area on the side of this big truck that was perfect to receive the image of a bank of brass calliope whistles that made the famous raspy sound. Using color to create the visual suggestion of cylindrical brass on a flat surface would be a challenge. Using the actual rows of pipes as reference, I observed how the reflections appeared on the forty-four ascending shiny brass pipes and the shadows between them. I attempted to replicate what I saw as I painted the faux pipes using subtle variations in color to add depth and light.

Starting with gold, I created the overall shapes of the whistles. I included the many multi-faceted brackets that allowed for the gap needed for the steam to escape and hit the sharp edge of the tube that made the sound. These were all carefully painted according to size. Because all these components were brass, the challenge was to paint something that would imitate the look of metal. Using delicate changes in the main color, shadows were implied and bright reflections on the shiny metal were established. Although this project was complicated by the sheer number of these reflections, the effect achieved simply by doing one stroke at a time ended up creating a compelling result.

With the calliope completed, I began to create the extensive Victorian scrollwork designs. Fascinated with my work, the big boss himself, Mr. Glenn Wade, volunteered to help. I supplied Mr. Wade with a brush and some paint and showed him where my guidelines were. As he concentrated on the areas he could reach comfortably, he soon became immersed in the work, slowly brushing his paint onto the areas I'd outlined. While he worked alongside me, his demeanor revealed much to admire. Mr. Wade took a personal interest in what was going on around him, including my daily life. As the patriarch of a huge carnival family, his regard for even the lowest of the employees nurtured a warm connection that many of these people didn't get at home. Glenn provided a safe place for everyone to be just who they were. The Wade Shows carnival supplied an environment that society simply could not match, and I was honored to be a part of this family, even if just for the summer.

The Fun House

When the White Horse truck was ready to shine, Jim Elliott directed me to my next assignment. Jo Clever, the office manager and owner of the fun house, wanted a fresh design. Since the unit played the same route every year, a change of appearance with decorative paint would imply this was a new attraction.

An illuminated wild west sign gave this walk-through attraction its theme. Playful images required a new kind of creativity. I began to think in terms of old ghost town features, western icons, and images of horses and saloon fronts to decorate the massive front. I drew a scale drawing that depicted the shape of the fun house and began to sketch ideas on my drawing pad. Inspiration came from recalling the animated characters of my youth - Casper, Wile E. Coyote and the Roadrunner, and Rocky and Bullwinkle. This project initiated the use of visual perspective in my art, that of a pictorial artist. I studied reference images from magazines and borrowed ideas to fill the surface with entertaining pictorials. Comic books became a rich source of inspiration. I learned implied action through graphic devices and stunning composition while I analyzed those pages. Soon, comical horses, cowboy skeletons, and western town features with friendly ghosts covered the front of the fun house. This was show business, a new beginning for me.

As the fun house neared completion, I found additional opportunities to create festive pictorial and lettering work with the endless stream of rides, game fronts, concession trailers, and ticket booths. The showmen kept me busy around the clock, my days filled with creating artwork from atop a ladder as I generated many

visual suggestions to influence and entice patrons to engage with each attraction.

The show owners recognized that my passion for creating art was good for everyone. Because of their regard for each person under their umbrella, Glenn and Red were good sports when I wandered away from their main undertakings to work on other projects on their show. I was enjoying the interesting work in a friendly setting, and I eagerly looked forward to making this a regular part of my painting career.

But the spring was a time of cold, intermittent rain in Michigan. In my new role as a show painter, I was at the mercy of the weather. Whenever it rained, I had to find an indoor job to focus on, such as paper patterns and small signs. When it was dry enough to be outside, I filled my time with the creation of decorative lettering behind festive images of clowns enjoying delicious fair food in pictorials so real they just lacked aroma.

The popcorn concession was operated by Jack and Sid. These guys were show business in human form. Because of their love for this occupation, they provided an endless stream of patter about what they believed would look good on the various projects I worked on. They also kept busy as matchmakers, introducing eligible singles to each other every chance they found.

Jack was the taller of the two and made himself busy with all the outdoor stuff - inventory, rolling stock, equipment repairs, and logistics. Sid always wore a big smile in his paper soda jerk hat and stayed busy preparing cotton candy and popcorn, keeping the interior of their stand clean, and simply enjoying life. Best known as a relentless source of fun, these men lifted the spirits of everyone on the show with their uninhibited antics and zeal.

On particularly cold days, they provided a warm place for me to escape into their popcorn trailer, always ready to share a hot meal from the crockpot with me. As a bonus, this area of respite became a place others recognized as a means to contact me. From their point of view in the glassed-in centrally located enclosure, my good friends Jack and Sid became gossip central.

"Oh my gawd," Jack said, bounding in through the back door. "I can't believe it!"

"What?" Sid squealed. "Pray tell."

"You know that blond boy on the Matterhorn crew?" Jack began. "He's hot for Cindy in Duke's grab joint!"

"What about the dime-pitch girl?" Sid wondered. "Has he forgotten about her already?

"Oh, Erica," Jack sizzled through his teeth. "It ends up she prefers the company of players on the other team."

As their conversation skittered on, I found myself immersed in a live-action source of entertainment and orientation of the latest drama and romances.

Midway Marketing

Many of the game operators had the traditional stick joints, or wooden-framed booths with canvas covers. Others had sophisticated trailers with flashing lights, buzzers, bells, and plush prizes hung high out of reach—all designed to add excitement to the game and entice carnival-goers to play.

When I was here two years ago, I decorated the Skee-Ball Alley trailer for Tim Bors. He was building a fleet of game trailers and shared his concept with me about what he wanted painted on his next acquisition called Happy Hippos. He welcomed my use of color to depict a story graphic that placed cartoon hippos in a fantastical environment.

Over the years, Tim Bors would design many festive and

cutting-edge games, all built in Tampa, Florida by Specialty Trailer and decorated by me. Because of his vision for the future, incredible attention to detail, and sharing his plans with me months in advance, Tim soon became my all-time favorite sign customer on the show.

The carnival, or midway as it was known in the industry, was often clumped in the same category as a circus. But, in fact, the carnival was a completely different animal. A circus used a big top to host various performances. The big-top components were simple - poles, stakes, rope, canvas, rigging, and planks. These all came together to create a safe place for the audience, who all received the same thing in the form of one big show.

At a carnival, the audience made their own way among many sophisticated attractions, making impulse decisions depending on the level of enticement. The aromas, visuals, and sensations unique to this industry created a world of competition rather than the camaraderie of the circus. Each twenty or forty-foot space had as much visual magnetism packed into it as possible. The rides, fancy foods, games of skill and chance, and other festive attractions all battled for attention with the combination of electric lights, sparkly fiberglass shapes, sirens, whistles, and tunes, and the overlapping voices of hucksters attempting to appeal to the passersby.

Though each carnival showman had his own idea of what worked, one thing they all agreed on was the allure of decorative paint and sign work. The year I spent as an apprentice sign painter had given me plenty of time to learn letterform, layout composition, and brush handling techniques that came in very handy on this scene. I had passion for the work, and I found I could truly thrive within this competitive environment. Because each vendor competed with each other, they also competed for me. Keeping me busy meant their competition didn't have access to my talents.

I involved myself with translating requests from showmen into painted combinations of brush technique, color relationships, and creating the illusion of form. In serving these savvy merchants, I also gained access to their individual philosophy of merchandising and sought to maximize on the premise they held dear. The marketing ideas used on the midway involved effective sign placement and the use of supporting flash - what carnies call visual product enticements.

As I became more and more acquainted with the many selling angles that worked for these showmen, it was clear that visual appeal was key in creating the draw that resulted in sales. Because of this, the field of hand-painted imagery extended far beyond the trade of forming letters with a brush, an endeavor that has had volumes written about it. Along with fancy lettering, I created happy images, visual suggestions and stimulation, subtle décor, and bold statements, all with the goal of commanding attention and attracting customers.

In the midst of immersing myself in providing this service to a unique community, logistic challenges also began to fill my awareness. With the assortment of components used on carnival units that moved to a new location each week, the lineup at each venue could be different due to a variety of considerations. This meant an unfinished project might not get finished if that part of the carnival headed to a different destination than I did. Some projects had looming deadlines; others experienced a long gap in production. I had to learn how to accommodate the weekly jump into my painting schedule.

I also did not always have access to every part of a project at the same time. The unfolded front of the fun house, for example, was unavailable after teardown until the piece was placed into position on the next lot. The same was true with much of the rest of the show whenever they packed up and rolled toward the next lot. Adaptability became vital to my ability to continue thriving. I began working on fifteen projects at once so I always had something I could switch to whenever necessary. I also learned to use any interruptions to accomplish other interests, like working with Bingo.

The Riding Stable

Miller's stable was situated on a farm in the vast flat sod of Mount Clemens, Michigan. The twelve-stall classic Arabian barn had rolling barred doors on each of the stalls and a concrete aisle down the center, along with an attached indoor arena. The stable operated year-round, boarding horses and providing riding lessons to regional aficionados.

Lane Miller, who kept their string of Arabians fit and trained, was of medium height with short, bouncy hair. Early every other morning while Wade Shows was close by, I would ride Bingo under her supervision. Occasionally, I would ride one of their Arabians. Though I'm sure my six-foot-four frame looked pretty funny on such a small horse, I learned to appreciate the fiery nature of an Arabian compared to the merits of my cold-blooded quarter horse. Still, there's nothing like riding your own horse who you have a partnership with.

"Good morning, Dave," she almost sang from in the stall as I entered the barn. "Get Bingo ready and we will start your lesson."

Bingo had been born in 1973 during one of the winters I spent training my palomino liberty ponies in Hugo, Oklahoma. His mother was a white and sorrel paint mare, and his dad was a buckskin stallion. They produced his spectacular color - a paint pattern of buckskin and white. He had a black mane and a spectacular tail with white at the base that morphed into black at the tip. I was completely enamored with the little colt.

Bob Grubb, the man who had bred Bingo, began early in training him to march and bow. Though Bob received many interested offers from cowboys who wanted to buy Bingo, he refused every one of them—he already had Bingo's next owner in mind. I was honored to discover it was me.

I now stood in this Arabian barn in Michigan, grooming Bingo while he ate before I laid the saddle on his back and cinched it up. Once his bridle was fitted, I exited through the door at the other end of the barn into an arena with mirrors on the walls for monitoring posture and the footfalls of the horse. As I blazed across the arena, Lane shouted her instructions.

"Keep your heels down," she said, launching into lesson criteria developed over years of teaching. "Relaxation in that area of your leg facilitates a comfortable connection with the horse."

I glanced down at my right foot, making sure only the ball of my foot touched the stirrup while dropping my heels.

"Look up!" Lane's voice pierced the air. "It's the same with looking ahead," she explained. "The horse can feel the subtle change of your head looking down."

Lane introduced me to a routine different from training for the circus, but this was the classic discipline that would create a solid foundation for achieving progress with my horse in every area. We concentrated on variations of trot work that activated specific muscles in the horse to promote the engagement of the hindquarters. Riding with haunches and shoulders in while bending through large circles made each session delightfully strenuous for me as well as for Bingo. I concentrated on keeping my legs in the proper place with my head up and shoulders back while maintaining a proper bend of the horse's neck and head. These were disciplines in proper posture begun with Clarence Hastings which Lane would help me perfect with time in the saddle. At the end of my lesson her next student, often a child of an affluent family, would show up, and I would return to the Wade Shows to paint, biding my time until my next lesson.

Time spent with horses offered an outlet for pent-up energy and enthusiasm. Seeking ways to stick around even outside of my lessons, I often helped with chores and was never shy when needed. I stacked hay, built stall walls, and joined in mucking, the term for cleaning out the stalls.

"Will you help Betsy unload that feed while I get my next lesson horse ready?" Lane asked after our lesson was completed.

Betsy kept her bay warmblood gelding in the stall next to Bingo. She was a college student who aspired to ride upper-level dressage, earning her keep through extra chores. As I placed a sack of feed on my shoulder, Betsy made her current complaint known to everyone in the barn.

"I don't know why it has to be such a secret," she bellowed past me, loud enough to be heard down the aisle. "Phyllis won't tell me what bit she uses in Boyden's mouth."

I kept my mouth shut, avoiding all involvement in the barn drama. Still, I couldn't deny the conversation among the mainly female staff and students was always rich and enlightening. I learned plenty just by listening like a fly on the wall while they carried on about their obsession for horses.

Outside of the occasional drama, this was a great outlet for my ambition and the perfect community to fit into. We all reveled in our common interest for these majestic horses and the time-honored skills each of us hoped to improve. Luckily, the location of Miller Stables proved to be accessible and convenient from many of the carnival venues I frequented, and it quickly became another haven for me.

As an occasional distraction from our strict training routine, many an afternoon was spent having a hilarious time on our horses. One time, Lane's father, Dutch, challenged us to a game of walking polo. The idea was to play the game just like the real one, only with a volleyball, and at a walking pace to prevent injuries. Due to Bingo's experience in the circus, he wasn't rattled when I swung the polo mallet from his back, nor was he startled when the volleyball came sailing into his side.

When evening rolled around after one such game, I helped put the barn to bed. Then Lane, Betsy, and I piled into the farm pickup and went to the local ice cream shop. Our chatter continued while we savored our sweet distractions, with the concluding challenge of the day to tie the cherry stem into a knot inside our mouths.

Mechanical Marvels

Even though I painted all day, each evening I would make my rounds to visit the many people who made up the show family. The SkyWheel was my favorite stop. Since this was the tallest ride, it was considered important as the beacon that attracted attention in whatever neighborhood we were in. The foundation for this ride was the twin trailers parked parallel with half of the massive tower on each side. This colossal structure supported two Ferris wheels mounted between either end of the giant revolving arms.

Joyce and Jerry were the foremen of this ride. The

dismantling process that evening was fascinating to watch while I had another late-night amber beverage. Keeping the load balanced during disassembly first required removal of the tubs from each wheel. The remaining components, rim rails, lights, and spokes were then removed a few at a time from each end to avoid the remaining structure from becoming top heavy. Otherwise, the suspended weight could collapse the whole structure.

The rim rail removal of the wheels reminded me how the bible-backs in the circus were loaded. Bibles were the platforms in the grandstand upon which reserved seating chairs were placed. Each platform folded like a book, thus the name. Men on either end would pick up the long bible and lift it over their heads to walk toward the trailer, which would have been brought into the center of the big top. They'd then hand it up to the men who stacked them. The pair who had relinquished their bible would smoothly duck down to go underneath the incoming bibles as if square dancing on their way to retrieve another. While the many crew members loaded row after row, the trailer would creep forward to facilitate their efforts. In this manner, many pairs of men would get the bibles loaded quickly.

Although the system wasn't quite the same as what I currently sat watching, the rim rails of the SkyWheel were removed by two crews of two men each, moving them one at a time. I popped open another bottle and took a swig while they carried them over the deck and placed them onto the rack. When that was completed, they began working on the spokes. This process required one man to be up in the air, draped over the central axle. I watched as he pulled the pins that held each spoke in the cheese (or the receiving manifold).

A block-and-falls set of rigging was managed by a second

man, who gently lowered the spoke assembly where even more workers waited to receive and maneuver each of them onto one of the stacks on either trailer. When all the components of the inner wheels were loaded, the superstructure on the trailers were lowered into traveling position and the main axle removed. Each week, the crew would go through these motions to develop muscle memory and the ability to accomplish teardown in better time for fair season.

After teardown would come the jump to the next town. With nothing left to watch and minimal teardown of my own to worry about, I gathered my empties, called Superdog, and turned in for the night.

The first of our affluent street festivals began when the show moved to downtown Dearborn, Michigan. During setup on those downtown streets, Bruce Cook had just joined the show and somehow befriended me. He was the foreman of the Toboggan, a ride with a central tube that stood vertically. Passengers would ride straight to the top in a car, where they were released to roll out and down a spiral track that orbited the tube, eventually arriving on a small roller coaster track that went around the base.

"Hey, Davee," Bruce's stealthy greeting chimed. "Walk with me."

He was an avid marijuana smoker. Instead of the expected small-talk conversation, we walked briskly around the block in near silence. Bruce looked each direction and then showed me how to share a joint in broad daylight in front of the busy merchant area. I preferred my drink of choice, but I still partook in his offer. Once around the block, we returned to the ride area and got to work. Now blitzed, Bruce began assembly of the Toboggan. There was always something going on inside his head. Although he was friendly enough, his reserved nature coupled with almost no eye contact made connecting with him rather difficult.

With so much mechanical equipment to keep in working order, it was inevitable that things would go wrong from time to time. One busy afternoon, over the noise of the crowd, the sounds coming from all this machinery, and the music that blared from several sources at once, there was a loud explosion followed by an erratic jet blast, commanding everyone's attention. Workers and fairgoers alike immediately wondered whether to run toward or away from the noise. As it turned out, the compressed-air hose that lifted the large round platform with passengers in tubs on the Tip Top had burst from its connection to release a high volume of compressed air. The hose beat erratically underneath until the source was turned off. The disabled ride sat idle while repairs were made, equaling hours of lost income for the show. With the size of this crowd, each hour lost meant thousands of dollars. Skilled with mechanics, Red was summoned, and in no time he'd investigated the cause and facilitated the repair using whatever he had on hand.

Teardown followed the busiest day of the fair. When the traffic stopped climbing on the rides and began to thin out, one at a time the ride operators morphed into teams of jockeys as they began the dismantling processes. Coming from multiple sources, music was also turned off one by one, leaving only the low droning sound of the diesel generators. The chatter of impact wrenches loosening bolts and the hammering of connecting pins became the primary sounds of the night in the mostly empty fairgrounds.

Watching as giant structures slowly assumed manageable shapes that the trucks could hook onto and move to the next town, I was fascinated by this weekly transformation. By day, the flashing lights added excitement and refashioned the mechanical diversity into a fairyland. Now they became the nocturnal illumination for the workmen preparing the machines for transport.

In the middle of all this activity, two men stood among the litter left behind by the crowds. Glenn Wade and Red Wood faced a long night of supervising their territory and these giant machines. But even greater than the machines was the sight of these two men who had made such a difference in my life. Their regard for everyone here, including me, filled the void of something I hadn't gotten at home. Truly giants among men, Red and Glenn left an indelible impression upon my soul that would last a lifetime.

A Gifted Man

Red Wood grew up in Kansas the son of a farmer. As a young man, he knew how to use heavy farm equipment to disc a vast section of land and get it as flat as a billiard table, yet farming bored him. Also a gifted mechanical genius, Red became fascinated with the specialty machinery used by the carnival to entertain passengers.

Glenn Wade quickly recognized that he could always count on Red to appear in greasy clothes in the midst of any problem on the show. With a gift for bringing a neglected and well-worn ride back to life through his relentless pursuit of restoring mechanical integrity, Red had special talents and his own brand of zeal. Not only did he have an aptitude for everything mechanical, his demeanor on the show with the employees was also admirable. He could motivate the help to the point that they actually wanted to work. It was these characteristics that influenced Glenn to ask Red to become his partner.

Red's restorative work took place in winter quarters where I was typically needed at the last minute. Many times after I put the finishing touches on a number of ride components, the pieces would be loaded wet. The paint would dry on the way to the first town. I discovered this was yet another standard part of show business procedure that I would have to adapt to. Despite the rush, I still found this sort of project rewarding due to the benefit of getting to work alongside Red.

He introduced me to his personal philosophy, infecting me with the enthusiasm that the rest of the crew had for working together and getting the jobs done. That attitude permeated the show and provided an indication of the management style of the show owners. A desire for connectedness and true teamwork prevailed, allowing an overall positive attitude to be fully present on the lot.

As springtime came to a close, the show would soon begin setting up on fairgrounds—the dedicated area in each county that shared a grandstand, horse track, barns for agriculture displays, and tree-lined avenues filled with concessionaires of foodstuffs and other products. Parades, contests, animal competitions, concerts, trotting horse races, and special daily considerations added to the momentum of activity around the carnival, making every day more interesting than the last. The W.G. Wade Shows made an impressive presence at the fair. The lineup included a Ferris wheel, the Matterhorn, Wild Mouse, Saturn Six, a large fun house, and many others. The recently refurbished rides and other large, heavy rides were only used at the big fairs.

As the major carnival ride attractions began to show up on the fairgrounds, merchants of every conceivable product lined up along the outside of the carnival territory. Referred to as independents, those concessionaires represented a huge opportunity for what I did. Seeing my work on the renewed rides and attractions, they kept me busy with sign work and decorating their concession trailers.

Among the rides owned by the Wade Shows was an extra heavy one. The bumper cars ride was essentially a large portable building with a flat steel floor for individual cars to drive around upon. One morning while headed to another project, I was stopped by Red to discuss a facelift for this classic ride.

"Davee, I want you to handpick the five people you want as your helpers from all of the crew," he said. "Then I want you to design a job that this crew can accomplish in one morning by giving each their own roller and a different color. When we get to the Mason County Fair, we will decorate the scenery."

The bumper car building was a big, heavy piece used only during the summertime fairs. It had scenic panels that surrounded the top edges to disguise where the steel building structure met the edge of the canvas top.

"All the panels are identical," Red explained, "so I want you to design a simple graphic and make a pattern that has large simple shapes that the crew can easily roll individual colors on."

"Sounds easy enough," I acknowledged.

I began to imagine the step-by-step process. On the day of

the project, the overhead panels would be removed and placed on saw horses. I would then transfer the pattern to the first panel with my pounce bag filled with chalk. At that point, each helper would take a roller and their assigned color to fill in the designated area. In this manner, the panels would be filled with a variety of colors, and when all of them were on, I would come in with a spray gun to refine the patterns by painting a line to hide all the jagged edges.

Understanding the project ahead and with my plan in place, I recruited my favorites among the many crew members to assist with the job. Among them, Joyce from the SkyWheel was my first pick, and Beanie, the wife of the Matterhorn foreman, was my second. Both of these women had positive attitudes that attracted others like the pied piper. Plus, they loved Superdog.

The morning of the event arrived. I opened the many gallons of paint requested and distributed rollers and paint pans. Two ride men took the first overhead panel off and laid it onto our sawhorse assembly line. As planned, I transferred the graphic pattern onto it and the members of my team each started their tasks, resulting in the festive and colorful design. I was happy to see the project moving along nicely as a fun rapport took over—the product of choosing the right people to surround myself with.

I went back and forth between pattern transfers and spray man with my chosen color of green. As the panels were each completed, the ride men seamlessly removed them from our work area and put them back into position. In no time, the bulk of the panels that went around this attraction sported new paint and were once again hanging overhead. By opening time, all the wet paint was up and out of the way of the customers.

After completion of the final corner pieces, everyone felt a sense of pride and satisfaction. We basked in the glory of our accomplishment, and just in time, too. All my help now had to leave to open the carnival. This project introduced me to creative possibilities available by organizing simplicity with a quality committee.

Left to work alone once more, I made quick work of the cleanup and added another feather to my show-painter résumé. Being empowered to orchestrate this project demonstrated another aspect of Red's character I had not seen before. More than ever, I valued his insight, regard, and ability to motivate others.

Chapter 2
Finding My Place

"It isn't necessary to have relatives in Kansas City in order to be unhappy."
—Groucho Marx

Fair Time

Fair season officially arrived in July, and every afternoon was filled with crowds. I discovered mornings on the carnival midway to be a magical time of day, especially since I usually had it all to myself. All that was missing was an occasional blowing tumbleweed and the stirring soundtrack from The Good, the Bad and the Ugly to transport me to the desolation felt in any western ghost town.

This was the perfect time for me to paint. In contrast to the peaceful quietude of the morning, the mass of people would populate every square inch of the fairgrounds once the gates opened. Any sign work in proximity of curious fingers needed to be completely dry by late morning. Therefore, the safest place for me to be applying wet paint while the crowds milled about was from the top of a stepladder.

As I formed the letters on another carnival sign, I wondered how I, the guy who didn't want people around me, had gotten here. As a child, I'd watched bullies pick on my older brother. His awkward behavior and complete lack of social skills made him an easy target. As a result, I wanted nothing to do with others; I blamed others for my fear. I withdrew from making normal connections and focused my energy on creativity. In the safety of my endeavors, I excelled.

In my teens, I became a drummer on the road with the circus. I found a place to be creatively spontaneous and receive approval, but I wanted more. I began entering the ring to perform. This sacred place surrounded by the audience gave me a sense of control. I had their approval and they remained at an arm's length where I preferred them to be.

It seemed as if a tug of war was going on inside. I was distrustful of people, yet at home in the midst of throngs, a recluse who needed a sea of humanity to thrive. Some invisible force had drawn me to this environment, but whenever the show was over the inevitable echoes of my wounds reappeared. I was back to being alone. They say God has a sense of humor. Maybe it's true.

Wanting to create something that would last forever and leave my mark on the world, I recognized that with paint, I could do just that. Here I am.

To push through the discomfort of being around others, I self-medicated with alcohol to quiet my inner tension. I always had a cooler full of beer in the van. All I ever wanted was to be calm, to wash away the bad taste of not being good enough so I could fit in. I wasn't interested in the oblivion found with my first drinking experience, just the elimination of the self-deprecating thinking. The beverage provided a calmness and gave me the ability to focus my attention on the task at hand in spite of the chaos of the midway going on around me—a feature useful for a man who needed to manipulate a brush like a surgeon to create distinctive shapes with paint. I discovered that the drink also made my reluctance to connect with others diminish. From the first sip, a sense of ease and comfort washed over me immediately, freeing me from my self-imposed chains. Aside from my faithful companion, Superdog, the drink became my best friend.

Unusual Sights

Working the fairs meant being in the midst of an abundance of unusual sights. One interesting sight that whizzed around the lot appeared to be a small chariot with a vertical tiller steering device. The driver simply stood upon this contraption and zipped through the crowds. Attached to the back was a two-wheel dolly used as a cargo trailer. Jim worked for the hot dog and sausage operation on the show and was constantly replenishing stock using this chariot.

The hot dog and sausage concession was run by a cheap and grumbly guy named Bob. In stark contrast, Bob had an attitude that didn't fit with the otherwise encouraging and friendly regard the rest of the show radiated. I tried to do business with him but soon learned that he did not want to pay for anything. Instead, he was always scheming about how he could get something for nothing. I was better off letting him paint his own stuff, which he did. The vowels in the crudely painted "Root Beer" on the side of his booth looked like he'd traced a trash can lid to establish the shape. Still, I preferred Bob who made his intentions clear from the get-go to the occasional grifter. Those scoundrels would try to employ some selfish motive during the work or change the terms we'd agreed to prior to the transaction. This prompted me to shut down, finishing the project as quickly as possible so I could move on.

Through these experiences, I learned to be discerning about which jobs to take. The right customer made all the difference. I found a plethora of independent food concessionaires who appreciated what I did and provided me with plenty of work for fair pay. They provided me with encouragement, and I became free to use my energy and imagination in a loving, productive manner.

Another interesting sight came at Cole's grab joint one night. A grab joint was distinct from a cookhouse due to its limited menu. This was where you would grab a sausage or a hot dog and a cold drink. The flash for this joint was a grill heaped with sizzling sausage and a pile of peppers and onions steaming at eye level of the passersby, luring them with the mouth-watering aroma. A savvy concessionaire, Cole wanted sign work everywhere. In addition to creating brilliant signs around the outside of his grab joint, Cole had me come inside and letter the interior walls. His trailer was a high-quality unit purchased used from the Freedom Train, the traveling railroad exhibit of historic documents that toured the country during our sesquicentennial year. It was a marvel to work on and Cole was a true character.

On the high traffic corner he enjoyed at this fair, he occasionally yelled out a loud chicken clucking noise as a surprise sort of ballyhoo. From his vantage point at the grill, his constant composition of the next sandwich also qualified as a show when he supplied the girls who flanked him at either service window with the sandwiches their customers had ordered.

I qualified for those delicious sandwiches while working for him. After my work was done each evening, I got in line for dinner. On one particular night as the busy throngs milled about, Cole's wife, a dark-haired beauty, made a quick surprise gesture intended just for me. In the midst of all the frenzy, she caught my eye and reached inside her blouse. Before I knew what happened, she'd revealed one breast, and just as quickly, had my sandwich ready to go. I was stunned into silence. In the moments that passed since that brief flash, I questioned in disbelief what I had seen. Maybe it was shock value that made her do that, or quite possibly she had another motive I was too naive to recognize at the time. It was probably for the best.

Nicknames

Many of the personnel around the show had nicknames. The small man who handled the dark ride was referred to as Leprechaun. An unlikely fellow with thick glasses, often unaware of what was going on, was called Lucky. I didn't know how Spook got his nickname, but I did know the use of an alias was a way of allowing these people to simply be themselves in a safe place.

Cowboy had a perpetual smile framed by his mutton-chops mustache which emphasized his receding gumline and lengthening teeth. His straw hat made a radical sharp dip that almost concealed his mirrored sunglasses. Constant enthusiasm was no doubt a contributor to his worn-out voice.

Cowboy operated the Scrambler. This ride had three main arms with a revolving set of four tubs on the end of each arm. The undulating action made a rapidly moving tub seemingly halt near the outside edge. Then it briskly swooped and halted around again. The Scrambler was hypnotic to watch.

From his vantage point in the midst of a vast array of other rides, Cowboy's charm attracted many lone girls who sought something other than the regular offerings of the midway. When a girl hung around with a faraway contented glaze in her eyes, we all knew that Cowboy had gone above and beyond the call of duty.

One day, as I sat inside my bus parked nearby working on patterns and lettering small signs at my bench, three curious town boys came over to investigate. They crowded into the open doorway to talk to me. It was innocent enough, but Cowboy strode over from his ride to make sure no foul play was afoot.

Looking over the top of these boys, he checked on me. I gave him the signal that all was well and he went back to his duty, but this gesture by Cowboy was a clear indication of the "all for one, one for all" atmosphere of the Wade Shows that made me feel like part of a family. Concern coming from others made me feel significant, fortifying that this was the right place for me.

The First Airbrush

My companion Superdog was always at my heels as I walked toward the next appointment of a quick lettering job. Once I settled with my paints into a particular area of the show grounds, Superdog would enlarge the radius of his territory to reach eager dog lovers who couldn't resist his charm. Many times, I would look over my shoulder from the project underway to find him surrounded by a group of patrons as he gobbled up their affection.

Superdog was best described as a fluffy white smile. He was an American Eskimo Spitz, and he was just as dedicated to me as I was to him. Both friendly and attractive, he enjoyed adventures as my lifetime companion, and the turbulence of our unique lifestyle forged an unbreakable bond between us. His stature and fearlessness coupled with road wisdom learned during our relentless travel and growing up in the circus had given Superdog a confident air that prompted admiration from the show folks and patrons alike.

"Hey, Davee," came the call as I strolled through the games area.

Shelly was especially excited when I passed her ticket booth that morning. The soft plush animals framed her smiling, freckled face, at ease among the blinking lights that flanked the alleys of the Skee-Ball game. Ever the charmer, Superdog took his cue and jumped up on one of the alleys, ducking behind her ticket box to receive some affection. This dog really knows how to operate, I thought. He was happily getting scratched behind the ears while Shelly began talking a mile a minute.

"Look what I found," she bubbled. Shelly held up a T-shirt with a purple, black, and pink unicorn painted on it. "An airbrush artist is set up next to the Himalaya," she announced. "You could actually do this kind of work, Davee. You paint beautifully."

Complimented, I pondered her suggestion. Years ago, my brain had been seduced by the colorful airbrushed fantasy photos I saw in magazines and the detailed scenes on customized vans. I went out and purchased an airbrush, thinking I would easily excel with it because I was so adept with conventional paintbrushes. I soon learned otherwise. When I tried to paint with the airbrush, I discovered a mysterious device. In the end, I managed to quickly cover large areas with color, but little else.

As I looked upon Shelly's beautifully decorated T-shirt, I

struggled to figure out how the artist had negotiated the finer details. I had all this painting experience with producing carnival graphics and characters to attract attention, but when it came to the airbrush, I was dumbfounded. Discouragement had caused me to shelve the airbrush, and as it sat my puzzlement only grew. Yet, here was an opportunity to finally get my questions answered. Captivated with the results before me that had been achieved with this device, I vowed to Shelly that I would go meet the artist and use the opportunity to discover how he created such beautiful work.

Later in the day, plenty of patrons milled around the show grounds as my workday wound down. I headed over near the Himalaya and found a worn orange wooden railing delineating the airbrush artist's territory. He worked behind a long line of customers. With shaggy hair and an air of confidence, he was putting on a show while the people pressed in for a closer look. Rock and roll blended with the screams, laughter, and other noises coming from the nearby rides as he made beautiful artwork among colorful clouds of spray paint. I was amazed. Watching him in action, I witnessed this man airbrush a three-color name on a shirt in a matter of minutes. Fascinated, I studied every little motion, how he handled the airbrush, and especially how he entertained the crowd. It was thrilling to watch him work, and he even made changing colors flashy. He would spray the last of the old, unwanted color onto the support leg of his shirt easel, forming an abstract pattern with a brilliant mix of colors. The splat grew with continual air pressure as he blew the color out. While he got busy putting in the next color, gravity took over the splat and caused the excess wet paint to droop and drip. Each successive color repeated this pattern, making his easel reminiscent of a Jackson Pollock creation.

He grabbed another T-shirt and got to work on a new design. I began to recognize the procedure used to create an image. First, a faint layout in yellow roughly established the position of the name and the decorative elements that went onto the tee. Next, the artist moved rapidly to create a series of black lines with the airbrush. Letters were either big block letters outlined in black or in a solid color wavy script. Block letters were typically red on the bottom, blending into yellow on the top half with a white highlight and a sparkle. Any added cartoon figures, such as Shelly's unicorn, also began with linework. Finally, the colors filled in the areas established by the lines and a light blue outline cast a halo over any stray color.

"That's fantastic," I gushed in admiration. "You are certainly in command of that thing."

"Well, thanks," he responded over his shoulder, keeping focused on the project at hand.

Like most showmen, this artist had a nickname. When he finished the latest shirt, I leaned in to read his signature - Tuna. Being in close proximity gave me the opportunity to introduce myself.

"I'm an artist too," I shared. "But I was never able to master the airbrush. I do a lot of the sign painting and concession artwork for Wade Shows."

That caught his attention. He paused in his work to look up at me and smile.

"The airbrush is a unique painting device," he said. "I can teach you."

Warm and friendly, Tuna did not view me as his competition. He took me under his wing right then and there, happy to mentor an eager learner. Tuna began his lessons on the spot, offering tips and advice while fulfilling his remaining orders.

Over the next few weeks, Tuna and I became good friends. He gave concise instructions for developing my hand at creating clear and spectacular freehand airbrushed details with precision. Under his tutelage, I became familiar with the finer aspects of operating this simple device.

"The airbrush is just another artist's tool," he would say. "But there is one thing that is really important for a T-shirt artist, and that is to be a good mechanic. When something happens and the brush doesn't work, you have to know how to diagnose the problem and fix it rapidly. Too much lost time can spell disaster."

Tuna's personal challenge to me was to never use a frisket or any type of stencil. He knew this would force me to develop artistic finesse rather than using what he considered a crutch. I am thankful for his advice, which matched my personal philosophy already in place. I preferred to avoid devices that robbed me of the opportunity to develop eye-to-hand ability instead entering into the heavenly realm where creativity takes place.

In learning to use the airbrush in the same manner, I received a spiritual lesson. All these years my pride had kept me separated from the truth concerning this simple spray device. In that moment, I was reminded that to walk in harmony and be receptive to inspiration required an inquisitive, playful mind. Jesus said to "become like little children" (Matthew 18:1 – 5). When I assumed an attitude of humility and asked for guidance from a mentor, I received a gift that grew into the miracle of creation.

Tuna changed my life. Not only did he introduce me to the airbrush, but his example inspired my mural painting style around the carnival to continue to grow and improve. His spectacular output on a few of the Wade Shows rides impressed me. In the details of his scenery, I studied the stroke he spoke of - the fluid motion that utilized his entire body combined with the paint needle moving rapidly in and out, influencing the start and ending of each stroke. I sought to imitate what I saw when he allowed me to complete the wintertime skiing scenes he had started on the Toboggan ride.

Once I learned a minimum of techniques, I began to include airbrush effects wherever possible as part of my daily decorating regimen. Highlights, sparkles, and shadows soon became almost effortless. The airbrush grew to be a valuable ally in my arsenal, catapulting me into realms of decoration that would have remained formidable without it. Little did I know, Tuna had bestowed upon me a greater gift than I even knew at the time. In just a few years, airbrushed murals would become my specialty.

The Big One

Walking through a packed midway and darting through people on my way back to my bus, I was reminded of the path of a pinball as it bounced around the machine. Being long-legged, I stepped rapidly through the mob to get where I was going, passing the free grandstand show with Marshall Tucker, the house of mirrors, and the rickety old Wild Mouse roller coaster. The Michigan State Fair was huge and pulled out all the stops, but I preferred the quieter part of the fairgrounds where the independent food concessionaires were set up.

I had parked my VW bus under the trees in the park-like setting to accomplish my sign work. Having learned about the need to be visible a few years ago, my bright mobile sign shop lettering was emblazoned on the roof of the bus, attracting attention to my services. The concessionaires already knew the value a well-maintained station could bring with a higher rate of customers. Because of this, they would proactively seek me out, and I almost never had to ask for work.

"I want broken letters."

I glanced up from my work to see a portly man wearing a white apron and a paper hat peering in the doorway of my van. I didn't know what he meant by broken letters, and apparently that was revealed in my confused expression.

"Please walk with me," he encouraged me with his European accent, "and look at my joint."

I followed him and saw a dazzling popcorn trailer sitting prominently in front of the main indoor exhibition building. His trailer attracted lots of attention with the sheer number of twinkling lights on the marquee sign. His illuminated display was cutting edge for that time; I had never seen so many lights before. Impressed by this spectacular display, I was complimented that he wanted me to contribute to his top-shelf operation.

The owner pointed at the existing lettering across the sides and marquee. The top half was red and the bottom half blue, with three little stripes in the middle to fill the gap. This combination made an interesting effect.

"Broken letters," he answered my unspoken question from earlier. Then pointing at the rub rail light housing below the fold-down counters, he added, "This is where I want serifed letters in a circus font with a special feature on top and bottom. Red on the top third, blue on the bottom third, with fragments of those colors in the gap between, just like the others."

He knew very clearly what he wanted and that included precision. I assessed the job. The letters would be small—about three inches tall—requiring me to be extra accurate with every brush stroke and making this a particularly fussy job. The project would require more time, care, and planning than the usual single-color lettering job. Plus, because he sat in a high traffic area, the wet paint on a busy day could get fingers stuck in it. I would have to start before the crowds got here.

After mulling these thoughts over in my mind, I had an answer for him. I may have never done anything quite like this before, but that wouldn't stop me from trying my best.

"Yes, I can do that for you," I announced. "And I can start right away."

Happy with my answer, he nodded and got back to his own work. I got busy cleaning the area, snapping my lines, and using Scotch tape to delineate the tops and bottoms of the letters down the lengths of each span. Then I carefully mapped out the shapes of each letter with a grease pencil, drawing each component to make sure my letter halves would jive. Finally, I could start the painting process, first one color and then the other. The job took several hours, but when complete, I had something to be proud of. The results were stunning, and the owner was pleased.

"Excuse me, mister painter."

I looked away from my newly completed task to see a grinning man.

"I have a lettering job for you," he said.

Perfect timing. I followed him to his large concession operation, visible from almost every point on the fairgrounds. As we spoke, I learned that Butch Netterfield supported the 4-H auction by buying the champion steer every year. He asked me to letter the prizewinner's name onto the four-by-eight sign he had on display in front of the livestock area.

I got that done quickly and easily, and then he offered me something even better. Butch revealed that he had transformed his father's operation into an elite fleet of highly decorated, well-lit popcorn and lemonade concession stands. The look of his fleet of trucks and concession trailers was the epitome of the pictorial artist's, sign painter's, and pinstriper's craft all rolled into one. He invited me to paint for him during the winter in Florida. I was complimented to become his painter and looked forward to a warmer location to wait out the coldest season.

All the concessionaires were competitive, always seeking to outdo each other with their flashy signs. They constantly studied each other's stands. Among the seasoned concessionaires, I became highly regarded. When the newer concessionaires saw my skills being endorsed by the established showmen, they, too, relied on me for advice to flash up their joints. Suddenly, I was an expert.

The Allegan Circus

The final county fair for the W.G. Wade Shows summer season was a classic. Considered to be the best fair in the state, the Allegan County Fair had been around for a long time and had seen the evolution of outdoor entertainment. The Wade Shows started here three generations prior with little more than a carousel, Ferris wheel, some side shows, a couple concession stands, and a few games.

After arriving at the fairgrounds with the rest of the show, I learned the circus was also in town. I made a beeline to the infield of the trotting track with Superdog in tow. Shortly, I found the familiar sight of elephants and other exotic animals, horses and ponies, the lineup of equipment, trucks and living trailers behind the grandstand stage. Superdog could hardly contain his excitement. I was elated, too. We were instantly transported into another era, reminding us of our years trouping with the circus. It felt like home.

While admiring the animal entourage, I saw a friendly redhead caretaking the horses. Joanne Wilson and her husband, Pee Wee Pinson, handled three elephants, the horses, and other animal acts on the show. Joanne stayed busy and connected with everything and everyone around her. She was the epitome of everything I admired in a young circus performer.

"I'm a circus guy too," I volunteered as she walked by. "I used to have a six-pony liberty act."

"I'm happy to know you," she replied with a friendly smile.

"We have a six-pony liberty act also."

The next thing I knew, we were sitting on a bale of hay talking about our mutual interest in horses, the circus people we both knew, and our experiences along the road of traveling circus life. I was in heaven, and the end of the evening came all too soon.

The next day, as soon as my paintwork around the fairgrounds was completed, I raced backstage to the proximity of the animals and Joanne. My favorite after-hours place became sitting on a bale of hay in the backyard with her and her animals while we chatted about horses and dreamed of upcoming circus tours.

Our conversations took on a life of their own. Joanne was very creative, designing and making wardrobes of all kinds.

She had virtually performed every type of act at one point or another, having grown up in the circus. When we returned to talking about our amazing horses, I felt a sense of comfort being in the presence of someone who shared my passion for performing with equine partners. Our conversations rekindled my interest in performing again one day.

But like most circuses, the Allegan Grandstand Circus

performed two days at the fair, and then it was time to head out for show dates in other places. Seeing them prepare to leave after their final show filled me with a sadness mixed with gratitude for the reminder of where I came from and what I was made of. In a short amount of time, a connection had been made, and this enthusiastic redhead had established a stronghold in my heart. I was thrilled when Joanne and Pee Wee invited me to visit their home in Gibsonton during the winter.

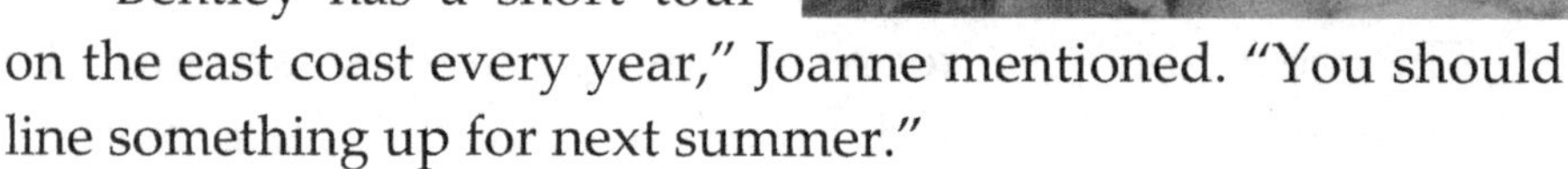

After I helped them load the livestock, I bid them adieu.

"Bentley has a short tour on the east coast every year," Joanne mentioned. "You should line something up for next summer."

"I'll be sure to check into it," I said.

As I watched them drive off the lot and disappear in the distance, I began to dream of performing with my horse again.

A Lesson in Fair History

The early morning gathering place at the Allegan County Fair was Gazella's cookhouse. The tall trailer opened up on three sides, flanked with stools and a counter on either side. An elevated grill commanded the center, and every item imaginable was on the menu. The cookhouse was one of the most rigorous enterprises on the fairgrounds, and the family who owned it worked day and night under the scrutiny of their strict patriarch.

Besides eggs sprinkled with coarse black pepper, toast, sausage, and coffee, the carnies also enjoyed the famous rapport that linked them to other showmen in this business both near and far. Many had careers that spanned decades and had witnessed the evolution of the carnival.

Because this interesting business covered the entire continent, there was always talk about what had happened at recent events in a litany of places. The diversity influenced their conversation, involving rhetoric rich with a language all their own. While listening in, I heard terms such as throw a hitch, set a roll down, clinch a deal, reave a block, buck a tub, lace a top, lay down a bead, and start a plant. It took time for me to grasp the meaning behind each of them, but I enjoyed the conversations, nonetheless.

"I heard Camel Rider couldn't turn a duke in Oklahoma City," one showman shouted over the din. "And that was after waiting two days to lay the lot. When they finally ran his lead, Camel couldn't turn a tip for the rest of the spot."

Everyone laughed at Camel Rider's misfortune. They'd all experienced similar difficulties. Such is the life of a showman.

The older well-seasoned generations also taught me about the evolution of rides.

"At the turn of the century, the first rides were simple and assembled on the ground from pieces unloaded from wagons," one of them told me.

He went on to explain, "the early versions rolled, spun, and revolved in various ways on an apparatus that went in the air.

As mechanical progress developed, new attempts to thrill passengers evolved. A major innovation occurred when showmen began mounting the central portion of a ride on wheels. They pulled this assemblage over the road, which eliminated handling and assembly of the heaviest part of the ride."

"Now all you see are trailer-mounted rides," another concluded.

These included various configurations that unfolded, hinged up, and spread out into the variety of spinning, twisting, and elevating passengers, saving tremendous time on teardown and setup at each location.

"And at one time, each ride was powered by its own gasoline engine, like the Saturn Six ride still is today," the second showman added to my lesson. "These days, most rides are powered by the central generator for the entire fair."

A remnant of that period of show biz, the Saturn Six had a prominent location on the Allegan County fairgrounds among the trees that determined the placement of certain rides. Though it was trailer mounted with six arms that hung at the sides of a central podium, it still supplied its own power source. Passengers navigated the walkway that surrounded the base to enter the multiple-passenger tubs. Once loaded in the spacecraft-style seating, the ride began turning. Using a cable-elevating mechanism inside and gunning the engine to produce centrifugal force, all six arms swung out together, and a regular rhythm commenced. As the sweeps rose higher and higher, the speed of the turning ride slowed almost to a pause and accelerated as the sweeps came down, much like how a figure skater increases her spin by holding her arms in close to her body or decreasing when her arms came up. The operator provided additional guns of the engine in rhythm with the tubs swinging out to perpetuate the elevation and experience of all the passengers. The loud engine belched out a steady stream of smoky exhaust, and at the apex of each upward swing the spinning passengers were immersed in smoke. Ah, show biz.

Farewell Fair Season

This busy county fair increased in momentum each day, with the weekend providing the biggest crowds of all. At the tail end of this profitable frenzy, a certain sadness filled the air. For the last time this summer, the ride men worked all night on the final teardown of this year's fair season. In the morning, geometric patterns of worn grass and various wagonloads among the remaining litter were all that remained.

The conclusion of the season had a different feel than all the previous Monday mornings. This time, there was no mad rush to get to the next town. Many members of the tired crew lined up at the office for their pay. Others rested against trees, on the ground, or on benches while those around them discussed plans to go different directions until the next season. Some had homes and jobs during the off season, and others would be commuting to a faraway fairground. There was a sense of loss as everyone said their goodbyes.

As I finished the last remaining sign project for the manager on his house car, or private living trailer, my concentration was interrupted by farewells from the fast friends I had made—I had been accepted as one of their own. They offered encouragement and the hope to see me next year. Then, one at a time, their trucks, rigs and cars inched their way toward the exit gate, pulling out of the drive and heading somewhere far away.

In the near-solitude of this ghost town, I watched as the last of the show equipment was moved into storage. Wade Shows wouldn't reconvene until next year, but for me, a convenient opportunity still existed nearby in Hillsdale.

Hillsdale

A different carnival company had rides set up for one final fair of the Michigan summer. Concessionaire customers who wanted more of my lettering work requested my presence, extending my work schedule into the first cold snap of autumn. By the time the fair started, I was bundled up as I painted.

On Sunday evening, I searched for a payphone. My parents were interested in what I was doing and encouraged me to call home frequently. They made sure to be home every Sunday night to wait for my call. We had worked out a system where I didn't have to worry whether I had any spare coins.

"Hello, operator. I would like to call collect, person to person, and speak to my brother John."

The operator dialed the number I gave her. When the phone rang on the other end, my mother answered.

"Hello," she said.

"Excuse me, ma'am," the operator began. "I have a collect

person-to-person call for John."

"Oh dear, John isn't here right now," Mother would say. "But he will be back soon. Could you please give me the number so I can have him call when he gets back?"

The operator would comply, providing the number of the payphone I was calling from. A few moments later, my parents called me back on their dime without the added expense of a collect call. My dad often did most of the talking.

"Hello, David," he would say excitedly. "Where are you and what on earth are you doing?"

"I'm at the Hillsdale County Fair in Michigan," I responded. "My sign painting business is doing great!"

Dad was eager to hear about my latest project, interesting occurrences on the job, curious aspects about show business, and my aspirations for the future. He had outgrown his role as the condemning parent of my youth I could never satisfy. These days, he demonstrated pride in my willingness to take risks and have them pay off. With artistic skills himself, Dad realized through my example that he could also paint signs to benefit his community in the Ozarks. Sharing a love for adventure, he was especially interested in the art I created for the carnival, living vicariously through my stories. Dad had never pursued some of his dreams due to the belief that he needed to make a positive impression as a professional. In boyhood, he'd secretly wanted to run away and join the circus. The only difference between him and me was that I had actually pursued my dream. In doing so, I gave him an outlet.

While fairgoers were seduced into buying or participating at any number of joints, my focus was on the paint. I already understood the importance of a sign being legible, having good critical distance, and conveying the right message at a glance to be successful. Since this show was different from the ones I had been around all summer, I could use my critical eye to analyze the new signs and artwork from other sources and learn from them.

While walking around the Hillsdale fairgrounds, I studied the composition, technique, combination of colors, and images of the festive art as inspiration for my own work. A fun house had been completely airbrushed by another artist who did an overall admirable job. He used bright colors for his depictions of faces and figures emblazoned across the front.

As I discerned how the artist had accomplished this feat, I also noticed something I didn't like that influenced my carnival artwork from that point on. After creating the large color shapes over the entire front, the artist had taken his airbrush and made it look cartoonish. The amount of black he used diminished the brilliance of the colors.

I never liked black. Each color had a specific meaning and an appropriate use. Black was not a good color for food signs. The lifeless, all-consuming hue reflected nothing. When my opportunities for airbrushing scenery began, I had started using brown for my outlines to soften them. Dark blue or purple was also effective in keeping the brilliance of the other colors intact. In later years, I would come across more recent work by this same artist and noticed he adopted my practice of using brown instead. I was flattered.

With the last few lettering projects at the Hillsdale Fair completed, the time came to pause. Superdog and I drove to Clarklake to share tales of our adventures with Hayes. In the comfort of his living room, I told him about my plans for the future as a show painter and the opportunity to paint for an elite concessionaire in the Sunshine State after Christmas. I also expressed how I would equip my new horse trailer to live in while on the road and begin regular practice with my horse. Pride evident in my mentor's face, Hayes beamed at me.

Chapter 3
Relativity

"Call it a clan, call it a network, call it a tribe, call it a family: Whatever you call it, whoever you are, you need one."
—Jane Howard

A Different Reception

My original friend, my little sister, was getting married. I hadn't seen Paula since our summer together at the circus. Now I was being invited to join the entire family for her wedding.

Upon arrival in St. Louis where the groom's family lived, I discovered this would be a union in a different religion than we had grown up in. The grand affair would occur at the Immaculate Conception Church. Prior to the event, those of us in the wedding party received specific instructions in regard to our participation, a moment that was incredibly revealing about the man she was about to marry.

"Since you come from an inferior religion to ours," Chris spewed forth, "you will only have an incidental role to play in the ceremony."

As another reminder of the shame and unfounded rejection received as a child, my response to his smug superiority and self-centered prejudice was angry withdrawal—the very method my sister and I adopted for survival in our frustrating childhood. I picked up the baton of resentment for his narcissistic inconsideration and stomped out of the rehearsal. Down the street, I found a friendly bar where the bartender's magic soothed my outrage.

I had been unfairly judged once again, this time by the "good church man." Chris' animosity set the tone for the eternal lack of relationship between us going forward. Perhaps the outburst had been orchestrated by his family, or maybe his church actually taught such behavior. Either way, he must not admire anything that Jesus exampled—where was the love, acceptance, and tolerance for others? Whatever the cause, my perception of Chris was firmly established from our very first meeting, and it became virtually impossible to see a single admirable quality in him ever afterward.

I remained alone in my frustration as an outsider in my own expanding family; it wasn't fair. Paula never spoke up on my behalf, and our subsequent separation spanned years. The gap became a chasm. Perhaps she thought turning her back on her family of origin was a gesture that would demonstrate dedication to her new husband and his self-centered ways, promoting connection in their marriage. All I knew was our relationship was growing colder by the day.

It was no surprise when I learned through Mom that Paula and Chris had settled in St. Louis. Chris was a hardworking, corporate-minded chemist with Monsanto, and Paula was free to work at home with her craft projects. Her job was to write stories and produce children. Michael was the first; then came David.

The few times I passed through St. Louis, my sister and her husband were not warm to me. I was considered an outsider of the wrong religion and not invited to holiday meals. Love, if it still existed, went unspoken.

In contrast with the visits to my sister's home, my arrival in Sulphur Springs was always a festive occasion. Unlike Chris and Paula, my parents and the many friends I made in the Ozarks were glad to see me, welcoming me with open arms.

Dad said I was home just in time; he wanted to get the roof sheeted before winter. It didn't take long for my schedule to become full from morning till night. We started each day listening to the early morning teachings of Father Janisch.

Although I was reluctant about the religion of the church, most of the spiritual teachings taking place at Shiloh made sense. The ongoing study of an enlightening book called A Course in Miracles augmented the spiritual path of everyone at the commune. The book claimed the two basic thought systems consisted of perception and knowledge, and reminded the reader that perception is not always based on fact. As I became familiar with this concept, it introduced a dramatic shift in perspective that would benefit the student, lifting me above my usual way of seeing things to see them in a new way with an emphasis on love.

After the morning study concluded, we enjoyed an enormous breakfast before launching into the construction, which easily filled the remainder of the day. What had been a hole in the ground with concrete forms a year ago was now a skeleton of a house being framed up. My dad's design involved two-by-six studs to allow for thick foam insulation and an extended eave overhang to relieve the relentless effect of the sun on the exterior that would become brick veneer.

While there, the horse trailer I'd ordered was finally ready for pickup. Having a home base allowed for the opportunity to build features inside the living quarters for my travels. Soon I had built a shower stall, overhead cabinets, sink, desk, and closet. I was ready for the road more than ever before.

New Wardrobe

The costumes that had worked for my liberty act presentations were not sophisticated enough now that my taste had developed through the riding community in Michigan. I began to visualize elegant costumes with a splash of circus that went beyond the classic jodhpurs and jackets of the dressage community. The wardrobe I admired on the other performers was decorated with sequins or glass stones. The reflective surfaces sparkled magnificently, but applying the multitude of small items was labor intensive and difficult to wash. As an alternative, I sought fabric with a metallic-content thread called brocade. This fabric sparkled all by itself without requiring the meticulous sewing of sequins. It was also easier to keep clean, but it was difficult to find. Specialty fabrics were best found in large cities.

Although my visit with my sister wasn't as pleasant as I had hoped, one good thing that had come from my recent trip through St. Louis was the ability to go downtown to the garment district in search of my object of desire. I found some brocade in a dramatic emerald green with an ivory and silver pattern that suited me just right. Purchasing several yards of the stunning fabric, I could already envision the beautiful circus wardrobe it would make.

Shortly after, I pulled out my sketchbook and became busy drawing a variety of designs for my wardrobe. Once I settled on my favorite ones, I just needed someone to make them come to life. Fortunately, while I was visiting my parents in the Ozarks, a lady in town told me of a seamstress who lived nearby, just across the state line.

I drove to her home in Oklahoma and found her mobile

home situated next to a wooded area. Walking up the wooden steps past the dogs, I knocked at the door. When it swung open, I was greeted by a tall, frail blond.

"You must be Dave," she said with a smile. "Please come in."

Zella's home was full of earthly delights—Schlotzly mirrored artworks, statuesque formal-attired dolls staring headlong into space, sturdy wooden furniture, and delicate glassware displayed in a handsome hutch. She also had a gaggle of children, who she bade me to sit with at the dining room table.

The kids were fascinated by my circus involvement, and they all became the perfect listeners as I described my ideas for new horse-riding costumes. Zella welcomed my unusual requests, providing the perfect setting for my imagination to flourish. In this warm environment, I showed her the brocade and my sketchbook.

Armed with my ideas, measurements, and the fabric, Zella referred to the many patterns she had in inventory and came up with a plan. The short drive into Oklahoma to check in on Zella's progress became a regular respite from the construction taking place at my parents' home. Over the next few weeks, she would carefully tailor beautiful jackets, matching vests, and trousers that incorporated the stunning shapes applied from my drawings. With Zella's sewing abilities and my designs, we

soon had a diverse new wardrobe with pressed creases and accurate seams. A perfect fit resulted from meticulous measuring and stitching. Zella had gone beyond all my expectations and even incorporated matching fabric covered buttons, reversible vests, and other innovative inclusions.

Besides the business talk, I had found a new friend in Zella. I enjoyed the time spent with her and her family. Her eldest son, Von, was a talented mechanic who ran the exhaust shop in Southwest City. Von was always drawing trucks. Knowing I could appreciate his work as an artist, he showed me sheets of school paper with his drawings on them. One particularly well done drawing displayed a semitruck going over a bridge while another appeared beneath. Both trucks were rendered in ballpoint pen, filled with minute details including speed lines that depicted motion and billowing smoke from the exhaust pipes. It was a wonder to behold.

Von came to mind not long after when my dad found a three-quarter ton Dodge pickup truck. Dad claimed its purchase was to haul block and supplies for his home-building project, but I later found out that he'd had me in mind from the start. Although he initially thought my career with the circus and carnival was silly, Dad gradually began to admire my having the guts to pursue my passion. He enjoyed using his gifts to do what he could to help me, and Dad wanted me to use the truck to haul my new horse trailer. The only problem was, while preparing the Dodge to pull my gooseneck horse trailer, I realized the best place to carry the spare tire would be over the cab, but I would need help achieving this vision. Luckily, the summer around the various carnival ride devices had inspired me when I'd observed the clever ways and machines carnival showmen used accomplished various mechanical feats. I was able to come up with the idea for constructing my tire rack, but its construction required talent I didn't have.

I drew my concept one evening while sitting at Zel's dining room table and gave it to Von, the perfect person to co-create this vision. I wanted the rack to span the toolbox mounted behind the cab in the bed and rise to a platform to support the tire being held over the cab, along with mounts for twin CB antennas. The rack would also have a streamlined feature to slice the wind in front of the tire. As I showed my vision to Von, he saw perfection in my strategy, and we came up with a plan to make it out of tubular steel.

I drove the Dodge into the service bay of the exhaust shop in Southwest City. Von immediately began bending exhaust tubing into the shape of a roll bar and making the two legs that would span the toolbox. We then had a platform for the spare tire. A minimum of welding secured these pieces together. Then he added flat plates at the base to secure it to the bed with bolts. The next part was the wind foil/deck pieces. As I watched Von study my sketch and perform silent mental calculations, an expression of confidence came over his face. He patiently bent the exhaust tubing to my specifications, fabricating one-half of the upper piece. When he rounded the second piece of tubing with specific degree bends in exact places, he made a mirror image of the first piece. He then added stretch in the tube to allow for overlap. When completed, the two halves fit together perfectly. Finally, a flat piece of sheet metal was fastened to the face, strengthened due to the curve. With the rack finished, my tire carrier/wind deflector just needed paint and installation.

As I watched all this happen, I couldn't deny there was a spark of providence at work in my life. I recognized the pattern of first having an idea and then meeting the right person to help make it reality. The beautiful costumes, the Dodge truck, and now the tire rack were all evidence of something divine taking place. As I began to grow in understanding, I also began to have a greater appreciation for my connections. I was learning to entrust my path to the divine that was greater than I am.

Ozark Signs

As I traveled into any region, I always made it a habit to observe signs and assess the level of ability of the local sign painters. Back in those days, all sign work was hand painted. The discipline of making a visual assessment learned as an apprentice allowed me to critique the advertising nuance that could always be improved upon. With my discerning eye, I studied the hand-lettered output on display at the various businesses and on the delivery trucks while in the Ozarks. The Sulphur Springs post office had some handsome Roman letters with outlines and a drop shadow on the large picture window signed by the artist Smitty. I found out later he was a lettering legend based in Wichita. Smitty traveled a large area to hustle sign work and create his well-trained lettering output. I also found out that his hobby was skydiving, and at eighty years old he set a record for jumps. That was proof enough that sign painters were crazy characters.

Opposite to Smitty's skilled work, another sign painter based in Anderson, Missouri had not developed much more than a casual quick-stroke style of plug lettering. His crude work filled the region as well, allowing me to recognize my artistic abilities were much more similar in talent to Smitty, which proved that I had a lot to offer this community.

Members of the Shiloh commune were delighted to have an accomplished sign painter in their midst. With my mother working in the Shiloh office, the commune commissioned me to paint their logo on the glass of the main entry doors. And, through the contacts my dad made in the surrounding area, I also lettered signs for a used-car lot in Gravette. Completing that job led to another at an auto-auction barn in Oklahoma. I also met the lady from State Line Liquor, who had me climb up on the roof and letter the large sign mounted there.

Despite the plethora of opportunity here, I knew there was a limited supply that would eventually run out in this remote and sparsely populated region. Shiloh would not be able to support a full-time sign painter forever. That was why itinerate sign men were the ones who left their mark in this area, and that was what I was on my way to becoming.

Holiday Lights

As the various projects in the Ozarks all made progress, the holidays loomed on the horizon. Christmas had always been a special time for my dad. He started to decorate as a child in an effort to impress his own difficult-to-please dad, and decorating with lights became an annual tradition. Unfortunately, with my parents' home currently under construction and living in a cramped situation, Dad didn't have a place of his own to decorate this year. Not to be hindered from carrying on his tradition, he took his collection of Christmas lights and hand-built nativity scene to the city park. There, my dad transformed the gazebo into a giant ornament, installed his nativity scene in front of city hall, and decked out various picnic shelters with colorful lights. He'd even fashioned a large twelve-foot wooden star with lights fastened upon it, and after he'd decorated the park below, he drove up a rugged gravel road with his creation strapped to the top of his car. He added lights high up on the bluff and stood his handiwork up in a clearing that made his Christmas star visible for miles.

Due to his love for the birth of our savior, Dad's efforts made this holiday as special as everything else around him, using his creative flair for everyone's enjoyment. The result of his industry was a festive sight for the traveler driving on the highway that sliced through the middle of this small town.

When Christmas Day arrived, Mom, Dad, and I enjoyed a special musical program in Shiloh, in which my mother sang. The worship service included the usual spiritual reflection on the reason for the season, and afterward we happily indulged in a spread of wonderful food.

When the community celebrations ended, we returned to my parents' temporary home. Because the compromised quarters made a full-blown gift exchange difficult, our swap was quite simple. Still, it was magical just looking into my dad's sparkling eyes full of pure joy for the Christmas holiday.

Netterfield's

Butch Netterfield loved signs. With the advent of the spectacular marquee signs on top of concession trailers, Butch took it a step further. His trailers sported flashy fold-up reclining clowns holding candy apples, cotton candy, and boxes of popcorn. There was even a fleet of flags flapping high over these illuminated signs, but he was looking for even more ways to spice it up.

Having met during fair season, Butch had settled on the perfect idea and requested that I come paint for him after the holidays. The winter quarters of what may easily qualify as the most elite, if not the largest, of the carnival concession operations could be found in Land O' Lakes, Florida. This would be the perfect destination to escape the cold winter, and it seemed like I might be there long enough to really enjoy it. Netterfield's Popcorn & Lemonade had a fleet of forty concession trailers with enough trucks to pull all of them, and Butch wanted every square inch of each trailer covered with lettering, decoration, and images of all kinds. I could hardly wait to get there.

The conclusion of the holiday festivities coincided with my rig being ready to make the trip to Florida to fulfill Butch Netterfield's big request. The Dodge was now equipped with my custom spare tire rack and a fifth-wheel hitch installed in the bed. My compact living quarters in the new horse trailer promised privacy and comfort on the road, although I would be leaving Bingo pastured under my folks' care during this maiden voyage. I attached my VW bus with all my painting equipment to the back, and then I was ready to roll.

My parents said adieu to Superdog, gave me a hug, and thanked me for all my help. Superdog loaded up in the seat beside me as we waved one more farewell before starting the truck. Then we headed south.

As I began the lengthy journey from Shiloh to Netterfield's winter quarters, I savored the thought of what I had become. Like a piano player, my fluency and finesse with a brush improved with every lettering task, bringing me another inch closer to mastery. Because the field of hand-painted decoration was so vast, there would always be another hurdle to jump and a new challenge to attempt, just like the airbrush. With my eyes open for alternate techniques or concept styles and armed with a growth mindset, nothing could stop me from becoming the best show painter east of the Mississippi.

As the miles passed beneath the tires of my new truck, my thoughts drifted to my great-grandfather, Otto Prosche, a fine artist trained in Germany.

A hundred years prior, Otto led a crew of journeymen painters in decorating the interiors of the Loews Theatres and painting murals in various municipal buildings. Because the jobs were spread in a patchwork of cities, his was an itinerate career just like mine. Back in those days, everyone traveled by train. Otto's crew journeyed to the job sites and wrestled the equipment out of the baggage car and onto a gilly wagon, then over to the theater from there.

Their lodging in each destination was in the local hotel, and sometimes the living situation would be less than admirable. Mother would laugh whenever sharing the story of Otto's complaints to one such hotel clerk about bed bugs.

"That's quite impossible sir," the clerk exclaimed. "The man who uses that bed in the afternoon doesn't complain about bed bugs."

Nonetheless, Otto's crew prevailed, and the artwork that survived to this day in those majestic theaters was testimony enough of their determination, dedication, and talent. I was filled with awe whenever I explored those hallowed halls still covered with floral décor, Victorian scrollwork, and the trompe l'oeil—effects that fooled the eye by suggesting a reality that wasn't there. Entertaining with a vastness that brought the outside in and touched the heart, Otto enjoyed including references to the forest, waterfalls, cloud formations, and the moon and stars.

Oh, how I yearned to create such awe with a brush and a few colors in the same manner as my great-grandfather. Motoring down the highway on my way to the mystery that awaited in a facet of show business, I knew my great-grandfather would be smiling down on me. Following in his footsteps, I was headed in the right direction.

As the highway smoothed out between palm and pine trees, Superdog intuited our destination was close. He perked up as I rounded the last bend, revealing the festive fleet in a picturesque setting. A multitude of concession trailers, travel trailers, and stock trucks with bunks inside were parked in neat rows surrounding a steel shop building. The multi-acre compound was situated by a pristine lake, encompassed with cypress trees with Spanish moss. I was fortunate enough to have a spot for the winter in this rolling abundance.

As soon as I landed among all the activity, the foreman supervised parking my rig in the lineup and helped me hook up to electricity. Colt was known to keep the crew busy, often creating trivial tasks just to keep them out of trouble. He used strict discipline to ensure they would be there when they were needed. His motto was, "If you've got time to lean, you've got time to clean." I would be no exception. Once my trailer was set up, Colt showed me the first project that we had to get knocked out in a hurry.

During the first few days after arriving, I found my routine. One at a time, the trailers were backed into the shop where five crew members cleaned it inside and out. After that was completed, they would zoom off to perform other duties as needed, including maintenance on trucks, moving inventory, adding new supplies to the preparation areas, and fabricating and repairing popcorn and lemonade signs. No matter what, Colt made sure they kept busy.

Once Colt's crew hurried off to the next project, the joint was ready for my touch. As I became familiar with the variety of disciplines and effects that this fleet needed and how to work in harmony with the crew, I used the mentality of the traveling showman to make my operation more efficient. While the crew cleaned and repaired, I made paper patterns to facilitate the uniformity and precision required for a quality job. I knew Butch would want delicate lettering and detailed pictorial work, so while preparing these patterns, I envisioned the colors and details to include for a stunning final product.

I had become used to making do with whatever situation I was in. On the road, the occasional rainy day often meant a change in plans. At Netterfield's, I was honored to have a dedicated place to organize my gear. With my paint kit and supplies set up in one corner of the shop, my work area was safe and dry no matter the weather.

To top it all off, Butch was a brassy, fun-loving showman as tall as I was, although a little plumper. Having grown up in this tough business, he used a tongue-in-cheek style of encouragement, mixed with clever observations of the many interactions he had with the vast network of relationships connected to this operation. The occasional turbulence in the company was quickly and quietly handled, and overall, things moved smoothly among the crew. It felt incredibly special to be part of such an elite operation.

Because Butch loved neon, he made a lot of his own electric signs. While I painted all day in the shop, he was busy fabricating new neon signs with his glass-tube bending apparatus upstairs. The occasional glimpse of these techniques fascinated me as I witnessed the magical creation of these delicate signs.

First, glass tubes were carefully heated over a propane flame. To prevent the collapse of the soft tube, while bending the molten glass the inside pressure of the air was maintained through a rubber hose that went into Butch's mouth. As another section of the glass was softened, it could then be bent into the desired shape.

I stayed in the shop full-time decorating the next of what seemed to be an endless stream of joint trailers. By late January, they started taking these trailers to the fairgrounds to get ready for the state fair. I continued my relentless routine of painting all day while they were gone.

By the time the fair started, everyone was away working the carnivals and I had the shop and property all to myself. During this time, I designed a new four-by-eight sign for a Michigan summertime fair, the same fair where Butch's dad had started this business by selling peanuts. My new sign boasted the antique peanut roaster still in use.

With that completed, my workday wound down on the now-quiet homestead. I often found myself at the edge of the lake enjoying the waning light, but on this particular night, I wasn't alone. In the distance, a kid was casting his fishing line from a small boat. He plopped his bait into the water at various locations around the lake, occasionally catching a small bass that he would release. I was fascinated. When he later returned to the dock, I started up a conversation. Although the Netterfields had no children, Scotty informed me they treated Colt and his girlfriend, Kim, like family. As Kim's younger brother, Scotty was also welcomed into their circle. Having grown up around the carnival, the preteen radiated a smart-aleck persona, referring to the cronies in the yard by their showmen nicknames, including Hollywood, Cowboy, Einstein, and the like. Motioning to the one-man bass boat, Scotty said, "Don't tell my sister, but I come for the fishing."

I laughed and asked, "Think you could teach me?"

Scotty happily confided to me his strategy. "As I drift around the lake, I just look for a likely location that a bass would be hiding—lily pads or a shady spot under an oak tree or a dock where an insect might drop from."

He went on to explain that he wanted his rubber worm to look natural so the fish would take the bait, literally.

"You can use my gear and take the little boat out if you want," Scotty offered.

I eagerly accepted, and soon found myself quite often in the little battery-powered boat after work. Attempting to master this peaceful new hobby, I surveyed the likely places that a bass might linger, just as Scotty had advised, and attempted to plop that worm in proximity of a hungry fish.

One evening while zigzagging around the perimeter of the lake seeking to entice a bass, I cast my bait into a one such location. The line ended up lying across the corner of the dock, so I began reeling the bait back in to try casting again. But when my worm went across the dock, a lurking cat ran down the length of the dock and pounced on it.

"Oh no!" I said, alarmed. The last thing I wanted was to hook a cat.

I stopped reeling, instead guiding the boat adjacent to the dock to safely retrieve my hook and bait. Gently taking the worm away from the cat, I reboarded the little boat. To my surprise, the curious and friendly cat jumped in with me. I guess I had a fishing companion. He was quite content to watch me continue to plop my worm into other likely places on our lazy tour around the lake. With my lucky charm by my side, I finally got a hit, feeling a spike of adrenaline. After a brief struggle, I hoisted a small hand-sized bass out of the water. Nothing matched the thrill I felt in that moment of succeeding in a new skill.

Motoring back across the lake to the dock where the cat had joined me, my feline friend was just as engaged as I was in watching the fish flopping on the floor of the boat. From alongside the dock, I pitched the fish way up on the lawn. My little good luck charm wasted no time in jumping back onto the land and pouncing on his meal. Who would have guessed I'd go fishing and catch a cat?

Show Town

Gibsonton, known locally as Gibtown, was the notorious home for showmen of all kinds. A sun-bleached hamlet along the gulf coast south of the Tampa shipping ports and delineated to the north by the Alafia River, what made Gibtown so special was its zoning codes apropos for the exotic and unusual animals, unique equipment, and exciting outdoor activities of showmen. Best of all, it was less than an hour away.

When I finally got all forty of Netterfield's Popcorn & Lemonade concession trailers decorated and ready to roll, I couldn't help but want to satisfy my curiosity about this town I had only heard about. I had enjoyed my experience around Glenn and Red's show in Michigan. I thought perhaps I could meet other showmen just as wonderful. Plus, I had been invited to visit Joanne who lived nearby. I hadn't seen her since the Allegan circus.

Traveling south from Tampa, I saw the Giant's Camp while crossing the bridge—a trailer park, marina, and restaurant owned by a real sideshow giant. I drove around and surveyed the area, much like how I had always investigated town after town as a circus man. But here, the neighborhoods had unusual features unlike any town I had ever been to before.

Yards were filled with rides under repair, game trailers parked in rows, and travel trailers in abundance. The people here swallowed swords, ate fire, and sent tigers jumping through flaming hoops. A visitor was just as likely to catch sight of elephants and camels as they were horses or cows. At night, you could even hear the occasional roar of a lion or tiger. It was in this exciting setting where I would seek out sign work while visiting with my circus friend, Joanne.

I made my way through the grid of streets among the homes of these oddities, finding the destination where another job waited—two ticket boxes that needed lettering. I saw my customer working in a yard filled with concession trailers. Bill waved to me and pointed to the open door on the metal shop building where he built custom equipment.

"There they are," he said when I rolled my window down. "The show owner wants bold red lettering with a gold accent."

"I can definitely do that," I assured him.

Parking my rig, I went to the shop to study his fabrication handiwork while Superdog investigated the yard. After measuring the available space between the lateral rows of lightbulbs on the marquee area, I made a paper pattern with my design of serifed Roman letters and playful negative shapes. Once the pattern was ready, I perforated the paper to transfer the design. Bill came in and made idle conversation as he watched.

"My son just installed a thirty-gallon water heater in his living quarters."

I could only glance at his clean-cut, chiseled face with thick gray hair on top while I worked; I needed to focus or the pattern wouldn't be set right. I secretly wished Bill would get back to his own work so I could focus on the task at hand, but no such luck.

"Oh yeah?" I said, not really caring.

"Yep," he said, chortling. "That way he can take long showers with his girlfriend."

"Hey," Bill said at the end of my workday. "I completely forgot what we agreed upon. I only collected this much from my customer for you."

Despite his words, he certainly didn't look remorseful or ashamed when he handed me the compromised amount. My heart sank. I had been warned about working for sly carnies by my circus friends, but my experience with the Michigan showmen had proven contrary to their words, so I had shrugged it off. Unluckily for me, Bill was happy to example what their warning was about. While opportunities for paintwork in the carnival were plentiful, so was the stereotypical attitude of sordid showmen screwing one another with every transaction. Sometimes these stealthy showmen used a clever ploy to get more from an agreement. Other times they just lied.

Sadly, not many showmen were of Red and Glenn's caliber, and I was not yet adept enough to hold my ground against con men such as Bill. I chose to leave the swindling to other show painters, taking my compromised payment and a hard-learned lesson with it. When I left Gibtown behind, I'd bring with me a new resolve to be more selective about who I agreed to paint for going forward.

Before saying farewell to this swindling town, I wanted to say hello to my special circus friends with an ennobling tack. I drove to the address I had been given the previous summer. When I found the wintertime home of Joanne and Pee Wee, I saw several adjacent lots filled with a fleet of travel trailers and ample room for aerial rigging, construction projects, and portable stables. It was there that I would meet the entire Wilson family.

"Welcome, Dave," Joanne said, radiating a smile that made the Cheshire Cat wax pale in comparison. "I'm glad to see you."

Her warmth melted away the ice that had formed on my heart after the interaction with Bill.

"Joanne, you're a sight for sore eyes!" I said honestly.

"Pee Wee is up helping Bill with his perch rigging." She gestured toward the aerial apparatus standing in the yard.

"They'll be done soon."

I involuntarily flinched at the name Bill, though thankfully she was referring to a different Bill.

"Dad just got back from the feed store," she added as she led the way. "Come on. Let me introduce you."

As I followed Joanne, her dad entered our proximity. Dime was short in stature, confident as a bantam, and enjoyed the constant rapport taking place with everyone in his family. He'd raised five beautiful redheads with his wife, all of whom became fantastic performers with virtually every circus specialty. Dime's language and mannerisms accumulated from the horse-drawn wagon era of showbiz reminded me of Brownie Silverlake. He came from the days when everyone on the show doubled in brass—after performing their acts, they would return to play an instrument in the band.

"Dave, nice to meet you." Looking at his daughter, he then drawled, "Sorry I took so long; I bet you thought I blew the arrows." Dime grimaced. "I had to red light that male goat."

After the standard greetings, Joanne continued to lead me to our destination.

"I'm real pleased with the little dog I rescued from the pound," she confided. "I want you to see him. I just love his positive attitude. He's going in my dog act." Joanne beamed as we walked. "He took right to being on his hind legs and it didn't take much to get a backward somersault out of him, either!"

As we neared her animal trailer, the eager barking of her dogs eliminated any doubt of the love that resided in this place. She let her latest acquisition out of his kennel and sent him to sit at attention on one of the pedestals in the practice ring.

"Seat, Roscoe," she commanded.

I settled onto my favorite place, a bale of hay waiting in position to be tonight's dinner for the show horses, ponies, goats, and llama. With one eye on her new dog, Joanne filled me in on some of the more remarkable incidents that had taken place on tour since I'd seen her last summer.

"Hubert booked a new Chinese acrobatic act that leaps through hoops of knives for Kansas City. Pretty flashy, too. Then, later in Montreal, Hugino broke his arm during the second shot out of the cannon, and his wife, a school teacher with no circus experience at all, stepped up to do the cannon leap for the rest of the ten-day run."

"You don't say!" My eyes widened at the thrilling and sometimes comical details of Joanne's stories. She moved to the center of the ring, nodding. "Oh! And here's something interesting—while socializing with the teeter board troupe backstage, I found out that back in Hungary, a kinker is called a spanglepratz."

Catching the attention of her new canine protégé, Joanne said, "Roscoe, come here." She gestured with her position in the ring and the little dog leaped into her proximity. "Up!" Her arms made a specific signal and Roscoe stretched up to bounce along on his hind legs. When his posture became perfect, she moved quickly toward him with an exaggerated arm movement and a crisp command, "Jump!"

I watched in amazement. The little guy jumped up in the air and bent backward away from her pose to turn a complete somersault.

"That's amazing, Joanne!"

My applause was augmented by other observant family members who knew to get the new dog used to audience noises. Joanne's accomplishment validated the use of genuine regard to enroll the animal and reflected true love. It was certainly a sight to behold the bond between a woman and her performing dog.

The friendly nature of Joanne and her family became more than just a safe haven in this town of extremes. Their example fired me up to resume the aspect of my career that, up until now, had lain dormant. I would once again perform in the circus, this time with my horse, Bingo. While I interacted with the talented Wilson family, I began to compose a plan. As if reading my mind, Joanne reminded me what she had mentioned last summer.

"Why don't you work for Bentley Bros.?" she suggested. "They have a short circus tour you could work this summer."

"I think I just might," I confirmed.

Determined to find out more about this opportunity, I would create a strategy to resume my performing career before I headed north to begin another season painting for the carnival. But for now, it was time to return to Arkansas, where I could check in on my parents' progress on their home, Zella's progress with my fresh circus costumes, and practice with my horse in preparation for the upcoming season that just might include a circus.

Getting Ready

Reuniting with my parents in the early spring became a festive time of rejuvenation. The flowering dogwood and redbud trees announced the birth of another season, and with it came changes in this ample commune called Shiloh. We celebrated new growth in more ways than one. Some of my friends had moved away, new ones arrived, people had died, and children had been born. The construction site of my parents' new home revealed evidence of much progress since I'd left for Florida and experienced my own growth.

When it became my turn to share, my ardent friends enjoyed my stories about my recent accomplishments. As I voiced a plethora of show business anecdotes, I noticed my dad was especially eager to learn all about my adventures. By this time, he had grown used to my itinerate lifestyle, revealing the secret desire he'd also once had of running away with the circus. I discussed my plans to prepare for a short tour performing with my circus horse after a triumphant return as a show painter for the W.G. Wade Shows. It was then that my dad surprised me with a request.

"I purchased a VW bus," he announced with a gleam in his eye.

Long ago, Dad had earned the nickname Speedy during his Army Air Corps years by combining a motorcycle and a two-day pass and traveling in a different direction every time. In the wake of my creativity, he recognized our shared passion for travel and adventure. Living a different lifestyle these days, Dad was eager for a vacation from building his home and told me he'd already equipped his new bus with a bunk. All he needed now was a thrilling adventure with his wandering son who lived an interesting life he'd only ever dreamed of.

"Do you think I could accompany you later this summer on the fair circuit in Michigan? I'd love to witness what you do with paint."

Beyond moved, I readily accepted. We had never connected on such a deep level before, and I was excited to share my unique lifestyle with him.

Chapter 4

Switching Gears

"The purpose of art is washing the dust of daily life off our souls."
—Picasso

Visual Coup

In the late spring, I drove from the Ozarks to Michigan to resume my role as show painter for the W.G. Wade Shows. The return to the Midwest felt like going home. Although the fair circuit wouldn't begin until summer, I had plenty of work to complete before then, and I could hardly wait for my dad to join me on the road later in the summer.

After the long trek with Bingo loaded in the horse trailer this time, my first stop was at the riding stable. My horse would spend the summer there, enabling us to resume our riding lessons and prepare us to perform in the circus. The Dodge and horse trailer would stay there, too.

Meanwhile, Superdog and I would work and live out of my VW bus.

Once I got Bingo settled in, Superdog and I went to visit a few friendly faces in Clarklake before my painting projects began. Hayes was always excited about my show business aspirations, and, as usual, he was eager to hear all about the faraway places I had seen since our last visit. I also stopped by the Beach Bar where my sign painting career had begun. The staff was always glad to see me, especially my friend, Jana. She even appreciated my early sign painting efforts, observing as I sat near the back and lettered the very signs that now adorned the place.

After catching up on my newly enhanced talents, Jana said, "Make sure to stop by and meet my stepdad. He restores antique fire engines."

I had passion for all things creative, and with her stepdad's wealth of information about decorative specialties, Jana had the foresight to connect us. She knew I would find his wisdom useful on my career path. His background with a multitude of skills would open my eyes to a vast new world of possibilities. Excited for the opportunity, I thanked my friend and assured her that I would go meet him.

I spent that evening preparing my portfolio with eight-by-ten photos of carnival equipment and concession trailers I had painted for the showmen, along with pen-and-ink designs for logos and signs. I was especially proud of the elaborate scrollwork, fancy lettering, and depiction of brass pipes I had painted on the old calliope truck last spring. I hoped Jana's stepfather would be impressed.

The next day, I found the curious home built into a hill, with a large cottonwood tree alongside. The only external indication about the curious contents within was an oval badge next to the door about the size of a loaf of bread. It was a relief depiction of two hands grasping one another covered in gold leaf to visually express the name "Hand in Hand." I went up the three steps to the entrance and knocked on the door.

A becoming woman who I recognized as Jana's mother greeted me.

"Can I help you?" she asked.

"My name's Dave. I'm a friend of Jana's and a sign painter." I introduced myself. "Jana recommended I meet Ken."

Jana's mom smiled and invited me to come inside. I entered the interior of what was once a one-room schoolhouse and discovered interesting artifacts spread throughout the home. Ken's collection of old firefighting relics and assemblage of components into useable curiosities gave the space a fascinating museum-like vibe.

As we waited for Ken to come upstairs, I received an orientation about some of the objects on display from my gracious host. One hefty wooden piece sported old gauges, elongated period lightbulbs, and a pair of large brass knobs elevated on shafts. This masterpiece had been lovingly crafted from old parts as a prop for the Frankenstein play directed by Ken's other stepdaughter, Gail. The device actually worked, producing eerie static electricity lightning bolts between the orbs.

Jana's mom showed me other inventions that fit with the antique furniture, leather bucket brigade buckets, firefighter helmets, old engraver's nameplates, and heavily carved frames with images of steam-pumper wagons and ladder trucks. One particularly curious piece of adapted furniture sported several innovative lighting effects from the fire engines of long ago. Arranged like a clock face, Ken had wired each of the examples in such a way that, when activated, the old clockwork mechanism sent a signal into each circuit in sequence. They would then begin their excited blinking, flashing, and signaling. In one case, a trio of lights twirled as the antique attention-grabbing device did its duty.

"We call this the antique fire engine light show," she announced.

As I studied all these fascinating objects, a tall bearded man with kind eyes emerged and invited me to sit down. After introductions, I took my portfolio out from under my arm and handed it to Ken. Seated at the other end of the table, he opened it in front of me. I busied myself by peering around the room filled with objects of the decorator's craft while anticipating his response to my best work.

As the sound of ticking from the old clock became more and more prominent, the manner in which he studied each photo of festive carnival signs, pictorial images of clowns, and especially my Victorian scrollwork indicated an interested, learned, and critical eye. After perusing my efforts, instead of entering into conversation, he remained thoughtful a moment longer. Pulling at his beard, he rose to find a book from the shelf filled with pictures of firearm engravings, hand-painted floral designs on china, and, of course, pinstriping and gold leaf on fire engines.

"I want to show you something," he confided. "This book discusses how carriage and wagon decorating evolved over the centuries. I believe you'll find it quite helpful in your craft."

He placed the large book in front of me, leafed through to a page, and pointed. I looked at the old image of an elaborate carriage, listening to Ken's story about old-time decoration.

"Proud tradesmen accomplished such intricate decoration for the purpose of implying precision and quality," he said.

Understanding this premise revealed an interesting reason for the elaborate filigree, but my lesson wasn't over. He reached for my portfolio, flipping to the photo of the antique calliope truck. Instead of kudos, he walked over to select several more large books from the shelf of curiosities and placed them in front of me to peruse. He took one and found a specific page, pointing at a particular feature in the visual example.

"See how that scroll element seems to twist around and flip back toward the viewer?"

I looked at the example and sure enough, the illusion of animation had been created using color. I was amazed, but unsure where this was going.

"Your scrolls are flat," he challenged. "I'd like to see you create some of these elements in your scrolls so they will have the illusion of form that flips over and turns back, just like these."

I gulped down my wounded ego and nodded. Although I had felt so proud of my work on the calliope truck, Ken certainly knew his stuff and I couldn't deny he had a point.

"You come back to see me from time to time," he offered, "and I will help you learn technique."

He found a couple more books filled with examples of carved rifle stocks, designs on fancy kitchenware, and even fabric patterns. As he pored over the images with me, my mind soon became flooded with a multitude of possibilities. I could continue growing and becoming even better every day, providing I kept my mind open to opportunities. I was grateful for the gentle lesson and Ken's willingness to share his years of accumulated knowledge as my new mentor.

As the summer progressed, so did my career as a show painter. I returned frequently to show Ken photos of my latest efforts. Being a historian of this niche of American history, he revealed the interesting sequence of decorative offerings, styles, and techniques that occurred throughout the decades as technology shifted, the market changed, or a style became in vogue.

Prior to the ability to print floral I on china and plateware, those designs were all painstakingly hand painted in the majolica fashion by a fleet of artists. When the printed production of kitchenware began, those hardworking artisans became unemployed. A few of them migrated to the fire engine manufacturing plants, launching the period of floral décor on fire trucks. As Ken and I grew fonder of each other, he shared more and more of the interesting history that warranted the extensive decoration of an era now gone.

"Firefighting companies were originally competitive service providers in the big cities." his gentle voice revealed. "In order to attract clients, the premise they sought to establish through elaborate decoration was that their equipment was the best. The extensive use of gold leaf, pinstriping, and artwork on the portable pumpers, ladder wagons, hose reels, and extinguishing devices would be included in regional parades. They wanted to impress the community and establish that their company was superior to all the others."

I was amazed. I had never considered the reason why old fire engines were so elaborately decorated.

"When a home or business owner enlisted the services of a particular fire extinguishing company, a distinct badge was attached to the front of their business or home." he continued.

'Hand in Hand' was one such brand."

The pride was evident in Ken's voice as he explained an era gone past.

"In a neighborhood where several firefighting companies existed," he went on to reveal, "there was competitive jealousy. It wasn't uncommon to witness a fistfight between rival companies in front of a burning house."

"Wow," I said, shocked. "So they just let the house burn?"

Ken nodded gravely. "Often, they were too late in settling who got to put the fire out. That's why firefighting gradually became a municipal duty, though the tradition of elaborate gold-leaf artwork remained."

Ken always seemed to know exactly what I was interested in. During another visit, he invited me to follow him as we threaded our way through a hallway lined with more artifacts and down the stairs to his work area. Filling the workbenches and floor was an eclectic arrangement of machine shop equipment, tables with various projects underway, a disassembled truck frame on jacks, and innumerable pieces of apparatus in various stages of restoration.

Giving me a tour of what was going on, he explained how his clients loved old fire engines. Several were in various stages of restoration, some from before the era of chrome.

For authenticity, Ken prepared select pieces for nickel plating, which would provide the stunning mirror-like finish. The red paint decorated with gold leaf, black, and ivory pinstriping held true to the traditional color scheme of that era. I saw extensive gold-leaf work everywhere. As I studied the long stripes of burnished gold and comprehensive scrollwork, I saw firsthand the effect Ken had challenged me to produce.

"Look here," he said, pointing. "Typical scroll designs in gold have leaves, curl-backs, flip-overs, and features that appear to be concave." Emphasizing his next point, he added, "It's actually a very simple technique—a tinted varnish loaded like a gradient in a brush, similar to the way flower petals are produced by a tole painter."

My intrigue was piqued. Ken walked over to the bench and picked up a small square of brass before grabbing a medium-sized quill without a handle. Dipping the quill into the varnish, he showed me how this was used to produce the stunning yet subtle effect as he made simple back and forth movements across the brass palette.

"The tint does not interfere with the brilliance of the gold."

Reaching for a can of asphaltum, he dipped just the corner of the brush into it. As he went back and forth across the brass once more, I saw that the tint was heavy on one side and transparent on the other.

"When the tar-like substance is mixed with varnish, the mixture is warm and transparent. By making a simple stroke across these leaves," he said, demonstrating the technique, "the illusion of form occurs and the scrolls appear alive."

While I listened to his explanations of various decoration techniques, it was clear this man had passion for his work.

"Let me show you something else," he said, moving to grab a framed photograph.

He returned to show me a picture of a fire engine that had been restored by someone else.

"This is why the fire engine decorators avoid using pure white," he explained. "It overpowers the gold. A softer ivory promotes harmony, so the gold remains prominent on the vast areas of red."

I was amazed yet again by another fascinating piece of Ken's wisdom. From all my customers, the admiring public, and well-meaning friends and family, I received easy accolades for my artistic efforts. With Ken, I had access to a discerning eye that could see beyond the current level of my efforts and encouraged growth.

His home transformed into my private schoolhouse as Hand in Hand became a regular stop during my summers in Michigan. My mind churned out fresh ideas for waiting clients back at the carnival. For years to come, I would stop by frequently to share photos of my completed projects and seek Ken's advice. Each time, a feast of encouragement and new knowledge occurred. Plus, I could admire the incredible achievements going on in his shop during each visit.

The Unforeseen

Motivated by my discoveries through Ken's mentorship, I resumed my role as show painter at the W.G. Wade Shows winter quarters. Upon arrival, the barn in Mason was filled with rows of colorful specialty equipment and teeming with activity. My enlightened state combined with a feeling of homecoming when I saw the crew, but my enthusiasm would soon receive an interruption.

As usual, Red was busy with another project in the barn. After making me feel welcome, he gave me a shock.

"Glenn and I sold Wade Shows," he announced.

The reality hit me like a ton of bricks, causing my heart to race. "What? Why? To whom?"

Red told me the new owners had been immersed in the carnival business elsewhere. Jerry owned a small carnival of his own in another area, and Frank had the giant game lineup at the state fair. I had never heard of either of them. The direction of all conversation narrowed to a singular topic - what would this mean for my career?

Seeing my distraught state of shock, Red informed me, "We do plan to continue in the carnival business, albeit on a smaller scale."

He explained his and Glenn's particular fondness for one man who had grown up in the business with them. In an effort to keep Jim Elliott with their show, they retained several nice rides and amusement pieces to form a small carnival company which would be called the Elliott Amusement Company. This would be a smaller operation made up of premium pieces.

"I'll have some work for you later this summer," he added, "but I don't have anything right now. You should go meet the new owners. I'm sure they'll have work for you in the meantime."

With mixed emotions on an overcast day, I followed Red's directions across the state. Still guarded from my experience with the con man, Bill, I held little hope for what I'd find there with the new show owners.

I guided my VW bus into the parking lot filled with carnival rides and attractions, parking behind Art's dark ride. Superdog jumped out as soon as I opened the door and we set out in this rugged fantasyland in search of familiar faces.

I saw Spook first and asked him about the changes to the show. He lowered his head and shook it.

"It's not good, Davee. I even tried to be friendly by offering Frank a cigar. You know what he did? He dropped it to the ground and crushed it under his foot!"

In one instant, Frank had utterly ruined Spook's gesture of kindness and set the tone for his business management tactics.

After chatting with a few other friends, I heard several stories that all drew similar conclusions. Fear-based leadership infected everyone under the new umbrella. Frank's arrogant oppression had expanded to replace the overall sense of togetherness and regard between all that had flourished with the old regime.

The crew who came with the new management were used to the putrid immersion of dysfunction in Frank and Jerry's style of dominance, but the established Wade Show crew members who'd enjoyed years around Glenn and Red had to either morph or go elsewhere. Instead of the usual coming together to unite as a team for yet another season, this new beginning had become a time of uncertainty and emotional upheaval.

Although my gut told me to run the other direction, I continued my search for the new owners; I needed the work. I saw Art pulling electric cables from the generator trailer and approached. He was being supervised by a tall balding man wearing casual attire that looked out of place in this whimsical setting.

Catching sight of me, the supervisor yelled, "Hey, that better not be a mean dog."

Intervening on my behalf, Art said, "Oh, that's Superdog." Stooping, he called, "C'mere, Superdog."

Superdog bolted for the familiar face and absorbed all of Art's attention.

"That's a good boy," Art said. "Davee is the show painter. A pretty good one, too. Davee, meet Jerry Vinson."

"I'm the new owner," the man quipped without taking my outstretched hand, "and I don't like dogs around the show." Apparently not one for pleasantries, Jerry turned back to the task at hand. Without looking at me, he added, "We're going to need to get this trailer repainted."

Unsure of what to make of the interaction that had taken place, I looked to Art for reassurance, but he just stared back at me apologetically.

Jerry walked off, calling over his shoulder, "You just remember what I told you about the dog."

In the morning, I joined Art, Dick, and Ron—the other early risers of the show—at a nearby restaurant for breakfast. While sipping coffee, they compared the turbulences that occurred with other shows that had undergone similar changes with their current experience. Their testimonies fortified how attitudes from the top always trickled down into the attitudes of everyone on the show, whether it be the harmony that blessed or the agony that infected. It became more and more clear that I needed to be on guard. Feeling discouraged, I simply aimed to get through this one spring painting for the new owners of the Wade Shows. Next year, I'd search for an alternative option. Returning to the show grounds, I drove my VW bus onto the midway to get into proximity of the next painting project. I'd barely stepped out of the bus when I was further introduced to the turmoil cultivated by the new owners.

"Hey," someone shouted at me, "get that thing out of here!"

"I'm the show painter," I said, trying to reason with the man and motioning to the trailer I'd be working on.

He wasn't interested in hearing my side. The self-centered, fear-based attitude radiated between all the workers, including this man. It was as if they were encouraged to only see the worst. Raw agendas replaced the altruistic teamwork concept that celebrated common sense. If the words of my friends hadn't already warned me, this should have been my red-flag moment. Instead, I tried my best to power through.

Another morning not long after, I returned from breakfast to discover the cargo door of my bus to be ajar. Startled, I noticed my sign kit was missing. I looked around the sleeping midway to see where it could have gone, hoping it was just a simple mistake. When it was nowhere in sight, I hiked to a nearby pawn shop to see if my box of painter's supplies had shown up there, but no such luck.

I never did find that kit. The loss of what I needed to thrive promoted a deeper fear of this place and these fellows. A new reluctance for my surroundings replaced any inclination to connect with this mob. I missed the old show where I had enjoyed a calm, encouraging environment that allowed my talents to blossom among trusted friends. Instead, I was here, amid aggressive enemies, helpless friends, and greedy business owners. My eyes had been opened to the ugly side of the carnival—senseless neglect, premature demise of mechanical features, dripping septic tanks, and relentless oppression.

The magic of the midway was gone.

In spite of the encouragement I got from the few lingering familiar faces, I seemed to be of two minds. Part of me was challenged by the advocacy of Ken to stick around and include new features in my work to create realistic form out of what used to be flat design elements. I wanted to become the best show painter there ever was, and that meant commitment. But this was also mixed with a desire to avoid as much as I could in this confusing and hostile environment. I retreated from any new social connections on the show and likely would have left after the loss of my kit had I not found another advocate on scene.

My wintertime customer, Butch Netterfield, had been in the right place at the right time, securing the popcorn exclusive when Jack and Sid vacated the midway under the new ownership. Now, the familiar fleet of Netterfield's Popcorn & Lemonade occupied all the strategic places, creating a sense of comfort and familiarity. I relied on my connection with the Netterfield crew to get me through this season.

Butch saw a huge opportunity for me on the show and encouraged me to try to fit in with this scary dynamic. Sensing

my hesitancy, he became my art director, a go-between so I wouldn't have to deal directly with Frank or Jerry. Butch even gave me a lavish travel trailer to live in. Accepting his generous assistance, I maintained distance by sticking with Butch and his crew.

Frank and Jerry's new office semitrailer came with a fancy bank teller window for business transactions. Parked centrally on the midway, fenced off, and under its own tent, the office served as portable headquarters for the show. Besides the yellow and white canvas that filtered the sun and filled the interior with sweet light, the trailer was rather plain.

The new owners wanted it decorated with fancy paintwork. Butch encouraged me to begin the creation of spectacular Victorian scrollwork down the length. My imagination was piqued and my mind filled with zeal. At last, I had the perfect outlet for the new skills and techniques learned under my mentorship with Ken. As I visualized spectacular results, I entertained the thought that this project may very well be my magnum opus.

I drew my designs on large pieces of brown butcher paper. With this pattern, my design would repeat in a regular rhythm and be identical on both sides. Once the design was transferred onto the sides of the trailer, the application of color began. I chose a large gray flat, a type of brush designed to flow easily over the lateral ridges of the corrugated-metal siding. Standing on a ladder and following my design pounced onto the surface, I began making tedious brush stroke after tedious brush stroke. While involved in this tedium, I became mentally immersed on an adventure of discovery. I am fortunate to be blessed with a vivid imagination. This gift compounded when my environment was filled with encouragement and enthusiasm. My hand calculated each accurate brush stroke. My eye visually reviewed progress that slowly became my best work to date. My mind was truly in the zone as I painted and dreamed about showing photos of the finished project to Ken.

And then Frank walked by.

"You'd better make sure you're accurate with the billable hours you turn into the office for this job," he spewed.

Stunned at this mistreatment, the magic that had previously filled my mind evaporated on the spot. There was no acknowledgment of my endeavors, no respect for my process, no appreciation for my talents. Just cold and bitter words smattering my spirit with their venom. The wounds experienced as a child rushed to the surface and I relived the piercing hurt that amplified my powerlessness while bullies picked on my older brother. I had no voice then, and I had no voice now. Just as quickly as he'd arrived, Frank moved on to his next unsuspecting victim. I came down off the ladder and walked away from the project. I wasn't going to paint for Frank and Jerry anymore.

After cleaning out my paintbrush and putting it away, I walked out onto the midway toward the trailer Butch provided for me. The usual fantasyland of sensual delights was narrowed into a tiny slit of bubbling hatred as I replayed Frank's unwarranted comment. Slamming the door of my trailer, I grabbed a beer.

Though I was alone in here, it was anything but quiet. My mind erupted into rage over the narcissistic bullying. My blood pounded. My brain shouted. I did not like what was going on. I sought to extinguish this maelstrom the only way I knew how—I downed the first beer and reached for another.

I had discovered the anesthetic effect of alcohol years ago. As the blurry sensation rose into my head, the intensity of the rage lost its stronghold. I began to formulate a plan to escape this madness. I was done with this show—I would never make another brush stroke on that office, nor would I ever see Frank again.

In the seclusion of the RV, I sipped the amber nectar to calm my throbbing pain. The mass exodus at the end of this spot would provide a convenient time to slip away. I would wait.

Up Here from Zenith

Finally free of Frank and Jerry, the gray overcast sky of early summer revealed patches of blue that offered hope as I returned to check in at the yard in Mason. The last of the rides and games for the new Elliott Amusement Company were being completed. Soon, these pieces would join the rest of the show already on the road.

I spotted Red and Glenn near the tubular frame of the Tip Top. They'd had it sandblasted down to bare metal and their crew was now spraying a fresh coat of blue paint on it. At the sight of these men I admired, my fractured spirit slowly began to heal.

Noticing my arrival, Glenn paused from strategizing with his business partner. My presence communicated the obvious; I didn't like the new owners and was in search of another opportunity.

"Davee," Glenn greeted, warmly gesturing for me to walk with him.

We strolled among the carnival equipment before he confided his desire.

"I want the Elliott Amusement Company to be the prettiest show in all of Michigan."

I understood and I welcomed his challenge.

I was needed on the lot right away to decorate the ticket box, letter various trailers, and make signs and décor. Combined with my passion, the atmosphere of like-minded, proactive teamwork would make for a much more productive and enjoyable spring. Zeal replaced the sting of the open wound left by Frank and Jerry.

Following Glenn's directions, I found the little show set up on a parking lot outside of Detroit. Several of the crew members who also couldn't assimilate into the transition of the big show were here. Among them was Beanie, wife of the Matterhorn foreman who'd run the dime glass pitch for Red for years.

Beanie now oversaw the games for Elliott Amusement Company. When it had still been Wade Shows, she'd often call out to Superdog while we traversed the midway on my rounds. Superdog adored her. Seeing us on the lot, Beanie invited him to jump into the joint as usual so she could pet him. United as outcasts from the big show, Beanie and I became fast friends as I found my place again.

The Meteor was a ride comprised of three round platforms with seats arranged like pie slices in a circle on each table. These tables revolved on three pivot points on a triangular support bracket that also turned. The entire apparatus was mounted on a semitrailer that required passengers to climb steps to reach the seats. Red had just completed new metal fence panels for each of the passenger tables and sought to give this ride a facelift.

"Davee, I want you to theme this ride," he began with a smile. "Then, come up with a list of possible names that suggest excitement."

Currently being known as the Meteor made a sci-fi or astronomy theme appropriate. The project became the topic of conversation with my crew friends who helped suggest new names. I accumulated a long list of possible names for the ride including Star Quest, Master Blaster, Space Flash, and Atomic Orbiter. When I saw Red, I shared my list with him.

"Well, Master Blaster is out," he said with a chuckle. "That sounds too much like masturbator."

I felt my cheeks redden at my oversight. After a little deliberation, we settled on Star Blast. Excited to have the name chosen, I knew what to do. I envisioned a diagonal stripe leading into the first letter of the new name on a repeating design that would be central on every other scenic panel. Hovering over a light blue background, the remaining space would be filled with dazzling constellations, futuristic space ships, flaming comets, and glowing stars. By combining sign painting techniques with the use of a brush and the airbrush, I could create both crisp and soft edges for the outer-space themed designs.

Excited, I began drawing designs for the graphics and artwork and made paper patterns to facilitate the duplication of my paint scheme onto all the pieces. When completed, the newly painted and renamed ride became a focal point in the small midway lineup. Though not the scrollwork project I had hoped to get that spring, the airbrushing on this refreshed ride provided yet another feather in my cap.

Speedball

The crossroads not only provided options for those willing to consider another direction for the trek they were on, but a place to stop, meet, and conduct this business of life. Recognizing opportunity, early trading places sprang up where these roads intersected. This infrastructure grew into the communities that currently dotted the landscape. The fairgrounds enjoyed a similar history, first as a place to trade, entertain, inspire, and, in my case, to find a niche in which to thrive.

At our own hypothetical crossroads, my relationship with my dad was slowly transforming from cold and awkward into one of warmth and intimacy. Initially resistant and dead set against my foolish plan to run away with the circus and become a traveling artist, my father now thoroughly enjoyed hearing my tales of adventure. He'd gradually acknowledged a similar longing inside himself. My dad was becoming my best friend, and I was thrilled to have him along for the ride during that summer of 1980.

After rendezvousing in Michigan, our journey began as we motored down a two-lane highway through Midwestern farm country. I enjoyed the reflection of his chrome-yellow VW bus in my rearview mirror, finding comfort in knowing he was with me. That summer would provide us with an unforgettable bonding experience. First stop - the Fremont Street festival.

The cornfields along the way yielded prominence as we neared the brick structures and business signs, beacons that silently announced our destination was near.

The streets of the small Midwestern town had been blocked off in preparation for the upcoming festival. Highly decorated trucks and trailers of all sorts were arranged in places that would normally receive a penalty for parking. As this sleepy town watched, downtown quickly became a flurry of activity while structural steel was unloaded and assembled into the geometric shapes that would soon provide amusement to these country folks.

Dad and I parked our buses well out of the way and hiked to where the carnival was setting up. Circus and carnival people had their own peculiar manner of conducting what appeared to be an unusual everyday life. Exhibiting the excitement and enthusiasm of a little kid, Dad peppered me with questions, one after the other. I was pleased to field this barrage of questions that only a few decades ago would have been going the other direction. Now I was the wise one with knowledge of conduct and advice on how to fit into this culture.

We entered the construction zone that would soon become the midway, pausing to appreciate its astounding wonder. Dad and I watched workmen unload and assemble pieces of steel and arrange arteries of electric cable for the highly decorated machinery with bright lightbulbs and beautifully painted scenes. I pointed out some familiar attractions that were proven winners and part of the traditional carnival lineup. Other machinery was new—the latest attempts that the ride designers hoped the public would enjoy and make popular.

Rows of illuminated booths were being filled with plush prizes—enticements to attract game players. Portable kitchens smothered with eye-catching sign work would soon belch out aromas to compete for the customers' appetites and dollars. In two days' time, this would become a fairyland of lights, copiously layered on various snowflake-shaped mechanical wonders that would capture the attention of all the residents.

As this area transformed into a source of fascination right before our eyes, I couldn't help but feel a swell of pride. I had found an outlet for creating colorful images, fanciful lettering, and having fun with paint. The carnival was my canvas, and I was content with the decision I had made. I was even more excited to share this world with my dad for the first time.

The manager of the show was busy directing truck drivers

as they maneuvered rigs onto location. During a pause in the activity, Tim Bors took the opportunity to welcome my dad to the show and give him a job.

"You'll be in charge of Speedball," Tim announced brightly.

The Speedball game was a large pipe framework covered with netting. This netting contained the baseballs thrown by customers. The target was a large white canvas with a painting of a catcher on it. Dad would receive his training from the concession boss later that day while I silently admired the compliment that my father was here with me.

By Thursday, Dad began his role with three baseballs and a change apron. My dad was used to being in the limelight, albeit at a pulpit. Now safely away from the judgmental eye of the congregation, he let his ego come to the surface, bold and fun. As I watched him transform into a fun-loving baseball huckster, Red took my attention away with a request.

"I want you to head over to the next town where the Octopus just finished being repainted," he said. "I want airbrushed decoration on it in time for the opening of the fair next week."

Seeing my dad was in good hands, I told him I'd meet up with him when the rest of the crew rejoined us in Holland, Michigan.

At the Holland fairgrounds the next day, I found the

Octopus ride intact with fresh paint, just as Red had promised. I got to work making paper patterns to ensure my decorations on each tub would be the same. After transferring my design, I began to paint. Before I knew it, the weekend was over and the show trucks started arriving one by one.

By the time I saw Dad's chrome-yellow bus pull in, the Octopus was completed and I had moved on to the next job preparing patterns for scrollwork décor on the Eli 16 Ferris wheel. As my dad walked toward me, I overheard my comrades on the show calling him Speedy, a nickname he'd earned during his military days that easily doubled in his role as the Speedball huckster.

"Speedy was amazing!" one of them told me.

"He's a natural," another added.

My dad beamed at their compliments and camaraderie. When the others headed over to the shower room, he couldn't contain himself any longer.

"Wait till you hear about the fun time I had," he exclaimed.

I was eager to hear his story, but it would have to wait.

"Speedy!" Red called out, getting our attention as he approached us. "I got another job for you, and the best part is that you'll get to work with Davee."

I smiled as Red gave me a wink.

To add some old-time flavor to the fair, Red had connected

an old farmer's steam-operated engine to the drive mechanism of the Ferris wheel. This source of energy was not necessary—usually an electric motor turned the big wheel—but Red liked to add showmanship wherever he could. This link to the past added to the festive essence of the fair as a point of pride for the owners of the show.

While I prepared the first of the tubs on the Eli 16 with the patterns I'd just completed, Red showed my dad how to operate this old machine.

"It doesn't take much to get the fire going in this old engine," he started to explain.

When Red gestured toward the firebox, Dad informed him of his familiarity with steam power. I didn't know it at the time, but my dad had a relationship with steam locomotives that began in his boyhood. During his seminary years in Chicago in 1948, he had a summer job stoking the fires in the locomotives used in the Chicago Railroad Fair show that celebrated one hundred years of railroading. Satisfied with my dad's knowledge, Red walked away and let us get to work.

Over the next few days, our morning routine involved our cooperative efforts. I placed the pattern on the tubs I could reach from the ground to transfer my design and my dad used the kindling and sticks provided to build a fire in the steam threshing engine. As I painted, my dad stoked the fire to get it hot enough to have a head of steam to power the engine. When the first tubs were completed, I stepped out from beneath the ride and my dad engaged the lever that started the belt and moved the giant machine. When I could reach the next two tubs, Dad stopped the wheel, and the whole process began again.

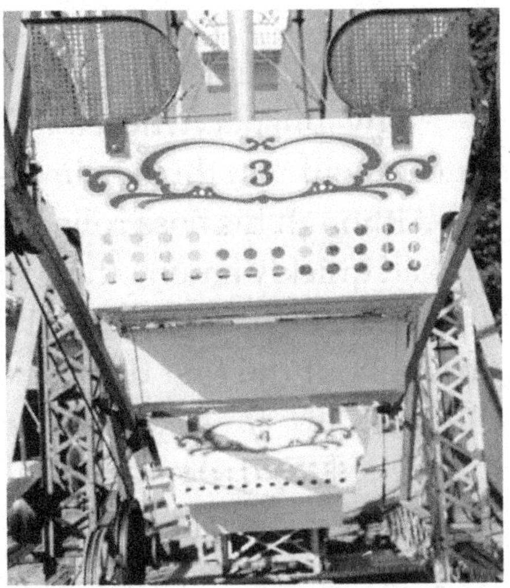

While I worked, he sat astride that mighty engine. Dad finally had the perfect time to share the story about what happened back at the street fair during my dad's first carnival experience.

At the Fremont Street festival, Dad's job had been to entice the passersby to attempt to win a high-quality major league batter's helmet with the team logo of their choice simply by predicting the speed of their third pitch. His carnie boss, Tim Bors, had told him the prize helmets were nice prizes that cost a hefty fee. The enticement was to get the customers to play without giving too many away.

But he didn't know my dad. Between Dad's love of having a crowd gathered around him and my friends on the show taking him under their wings and offering encouragement, he was inspired to create his own clever patter. Dad aimed to engage as many passersby to try his game as he could in an attempt to have a crowd around him at all times.

"Step right up and pitch a winner," my dad's mantra began. "Predict the speed of your third pitch and win a genuine major league batter's helmet."

In front of a growing crowd, my dad was further inspired. In order to draw additional players, he came up with a fresh marketing scheme.

"Any pitcher who can throw three consecutive identical pitches will win three helmets!"

Although his boss rolled his eyes when he heard this, word spread quickly among the patrons. Tim got over it when he saw the size of the crowd this promise drew. Many times throughout the first days of the street festival, clumps of men stepped up to ask about this challenge. Every time this happened, Dad would boldly announce it again.

"Throw three consecutive identical pitches and win three major league baseball helmets."

Tim was even happier when the final day at this location rolled around and no one had won this grand prize, despite the fact that business was hopping. The excitement among the baseball aficionados had built all weekend, garnering repeat customers and new ones alike. The feat of winning three helmets was clearly the goal of the customers, and by now his boss was pleased with the receipts he turned in.

By Saturday evening, Dad's experience contained an energy and enthusiasm that built with each passing moment, much like a song's crescendo. With the busiest crowd of the week packed in as close as they could get, Speedy repeatedly bragged about the challenge again, and still no one won.

Close to closing time, the peak of the ride traffic had passed and the crews began to dismantle the large steel rides. But the games and concessions continued until the last patron was satisfied. The biggest crowd surrounded Speedball, with my dad as the man of the hour.

Then it happened. A stocky young man in a gray T-shirt stepped up and handed Speedy a dollar. A few of the onlookers noticed something that my dad did not. One of them asked again about the challenge. Oblivious, my dad stepped front and center, repeating his choreographed marketing coup.

"Any pitcher who throws three identical pitches will win three genuine major league helmets."

Affirmed, the onlookers stepped back to allow this newcomer to try his hand at the Speedball challenge. My dad handed a ball to his waiting customer. Everyone grew quiet as an ominous feeling filled the air.

The gray-shirted player wound up. His first pitch went 100 miles an hour. Astounded, my dad's mouth dropped open. He handed the man another ball and scanned the crowd, starting to feel suspicious. He caught sight of the smugness of those who knew this contestant, whose second pitch yielded another 100 miles an hour. The crowd applauded and my dad realized with certainty he had been duped. This had to be a professional player. As the crowd became deathly quiet in anticipation of the third pitch, the steady drone of the electric generators and the clanging and hammering of the teardown process was the only audible atmosphere. There, on that street corner, a magical transformation took place, but the crowd's entire focus was on Speedball. Pressed in tightly, the crowd stared between the contestant and my dad. It was a showdown! The moment of truth had arrived.

In a show of good sportsmanship, my dad held the final baseball high in the air. He strode in front of the encircled crowd as if to tease them, and then handed the ball to the contestant. The man rolled the ball in his hands to warm it up. Then, with a mighty windup and a pitch that smacked the canvas backdrop banner, the victory was as clear as the reading on the radar gun - one hundred miles an hour.

The crowd went wild, cheering and applauding their hero.

In front of that crowd, my dad assumed humility and responsibility to the winner, handing over three helmets as promised. Secretly, my dad was happy too.

"I actually wanted the players to win," my dad confided in me. "But in that moment, I was worried what the boss would say about losing three helmets for a dollar."

As the crowd dispersed, their faces showed clear satisfaction with the deed accomplished at last, even if it had taken a professional baseball player to do it.

On this road of life, many lessons occur. The true value often lay with something we initially reject. Years of standing before another kind of people in a different role as clergyman, my dad had at one time sported contempt for the stereotypical low-life traveling showman. Now softened by the reality of the breakdown of the synod system, he had eased into becoming interested in the venue that provided his wandering son with a multitude of opportunities to follow his passion. My father resigned his contempt and joined me.

Released from his prejudice, my dad looked into the hearts of others at the carnival and began to understand the distinct challenges undertaken in a unique culture, one that accepted him just the way he was. The sparkle in his eyes showed the amount of joy he had found in his brief experience as a carnie and his understanding as to why I chose this path. In the illumination of halogen lamps surrounded by the multiple stimuli of amusement attractions of every kind, with blasting hucksters and blinking lights, my dad had found his place on top of the world.

Chapter 5
The Entrepreneur & the Circus

"Success comes to those who dedicate everything to their passion in life. To be successful, it is also very important to be humble. and never let fame or money travel to your head."
—A.R. Rahman

The First T-Shirt Stand

Evolving from a primitive crossroads where folks traded goods and had fun, the carnival midway provided patrons with an infinite number of treats, mechanical stimulation, entertaining marvels, and wonders to behold from around the world. Over the years, traveling merchants came to rely on effective advertising to compete in an ever-changing environment.

I had found the perfect arena to develop my emerging skills as a young artist with brushes and paint where the patrons eagerly consumed what I aspired to produce - creative, entertaining, hand-painted works of art. Personal dedication and an obsession with this genre fueled me forward among the showmen.

My small VW bus emblazoned with Krazee Davee was easy to park in the proximity of most projects within the crowded fairgrounds. Having the ability to generate these works in the midst of the hustle and bustle of the fair was a big contributor to the demand for my work. In addition to unique marketing for my services, it drew a crowd with live entertainment. The merchants wanted to draw that crowd to their own stands, increasing sales and getting a fresh custom paint job in the process.

In this environment of carnival culture with an ever-changing movement toward bigger, better, brighter, I found my talents thriving as they morphed into new ideas and concepts. The addition of the airbrush to my arsenal of painting tools expanded the variety of effects I could provide to my customers. As my ability with the airbrush developed, another logical direction to become a true fairgrounds entrepreneur arose.

The carnival showmen appreciated my talent as a creative sign painter. So much so that when I kicked around the idea of a T-shirt stand after learning from Tuna, they were full of encouragement. But now that the time had come to launch this new venture, I was hesitant. I was confused about when and how to begin this new endeavor. What if I failed? What if it didn't go according to plan? I needed someone to talk this through with. I would also need to find an assistant—my dad would be busy with his game joint at another fair. He was having fun; I didn't want to take away his chance to fully enjoy his experience.

Instead, I shared my dream with my long-distance friend, Mary. I had met Mary during my stint as the 24-hour man on the Clyde Beatty Cole Bros Circus two years before. We remained pen pals, and Mary offered to help. Her college schedule was free for the summer. She firmed up a date she could begin, which made the Genesee County Fair the logical starting place to launch our new business.

After picking her up at the airport, we went straight to Kmart to buy some plain T-shirts for our inventory, and then scrambled to get back to the fairgrounds. An area was selected for our booth in one of the long rows of rides and concessions. We set up between the Rock O' Plane and the Star Blast with its fresh custom paint job. Parking the van between the two rides, we tried to determine how to set up our official shirt business headquarters.

A good showman knows how to make something out of nothing— sage advice a carnival mentor had once given me. Red was right. Necessity was the mother of invention. Keeping his words in mind, Mary and I set out to accomplish just that.

A bare minimum of equipment and supplies fit into my VW bus. The area inside the van became both our work and living area. I borrowed two sections of ride fence to support a spare piece of plywood, which became our counter. Mary readied the inventory by removing shirts from the packaging and sorting them by size. A lean-to easel against the side of the van would act as my work area.

Though pieced together, the booth was ready at last.

The sun shined down on us during our first official day at the fair, creating an encouraging atmosphere for our new venture. The first order of business was to create flash, or display artwork, for the customers to select from. I had learned several flashy alphabets from Tuna while I'd watched him in action the previous summer.

I tried to keep up as my ideas came rapidly. I knew two names with a ribbon and a heart was a big seller. I also painted examples of unicorns, butterflies, and trucks with big tires. I suspected the 4-H kids would want a picture of their horse, chicken, or hog, so I added a few of those. Before I knew it, I had several flash shirts completed and ready to put on display.

During this process, onlookers began gathering. Mary fielded questions that turned into sales, proving her assistance invaluable. While I painted one shirt, she would gather the necessary information for the subsequent customer, including shirt size, particular request, correct spelling, and preferred colors.

"How much is a shirt with the name Shirley?"

"Can he paint a picture of my tractor?"

"Do you have a goat design?"

"How much extra for a name with a flower?"

Young and old alike gathered to watch the creation of each design. Watching a multi-color moniker come to life in a matter of minutes was pure entertainment. We caught on that watching the artist was what sold the next shirt. Soon, our first paid designs were visible on hangers in every available space, adding to the visual appeal and making it official. Our joint was up and running!

The procedure for each shirt was essentially the same. A small piece of paper was attached to the correctly sized shirt containing all the information Mary had jotted down from her discussion with the customer. Once familiar with the job, my mind began to visualize the design. I stretched the shirt over a large piece of cardboard for a flat surface. I placed this on my easel, and then found the center of the shirt so the design would be in the correct location.

Fairgoers watched me create a plethora of designs on a relentless stream of shirts—names of pets, rainbow unicorns, images of John Deere tractors, couples' names inside a heart, and so on. Business was booming. Several times, Mary had to beg a ride to Kmart from one of the carnies to get more shirts. Day in and day out, we found our rhythm that resulted in swift production.

The working conditions at the fairgrounds were challenging at best. There was steady background noise coming from the diesel generators that provided power to the rides and concessions. Each ride had additional motors that produced noise, and each piece of equipment had a unique sound such as clanking, whining, or roaring. Coupled with countless screams, shouts, and giggles of the patrons that blended with overlapping rock and roll music and the huckster's mantra, all of these sounds combined to create a rather chaotic environment that only a few would want to work in.

The carnival had become like my second home, so I was used to all of this and accepted it. Still, concentrating on the design for the next shirt amid such stimuli further complicated by a question posed by an ominously close onlooker wasn't easy.

"Excuse me, mister?"

I glanced up to see a freckle-faced kid. Mary usually intercepted these distractions, but there was always one or two that snuck past her. When that happened, it was good business for me to answer their questions cordially, even though I was incredibly busy. I nodded to acknowledge him and continued painting.

"What happens if you make a mistake?" he asked.

I paused to aim the airbrush gun at my temple, earning a laugh from the crowd.

After an intense and productive first day, the quiet serenity of the early morning was a welcome respite before we began another busy day. I opened the side door of the VW to let Superdog jump out. He was happy for the opportunity to run around. I stuck out my cowboy-boot-covered foot and stepped out after him, a toothbrush hanging in my mouth. Glancing around at the sleeping attractions—no noise, no commotion, no voices—I sighed peacefully and stretched before brushing my teeth.

On most fairgrounds, there was a rule that dogs must be on a leash, but no one was here yet. Besides, I observantly watched my dog at all times. Unfortunately for me, a police car happened to be cruising the perimeter of the midway that morning. Upon spotting my dog running around off leash and having a happy time, the officer slowly worked his way down the midway corridor where I was parked. I approached his car and went around to the driver's side to address him, but before I could speak, I had to do something with my mouthful of toothpaste suds. I turned away to discharge the minty mess. At that exact moment, my happy-go-lucky dog raced by me, earning a stripe of white toothpaste foam decorating his entire length. Stunned at my luck, but with my mouth finally empty, I turned to acknowledge the policeman.

"You just spit on your dog!" he announced as if I'd somehow missed that detail.

I stared in silence while he laughed, his stern demeanor melting away. After taking in his unique surroundings, the officer shook his head with smile.

"Make sure you wash that dog," he said with another chuckle before driving away.

Wearable Advertising

Walkaround publicity began with the sandwich board during an era long ago. A person wore hand-painted sign boards and walked up and down the street in a busy urban area to advertise a merchant, product, or event.

In the 1950s, two separate artists on opposite coasts with similar nicknames yet completely unaware of each other took this concept a step further. Karl "Big Daddy Rat" Smith and Ed "Big Daddy" Roth each created the first images on T-shirts. Having launched the trend of lettering names, drawing cartoon monsters, and painting hot rod pictures on clothing, these two artists caught the attention of showmen everywhere. Carnies, promoters at sporting events, and merchandisers at car shows were all quick to grasp the novel marketing coup that transformed the plain undergarment into the sensational and attractive social media of its day.

Artists like Richard Green, T-Shirt Larry, Henry Gerson, and Nick the Jap imitated their concept, initiating the first wave of sensational clothing that swept through the carnival world.

Although simple silk-screen printed designs and mass-produced iron-on transfers eventually captured the bulk of the market, the airbrush artist remained the only one able to provide individual expression, custom creativity, and entertainment on the midway by rapidly creating one-of-a-kind images on a T-shirt right before the customer's eyes. Soon members of every crowd sported personal visions, endorsed their favorite rock bands, donned witty icons, and plugged comical phrases. As demand increased, one-of-a-kind custom shirt painters thrived at vacation spots, tourist destinations, and fairgrounds, paving the way for artistic entrepreneurs such as myself.

By the time Mary and I launched our enterprise, this trend for custom T-shirts was firmly established. There was no better place that existed for me to develop my skills as an up-and-coming airbrush artist. The steady stream of T-shirt buyers provided an opportunity for me to develop finesse with this new painting device. Each challenging request propelled me along the learning curve toward becoming an accomplished airbrush artist.

Seeing a colorful work of art come to life was the "walking" advertisement of our business, a true source of fascination for throngs of fairgoers. The whole process was fascinating and had the ability to keep the audience's attention for hours on end. They stood and watched as shirt after shirt received the personal touch that only came from the hand of a live artist.

One reason airbrushing was so mysterious and appealing was because it was fast-paced. A three-color name, for example, was completed in just three minutes. Like magic, a plain T-shirt was transformed into a custom colorful creation. Even flushing the old color out of the airbrush and changing colors held appeal. As long as I painted, we had a crowd.

By the end of the fair, the grass that surrounded our little enterprise had been trodden down to reveal bare dirt, now shiny from the polishing received by the soles of countless shoes.

"You'se in da way."

I looked around to notice what this man was talking about. Teardown had begun, and our van and all the shirt painting supplies were in the way of his ability to lower the towering ride next to us. We still had customers waiting, so the only thing to do was to pick up the pace.

"Okay," I offered, shifting into high gear. "I'm on it."

As I finished the last of the shirts, Mary gathered up the ancillary stuff and packed it away in the van. As soon as I handed off the final still-wet shirt to the waiting customer, I helped pack the van with the remaining items.

My first task was to dismantle the board clamped to the ride fence and remove those pieces. Putting away the colors of paints would have to wait. With the overhead amusement apparatus partially dismantled and the foreman looming, we had to get out of there pronto. When the last of the gear was stashed in the bus, I started it up and drove out from under the ride through the labyrinth of carnival vehicles maneuvering to get their loads ready for transport.

Once beyond the edge of the midway, we found an out-of-the-way place to park. There we found peace and contentment after the final rush of the fair. Having emerged from the envelope of lumens, energy, and noise for the first time all week, Mary and I were at last able to inventory our experience, validating that the event had been a huge success.

This would certainly be worth doing again. We celebrated with an amber beverage each, making plans to relaunch the following season. I began to visualize an even better operation with the fabrication of a more sophisticated T-shirt stand that would shout success at first glance. Between now and next year, I would get this booth under construction.

The Tip Top

Back at the barn, I saw evidence of Red's busy summer. With no major rides on the Elliott Amusement Company, he planned to make one particular ride spectacular to serve as the missing centerpiece on the little show. The ride pneumatics had been rebuilt, the structural steel sandblasted and repainted, and the time arrived to accomplish the cosmetics on the project that had become Red's pride and joy.

"Davee," Red greeted me as I walked into the midst of the production. "I need your special touch."

The Tip Top was essentially a round table with tubs attached around the perimeter that got twirled by the passengers. The tall, central tower enclosed a large pneumatic ram that went up when charged with a high volume of compressed air and down when released. With the addition of lights, flags, and music, this ride would serve as the jewel of the midway for their little show.

Aluminum extrusions with multiple bulb sockets were mounted vertically at even intervals along the rear of the ride to create a back wall of light stringers, adding twinkle and animation. Red's plan also included a music system with DJ-style interactions to heighten the experience for the riders.

"I'm thinking of a tropical ocean paradise theme with pirates," he explained to me.

Red always sought to create a special theme for his acquired recycled rides in order to suggest newness. After some discussion and tossing out ideas for the ultimate vision, the SeaWave was born. I had my mission.

I studied reference pictures from several sources and began creating images of pirate girls, treasure chests, parrots, palm trees, and ocean vistas on the panels that hung underneath the walking platform and encircled the ride. On the sign that stood prominently over the entrance structure where the patrons got on the ride, I created a special design and proudly placed my artist name, Letterfly, in the corner.

Red had three children. Among them was a gangly preteen who shared his signature red hair. Prior to the age of responsibility, Glenn Patrick seemed to be constantly screwing around instead of getting his work done. The love between him and his father was evident. He watched me work, observing the process used for airbrushing images of pirate girls on scenic ride panels, and later made an enthusiastic report to his dad.

"When I grow up," he announced, "I want to be a show painter because they get to read comic books all day!"

I laughed. "If only it were that easy, kid."

The upside-down tubs for the Tip Top ride were gathered in the yard to get new electric brake magnets and be sanded down for paint. When those procedures were completed, I was recruited to make them look like wood grain with my airbrush.

On a postcard-perfect day, I succeeded with the application of a perfect layer of yellow paint glossed out to an admirable shine. Once dried, I would add in the finer details to make them appear wooden. But as if to prove my point that being an artist wasn't always sunshine and rainbows, one of those famous Michigan rainstorms came out of nowhere.

Before I had a chance to protect the tubs, a stiff rain poured down on my fresh paint. Forty minutes later, the sky was crisp and clear once again, but the damage was done. The finish on the tubs was now as rough as a corncob. A shame, too. This ride had a deadline to meet and a repaint did not fit into the schedule.

As an artist, I had learned that things didn't always go

according to plan, and as a showman, I knew that the show must always go on. Disappointed, I approached Red for how to proceed. With his encouragement, I used the airbrush to go ahead and paint the wood-grain linework and make them appear like wooden barrels. It worked out okay in the end, but it certainly wasn't one of my proudest achievements.

The next day, all the completed ride pieces were loaded and this trailer-mounted ride was finally ready to ship to the show. I followed the load to the small county fairgrounds and joined up with the others, including my dad. As my new biggest fan, Dad lifted my spirits by exhibiting pride for our new showpiece, despite my discouraging setback.

Those last few weeks of my dad's escape to the carnival went by all too quickly. While I painted, Dad ran the machine gun joint. His job meant he had to stay put, but he was eager to check out the scenery at our new digs. Expressing his gratitude, he didn't hesitate to accept when I offered to cover for him so he could go on an excursion. I was glad to help, and even happier knowing he was fully enjoying being immersed in this new culture.

Later, when I finished decorating the main portions of the Elliott Amusement Company, my mission was at last completed. The ticket box, stock truck, kiddie rides, and merry-go-round trailer were now attractive features on the fairgrounds. Pride swelled in my chest at my overall success. I had satisfied the quest given to me by Glenn Wade to make this "the prettiest show in all of Michigan."

When the drone of activity quieted down that evening and the moon hung full in the sky, my dad stared longingly into the distance. He was beyond proud to witness my achievements in this unique lifestyle, but he also missed his tradition with my mother. They'd regularly take their boat and a picnic dinner to Beaver Lake to watch the sun go down and the moon come up. More than that, he missed being in her presence.

Dad and I had accomplished much together that summer. Working hard and having fun had brought about healing and laughter as we formed a bond that would be with us until his final days. But he'd had enough of show business and was ready to head home. I understood; not everyone was made for a life of adventure on the road. Dad made his plans to return to Arkansas right around the same time I made my plans to return to the circus.

One thing was for certain: I'd never forget that summer when Dad became a carnie.

Wake-Up Call

"What the hell you doing?"

I looked up from shampooing my buckskin behind the grandstand to see a short, plump blonde with a feisty commanding attitude. Quick to teach a lesson in manners, her arms waved like a windmill as she made her way over to confront me.

"Look at this mess," she said, gesturing toward the ground.

She was referring to the sudsy mud where raw, dusty dirt had been before I began washing my horse.

"Other people have to come through here, you know! Why don't you wash your horse over there?"

She gestured to an area away from the variety of rigs that had transported the other horses, dogs, elephants, tigers, and performers who came here to produce a twice-daily show on the upcoming circus tour. Realizing she was right, I felt my cheeks redden with embarrassment.

I had just met Evy Karoli, albeit without a formal introduction.

Later that day, our first performance began. Evy would perform with her dancing horse and dog acts. As with most circuses, all the animal trainers soon developed a bond. Despite our rough beginnings, Evy recruited me to help her. Her dog act included an assortment of happy, bouncy dogs that were eager to jump hoops, roll a barrel, roll over, and somersault. She also had a pony that would run under a platform from where the dogs could jump onto the pad on the pony's back. The dog would then ride halfway around the ring, only to switch places with another dog waiting on the other platform.

Through working side by side, Evy and I quickly became friends and I learned all about her personal history originating in Holland. Evy was born into a bareback-riding family in Europe. I heard childhood stories about her sneaking into the barn where she could hide and watch her grandfather train the horses, observing his closely guarded secrets. As a confident youngster, Evy impressed audiences enough to be invited to travel to this country as a teenage performer in the Ringling Bros. and Barnum & Bailey Circus. I soon discovered for myself the command she had over of all aspects of training, living, and traveling with animals in this unique community.

Her son had risen through the ranks to become the principle bareback rider for the Hanneford Circus, owned by another established circus family known for graceful athletic feats on the backs of galloping horses. As it turned out, I had met Evy's son, Mark, several years prior during the fallow time when I had no truck with which to haul my horse and liberty act.

Bingo was being boarded at Hayes's farm when I found out the small three-ring tented show called Sells and Gray Circus was going to be nearby in Brooklyn, Michigan for a day. With hope in my heart and time on my hands, I rode my horse several miles that morning for the chance to show off. Arriving late morning, I found quiet grounds with setup complete and all the personnel off resting somewhere. The only soul visible was a kid near the large draft horses tied to a truck in the backyard. I wasn't going all the way back without doing what I came here to do.

"Hey," I called out to the boy. "Want to see my performing horse?"

"Heck yeah!" His enthusiasm bubbled as he approached me. "Let's see what he can do."

Mark was barely a teenager at the time. Under his mother's watchful eye, he was still developing the bareback-riding skills he would later become known for. On that day, he made up my entire audience as I ran Bingo through his paces. I had my horse perform the march, bow, lie down, sit up, sidepass, and rear. To my delight, Mark was amazed.

"Hey, Mom!" he exuberantly called out. "Come out and see this circus horse."

I didn't know whether she was busy or simply couldn't hear him, but Evy never did come out of the trailer.

Now several years later in another part of the country, I had finally met her.

Our tour began in the east. The act I learned with Bingo began by riding into the ring to salute the crowd. We trotted around the ring, then into the volte or small circle, followed by the sidepass where the horse traveled diagonally. After that, we switched directions and repeated before stopping in the center of the ring to take a bow, but we were just getting warmed up.

We then began another circular path around the ring, entering into the three-step, or a foreleg extension on every third step. After this, we changed direction through the middle of the ring and I asked for a Spanish march, or a foreleg extension on every stride. While marching around the ring, the prop man set our pedestal in the center and we marched up to it.

The horse placed one foot on the pedestal first, then the other to mount with both his front feet. At this point, we turned on the forehand, where his back legs stepped sideways to encircle the pedestal. We paused to style for applause, then backed off the pedestal and into the bow. In this pose, we styled again—show business is all about being showy.

Next, we moved forward at a vigorous pace to encircle the ring a few times before coming to the center. I asked Bingo to tuck both forelegs beneath him into a kneel. From this position, I coaxed him to lie down.

As he did so, I stepped out of the saddle and up onto his rump for another style. While situated behind him, I asked him to sit up. He rolled up onto his rump with both front legs stretched out in front while I took another bow.

When that was completed, I asked him to stand and bow for me to remount. While in this pose, I placed my foot in the stirrup iron and swung my other leg over him before he rose

back to a standing position. Once back in the saddle, we resumed circling the ring with several canter rears, a fancy term for a couple of strides at the canter followed by a halt and a rear, where the horse stood on its hindlegs. For our spectacular conclusion, we found the center of the ring and bowed once more to receive our hard-earned applause. It was good to be back!

Circus Equestrianism

During the heyday of the circus over a hundred years ago, horse acts filled the program. One display included dozens of horses and riders cramming into the performance arena consisting of three rings and the hippodrome track. This multitude of horses and riders called manège horses performed a choreographed routine to music where they all marched, bowed, lay down, and sat up in unison, similar to the routine Bingo and I did solo.

The sheer number of horses doing amazing things in time with each other was the prerequisite for the classic haute école, or high school horse display, which was the epitome of classic horsemanship. The main difference between the two was that the high school or dancing horse performed movements judged by fluid achievements within the movement—height of leg extension, engagement of haunches, span of hesitation, distance between footfalls, etc.—while the manège horse posed, meaning the rider requested the horse to arrive at and hold a specific pose.

After the manège display, individual dancing horses performed solo in each of the three rings. These horsemen had

the ability to enter into an admirable, harmonious union with their horse and were considered the highest regarded performers of the circus. Demonstrating the upper-level horsemanship feats, including the piaffe, passage, high trot, Spanish march, backward three-legged canter, flying lead changes, and other incredible feats, it's no wonder the high school riders resided on top of the performer's hierarchy.

Since discovering this style of riding, I aspired to climb the social structure of the circus by developing and refining my skills as a horse rider and trainer. But as I learned more about haute école while working with Bingo, I soon realized the physical limitations of my quarter horse made his breed unsuitable for the advanced work it required. Being a quarter horse, Bingo was considered cold-blooded. Unfortunately, these horses were not naturally inclined to want to move out like their hot-blooded counterparts. The eagerness to move made the hot-blooded horse a far superior choice for a dancing horse.

When I sadly concluded that the handsome Bingo was simply not ideal for my aspirations to become an elite high school rider, I began searching for the perfect breed. Evy had a bay-colored Saddlebred gelding named Chip who would passage and piaffe, march, three-step, and rear. I set my sights on one day owning a Saddlebred of my very own.

Class n Sass

When a Monday off coincided with travel through southeast Pennsylvania, Evy approached me excitedly.

"I know the perfect place to spend our day off."

Aware of my growing desire to obtain a Saddlebred, Evy was also ready to add a second horse to her own lineup. After our Sunday matinee loadout, we drove to the New Holland sale barn where horses of all types were auctioned off every Monday. We arrived after dark, but Evy knew where we could park our rigs for the night.

After unloading and checking on our livestock, we ventured into the massive barn that surrounded the sales arena, an ancient wooden structure with a café underneath the elevated seating. Tie stalls flanked aisles that led labyrinth style from the shifting pens outside into the holding area adjacent to the sales area. This was where interested persons could look at the horses that waited to be sold the next morning.

Wandering the aisles, we looked at ponies and horses of all kinds, and another aspect of my new friend was revealed. Evy had a sharp eye that could find the defect that was often the reason the animal was being sold. While we inspected these animals, she pointed out and explained her observations to me. Under her tutelage, I learned much about the value of the visual assessment while Evy pointed out characteristics, both promising and problematic, about each equine specimen we perused.

After a good look, it was time to get some rest. We'd return in the morning to join in the excitement of the auction.

The next morning, we enjoyed strong coffee in well-worn china mugs, fried eggs, potatoes, and toast. When our bellies were full, Evy found us a perch over one end of the sales area where we could observe the activity. The horses were led into the sale in a single-file path that split the abundant humankind covering every square foot of available floor space. Occasional outbursts from a skittish or uncooperative horse instantly created a hole in the sea of humanity within the proximity of the threatening hind end.

Evy inspected each horse that came by. As she pointed out interesting facets of equinedom to me, she revealed another facet of this mysterious world I was fascinated with. The audience that surrounded us was just as interesting a cross section as the horses. Farmers, sportsmen, cowgirls, Amish, and successful horse trainers all shared space along the rails, perched on gates, and populated the expanse of seating.

The scourge of the populace was easy to pick out. Dressed smartly and adorned with diamonds were the killers—men who bought these majestic animals at minimal prices to turn a quick profit on their meat and by-products. With a poker face and economy of signal, they bought everything they could. There was the occasional exception when the announcer forbade their participation with a valuable buggy horse or an obviously well-trained animal ideally suited for family pleasure.

The auctioneer's dribbly monologue filled the air, punctuated by the spotters on the floor who maintained eye contact with the buyers. Their job was to call out a crisp "hup" every time they saw a gesture indicating a bid. The drama unfolded with the handlers on the floor wanting to show the assets of the horse they led, encouraging a nice trot back and forth in the small area or having them park out in style.

It was the Amish who put on the best show. Admirably adept in the world of horses, they laid a harness on the back of a horse with lightning speed and hooked him between buggy shafts within seconds, trotting the horse down the aisle cleared for just this purpose. Then they unhooked the apparatus at the other end repeated the process with another horse.

All the while, the auctioneer's long garbled song continued to run interference with the dusty, stifling mix of men, muscle, and horseflesh. Like a little kid watching the interesting processes at Santa's workshop, I absorbed as much of the experience as possible, enjoying every second of it. But all good things must come to an end. After our day-long diversion yielded no additions to our herd, we returned to our overnight parking, loaded Bingo and Chip, and headed toward the showgrounds at our next town.

During our second excursion two weeks later, Evy struck up a conversation with an Amish horse trader and his partner. Hanley and King claimed to have horses just as Evy described, so that afternoon, we left the auction to climb into our new friends' pickup and go have a look. Outside of town, the gravel road led to a clearing on a wooded hilltop with a large horse barn in the center, flanked by fenced paddocks. Their border collie greeted us as we piled out of the truck to go inside the barn.

The ancient wooden structure had a palpable comfortability confirmed by many nickers from the equine residents. As I stood in the sawdust of the aisle way, Mr. King, a white-bearded Amish man dressed in appropriate garb, went to a particular stall and brought out a sorrel Saddlebred mare. Evy's face immediately lit up.

While she inspected this fine specimen of horseflesh, I couldn't deny the attraction I also felt for this stunning Saddlebred. Standing at sixteen hands with kind, observant eyes containing wisdom, I was captivated by the mare's elegant neck that provided a firm foundation for her handsome head. I imagined what it would be like to own such a horse, recognizing how she'd even met Evy's approval.

When they brought out another Saddlebred horse, this one a liver chestnut, Evy's smile brightened up the interior of the barn. Upon her inspection, it was clear this mare also met her approval and I wondered which one she would purchase. As the afternoon faded, I wished I had enough to make the chestnut mare mine.

While Evy held a conversation with the bearded duo, I opted to give her privacy while waiting by the horses. I wasn't completely privy to what was said until Evy rejoined me a few minutes later.

"Congratulations!" she announced. "You just bought a horse."

My jaw dropped. "What? How?"

She waved her hand to dismiss my questions. "Don't worry.

You can pay me back later."

Riding a natural high, we returned shortly with our own rigs, loaded our new mares, and headed back to the auction. Now that we had new horses, we would need some training equipment. An old-time friend of Evy's sold tack at the sale barn out of the back of his pickup. She told me to go find Mickey and buy the bitting rig that was among his assortment of stuff. We'd use that to teach our new horses to accept a bit and bridle. It would also be useful in developing the proper muscles for our particular type of equestrianism.

Still in shock when we headed toward our next town, I gradually let the thought settle in. I was the proud new owner of a stunning sorrel Saddlebred horse named Class n Sass.

Back in the circus, the training for the new mares began immediately. Evy started by leading them both around to discover what they already knew, and making a note to add the fundamentals required for circus horses. Early the next morning, she harnessed Sassy first to begin the training in hand. The bitting rig was essentially a girth that went around the horse's barrel with a backband that connected to the croup that fit under her tail. It also included checkreins to snap on either side of the bit on the headstall. Evy added a pair of long nylon lines onto the bit, similar to reins for a buggy horse. This allowed her to encourage the horse to move in a wide radius around her. Tacked up with her training gear, Evy urged the mare forward to trot in a circle around her and had her change direction with the use of these long lines. Sassy learned to yield to the command to stay in hand as urgings from Evy continued to ask for something new. It wasn't long before our horses could remain animated in place, producing the slow, elevated trot known as the passage.

Training the new mares was a team effort. While Evy stood

in the center to observe and give direction, it was my job to ride them. I saddled them up one at a time and practiced the trot work, lateral movements, halt, and backing. Evy's preliminary groundwork combined with my time in the saddle to establish a solid foundation for our dancing horses. While she stimulated front leg extensions with her pointer whip from the ground, I gave the hand, leg, and seat cues to achieve the combined result for the march.

Although Sassy showed us an occasional streak of defiance, she willingly submitted to the processes introduced. As the horses became proficient with these new movements, the time came to teach them how to perform the passage, which would become Sassy's greatest asset. Evy's efforts from the ground stimulated engagement of the haunches, while I drove with my legs and held with my hand and seat. Soon my mare had an admirable passage that, once initiated, became unstoppable.

Evy seemed pleased with the results, and I was ecstatic. I couldn't ask for anything better—my already willing-to-please mare actually appeared to share my passion for haute école. I could already envision the marvels that wondrous mare and I would achieve together.

Sensational

Bentley Bros. Circus was the product of a gay retired highwire walker who was mediocre in his profession at best. Tommy Bentley was elderly and rotund with a wardrobe full of square-tailed pastel shirts with twin vertical embroidered stripes designed to distract attention from his massive midriff. Large glasses disappeared on either side of a plump walnut-shaped head covered in a curly salt-and-pepper Afro.

With flamboyant gestures, his sexual preference was always on display and never in doubt. He used his arms like semaphore flags, assumed provocative poses as he talked, and effectively communicated to his audience that he wanted all the attention all the time. He surrounded himself with pretty boys who all seemed to have the name Sally. They made up Tommy's staff, clown alley, band, and wardrobe departments, busying themselves with lots of banter.

His flaming ego had a place to fly as the owner and director of this grand show, yet he visibly allowed emotional desires, selfish demands, and accumulated resentments to influence decisions that sometimes resulted in detrimental effects for his staff. I observed all of this while being coached by the wise troupers in the backyard to lie low and avoid being visible, lest I become a target for Tommy's flaming wrath.

The Bentley Bros. Circus program began with what was called spec, a spectacular parade made up of the entire cast. With one horse, life had been simple; I saddled Bingo up and waited in position until spec began. Then I rode Bingo through the parade route around the three rings, exited, and returned to the backyard to help with Evy's dog act, and later get ready for my own act.

Now with two horses, I used spec as an opportunity to get Sassy used to the sights, sounds, and smells of the performance, but this meant Bingo sat unused. In addition, Evy was absent during spec, being poised by the chute to help get the lions and tigers in and out of the big cage for Alan Gold, the first act after spec ended. That meant both of her horses sat unused as well.

The show owners were excited about our new horses. We had extra saddles to fill and two eager riders. Despite the others having warned me to keep my distance, the next thing I knew, I was saddling up three horses each day so Tommy and Clancy could ride in spec. Clancy knew the least about horses, so I put him on Bingo, the safest of them all. Since Tommy fancied himself a horseman, I trusted him to ride my new mare while I rode Evy's liver chestnut mare.

After their first ride, everything seemed just fine. Although I hadn't forgotten what the others had warned me about, we continued in this manner every time we did spec. I hoped it would gain us extra points with the difficult show owners.

Because I got to ride Evy's new mare in spec, she gave me a mission each day to test her out. From her vantage point by the cat cages, Evy observed each horse's behavior as we rode past. While her horse continued to get acclimated to the rigors of exposure, she began to show real promise. I enjoyed the challenge as these lessons blended into our training between shows and became an exciting time of exploration as we familiarized ourselves with our new horses.

"Keep her quiet going into the building," Evy directed one day, "and as you go down the main stretch, start to drive a little harder while holding her back at the same time."

With today's mission in mind, I helped Tommy and Clancy get on my horses, then mounted Evy's horse. Falling into position for spec, I followed her directions, keeping the horse quiet as we entered. Once we made it into the performance area, around the props, and onto the track in front of the three rings, I began to squeeze with my legs to encourage her to move forward while holding her back with my seat and reins at the same time. I continued to get more and more aggressive until I eventually felt her give me a rocking horse sensation.

I glanced at Evy in position near the cat cages on the other side. Her face began to beam, but I wouldn't know what happened until we had a moment to talk later.

"At first, her posture became extremely engaged," Evy explained, "and then she went into a slow canter, almost in place. It was beautiful."

Class n Sass was an elegant sorrel mare with a full mane and a tail that had been set, meaning it was surgically altered to remain elevated when the horse was working. I also discovered that she had been gaited. Right out of the box, horses come with three gaits - walk, trot, and canter. Man sometimes taught an additional four-beat variation of the trot to a saddle horse for comfortability. As a result, Sassy produced a four-beat gait known as the rack. The only time a traditional two-beat trot appeared was during the passage.

The one exception where caution was needed with Sassy was during saddling. When I laid the saddle on her back and prepared to girth her up, her ears pinned back and she bared her teeth as she tried to reach around and bite me. But because she was otherwise agreeable, I made a vow to never respond negatively to the fierce behavior she exhibited during saddling. The result as the years went by was that this behavior turned into a harmless game. Eventually, as I laid the saddle on her back, her ears still went back and she'd reach for me with her mouth, only now when she got close she licked me affectionately like a dog. As we bonded, I even went so far as to put my hand in her mouth while she gummed me lovingly.

I also took full advantage of exposure therapy to get Sassy accustomed to the exotic sights, sounds, and noises while on this circus tour. Bill and Cindy had an outstanding and rather unusual elephant who actually liked horses. Incidentally, Jewel was also the star in the movie Smokey and the Bandit. Each day in the backyard, as all the performers waited for opening spec to begin, I sat on Sassy and talked to them in the proximity of Jewel. As the summer progressed, my horse learned to relax around the many exotic animals, even the oversized elephants.

I was in love. Between her astounding growth and our developing bond, Sassy and my future appeared limitless.

As the season progressed, so did our horses—a detail that was not lost on the owners of the show who were personally familiar with them from riding in spec. Our two new horses learned more and more dancing skills and commanded the attention of our peers. Plans for additional seasons in the future seemed hopeful.

While surrounded in the backyard by other performers, Tommy recognized an opportunity to step into the spotlight.

"Training a dancing horse takes years," Tommy began his unsolicited advice. "The bareback horses around the Cole show never needed to be prompted. They've done the routine so many times, they know the music and automatically begin the routine." His focus honed in on me. "You keep practicing with this horse, and someday you will have a nice act."

It seemed my instinct had been right—allowing Clancy and Tommy to ride our horses had proven fruitful. Somehow, I had avoided his wrath and even gotten on his good side.

Chapter 6
Bigger, Better, Brighter

"All children are artists. The problem is how to remain an artist once he grows up."
—Picasso

Behind the Scenes

When the circus tour was over, I returned to Michigan to resume my routine as a show painter. While I would be boarding my horses for the rest of the summer, Evy had secured another set of circus dates and headed west. I hoped we'd get the opportunity to work together again someday and vowed to stay in touch. I would be forever grateful to Evy for connecting me with Sassy and helping to build a solid foundation in our performance career.

But for now, it was time to create clever sign work and scenery for the showmen. At that point in my career I was fascinated with all forms of show business. I was fortunate to have found a big market for my painting skills. Red was especially interested in my success, and opportunities expanded with his help. In October, he encouraged me to go with him to the State Fair of Texas, where he took several rides every year and knew all the other independent ride operators.

When Superdog and I got to Dallas, Red introduced me to his friends. Soon I was elbow to elbow with other successful members of this industry. Steck and Staph had rides to paint, Newport Concessions had signs to letter, and Wicked Wanda would soon proffer a collaborative proposition with her T-shirt stand. Plus, Billy Baxter and J.D. Floyd wanted me to come to their amusement park in the spring, and Butch Webb had a project for me right after the fair. These showmen had work that could round out a full year of paintwork. I was finally thriving.

When the fair was over, I rendezvoused at a premier concession operation headquartered in Kansas. Outside of Wichita, I found a large block building with carnival equipment parked all around. Inside was a brand-new concession trailer, on which Butch Webb wanted some special paintwork. The finished trailer was headed for an amusement business trade show before it went to the Kansas State University stadium for its career.

The first thing I did was get the whole thing clean and tape off my graphic stripe shapes for paint. Then I got to work creating a three-color metal-flake paint scheme, lettering the overhead sign faces, and adding decorative pinstriping wherever I could. I even made the removable hitch elaborate. I had it all completed in plenty of time for Butch to take it to the big show. With that project on display, the name Letterfly would be in front of even more members of the carnival and amusement park industry than ever before.

As promised, I kept in touch with Evy and learned that in addition to providing her horse and dog acts on her distant circus tour, she also began to assist with a bear act. She planned to winter in Texas at the circus winter quarters of Donnie Johnson. His place housed all kinds of animals—elephants, bears, baboons, lions, tigers, dogs, and, of course, horses.

After Butch took his freshly painted trailer to the trade show, I returned to Michigan to get my horses. Now that I had new carnival clients, my plan was to work year-round in my role as a carnival sign man. In the meantime, I would take the livestock to Texas where Evy offered to care for them in my absence. She had stopped by to haul my VW bus to Texas so I could visit in the downtime before my next job. I had hoped the visit would include some training sessions, but I would soon be struck by the reality that the off season, for some, was a time to grow lazy and careless.

The circus winter quarters were ghastly. Clowns, jugglers, acrobats, and musicians were gone; only the animals and their keepers remained. The hectic pace of the road did not exist here, nor did the usual regard for appropriate behavior. The keeper of a big box truck filled with monkeys simply swept the shavings and debris out the door into a growing manure pile that swallowed up the steps. No one watched. No one cared. I was disillusioned before I'd even turned off my truck. One thing was for certain, I didn't want to be here long.

Sassy and Bingo joined Evy's new Saddlebred, her pony, and Chip in tie stalls along the outside of the main barn. I was eager to train my new horse and ride in the practice ring, but with nothing pressing, even Evy didn't share my enthusiasm. This was not at all what I expected after our interactions during the tour. My energetic pace simply didn't fit with the slow, anemic off-season pace these animal people seemed to share.

Disappointed with my winter quarters, I was grateful for the distraction a few sign jobs in the area provided. When those were completed, I packed the VW for my painting tour of Florida. Just before Superdog and I headed out, another showman wanted some sign work. Hungry to grow my painting career, I couldn't turn him away even though I really should have been getting on the road. Showmen often had pressing deadlines and show dates in distant places that displaced sleep. This was just another one of those times. In order to stay on schedule and pocket a little extra income, I decided to complete his project and then drive all night to my destination.

The extensive purple decorations were completed by nightfall and the client was pleased. Happy the extra income would help fund my lifestyle and feed my horses, I loaded up and hit the long road ahead of me. Although somewhat tired, I was determined to stay on schedule. Between my legs, the piercing sound of another pop top soon promised to quench my thirst.

From the Wreckage

The rumble strips on the edge of the road startled me awake. Seeing I was off course, I quickly yanked the wheel to steer the bus back onto the road. The extreme turn caused the bus to rock violently back and forth several times until it rolled over onto its side. After skidding to a halt, I was wide awake. I stood up, pushed open the passenger door over my head, and crawled up onto the side of the bus. When Superdog's and my feet were safely on the pavement, I assessed the damage. Thankfully, neither of us had sustained any major injuries, but in this remote part of Louisiana with the stars filling the sky, my surroundings were as quiet as a morgue. There weren't any passing cars who could help.

I looked around, trying to figure out what to do next. After a few minutes, distant headlights loomed. A big rig entered my proximity and slowed down, stopping to shine his lights on my immobilized vehicle lying across the road. Hopping down from his cab, he called out as he walked up to me.

"Hey, there!" He waved. "Are you all right?"

"Yeah," I said, embarrassed. "I guess I nodded off."

"I'll radio for help," he offered, turning on his heel.

My thoughts filled with a mixture of panic and uncertainty. This would interrupt my plans, but at least we weren't hurt. That kind driver stayed with me until police arrived, and then continued on his own journey.

"Have you been drinking?" the officer asked when we were alone.

"I guess so."

He clenched his jaw and called for a wrecker.

"I'll need to bring you back to the station," he said.

My heart sank. How would I explain the delay to my next customer?

Illuminated by blinking lights, a cable was draped over the top of my damaged bus, the winch was tightened, and gradually my fallen VW was pulled back up on its wheels. My heart wrenched at the sight of my righted vehicle. The entire driver's side of my beloved van was flattened with diagonal scrapes ripping through the decorative paint job I'd worked so hard on. Purple paint from my last project was strewn throughout the inside and all over most of my belongings. The driver's door would not open, either; I would have to adopt a new technique of getting in and out of the bus from the passenger seat. In frustration, I kicked a small rock at my feet, eyeing my worn-out cowboy boots and thinking about how humbling it would be to drive the bus in such a condition. Unfortunately, I had no other options. To top it all off, now I wouldn't have enough money to replace my boots.

I was released by the authorities after losing several hours that should have been spent on the road. The officer must have taken pity on me. The report merely said, "Failure to maintain control of a motor vehicle," but I received no penalty besides the wrecker fee. Shortly after resuming my drive, the sunrise greeted me. I should have been in Florida by now, but instead I still had a long way to go.

Finally arriving in Florida, my first stop was to see Mary at Eckerd College. Our love had grown as we kept in touch during my travels, and in this moment of tragedy I needed to see a familiar face who could lift my spirits. The condition of my vehicle told the story of the driver being incompetent. I was embarrassed. I knew I would have to replace the bus at some point, but I didn't have the money to do that right now.

After a brief visit on her college campus catching up on fun, family, and ambitions, I left to accomplish the work that should have been well underway by now. Joe was a friend of Butch Netterfield and he wanted a huge sign for the front of the cookhouse stick joint he'd inherited from his father. After apologizing for the delay, I acquired multiple four-by-eight pieces of Masonite, (tile board with a white finish) which was an inexpensive material ideally suited for signs.

The composition of Joe's sign was daunting due to the large amount of copy he wanted. Once confident I was on the right track, he left to pursue other interests. I worked in the shade of the large pine trees in the backyard of his rural home, feeling myself relax after my harrowing journey. Little did I know, my wreck wasn't the only problem I'd encounter with this commission.

When the time came to get paid, Joe had disappeared. No one knew when he would be back. I suspected his behavior was influenced by drug consumption, but having been jilted on my fee before and needing it now more than ever, I came up with an idea. I had seen an orange VW bus for sale on my way to Joe's. Between what I had on me and what Joe owed me, I would have just enough money to purchase it.

I loaded the four-by-eight panels in the back of my bus and went to the used car lot. Putting a down payment on the bus, I stored the sign panels inside. That clinched two things; the bus was mine and I would eventually get paid for my signs. Since the remainder due was exactly what Joe owed me, I informed the salesman that he would be by to pay the remainder for the bus, at which point the salesman could give Joe the signs stored inside.

Hoping I was right, I left to serve another showman. Wayne Pies wanted his Corky the Pig sign renewed with fresh lettering. I enjoyed a productive time working for this nice guy at his home and was relieved when this project went off without a hitch and was paid in full.

With another successful project completed, I headed toward the used car lot with butterflies in my stomach. Unsure of what I would find, I was elated to see the salesman appear with a big smile on his face.

"He really wanted his signs," he announced as he handed me the keys.

I cheered inwardly at my bold move and told the salesman I'd be back soon to drive it off the lot.

With the orange bus secured, I left in my old, busted van to visit the home of Corky and Jean Shrewsbury, game operators from the old Wade Shows. I recruited one of their guys to drive the new bus and follow me to the Volkshop in Sanford. There, my old friend Marvin helped me swap my stuff into the new bus so he could acquire my old, crippled bus for parts.

With these problems behind me, I was ready to paint my name on the new bus and resume my quest as a sign painter with the other projects I had lined up, including western motif signs for a fairgrounds hat booth, lettering "World's Largest Horse" on another show front, and creating sign work for various showmen in a variety of locations all throughout Florida.

In the spring, I ventured back to rejoin my horses in Texas. I hoped to be pleasantly surprised, but when I arrived, my first impression of this place was confirmed. There hadn't been much productivity going on at the winter quarters.

Evy came stomping out to meet me when I pulled in.

"That blasted quarter horse of yours kicked Sassy," she fumed.

"What happened?" I asked.

"There was a ruckus and he got excited," she spewed. "He kicked out right into her side. It made me so mad! I hope she's not hurt."

Feeling like something was missing from this story, I tried unsuccessfully to get more details. The other trainers weren't offering any more information than Evy provided, uncertain of the ins and outs of what went on in my absence, I was glad to be reunited with my horses, the Dodge, and the comfort of my horse trailer. At the same time, I was relieved I had been away during the apparent chaos. The instant spike in my stress level upon being back in this rundown environment caused me to want to flee again. I stayed just long enough to practice my horse act with Evy for a few days—she'd finally found a little motivation.

When that fizzled out, I was glad to have an excuse to leave, explaining that friends of Red had an amusement park that needed signs painted near Chattanooga. And yes, they had room for my horses at the park. Thank goodness I wouldn't have to leave them behind in this hell hole. I loaded up my horses and bid Evy adieu, this time on a full night's rest. As I pulled out, I shivered at the sight of a horse skull lying behind the cat barn. Relieved to be leaving that curious mix of animal trainers, I ventured east and vowed never to return.

Lake Winnepesaukah

With my livestock on board and the orange bus in tow, I headed toward the amusement park. I would arrive early to help get them ready prior to their annual opening in the spring. After the final bend on the last road, I passed through the entrance to the quiet park and found Glen Bergethon, who was the manager of this fun park and a gracious host to boot.

After offering one of the many picnic shelters as a place for me to keep the livestock, he pointed out several projects for me to work on while giving me a tour.

Being familiar with the components of a working carnival, what I found at this amusement park expanded my understanding of this unique business. Lake Winnie, as the locals lovingly referred to her, was a quaint, folksy place. A regional favorite, the park had many permanent attractions inside buildings, along with an impressive lineup of both permanent and portable rides. Being set in a permanent location without the need for travel, the park had features that did not exist on a traveling carnival in addition to the old favorites found on every midway.

Among the permanent attractions at the park were a flume ride alongside the lake, a large dark ride in a building with two roller-coaster-like dips across the front, an elaborate forty-horse carousel, a railroad that went around the whole lake, the Sky Ride that went across the lake, and a wooden roller coaster. Other portable rides were set up in every available space around the park, making for an impressive atmosphere.

Off the main thoroughfare was a road that went behind the attractions, between the picnic shelters, and up to several large out-of-the-way metal buildings. A variety of support equipment, park components, partially completed projects, trucks waiting for service, and semitrailers of all kinds were all parked haphazardly around this compound. In the middle was the shop where the work took place. Inside the dark shop building, I saw the crew busily accomplishing various tasks.

One old man had a comfortable workstation in the corner and a single task. Old George rebuilt bumper car motors full time. Superdog loved old George. A friendly fellow, he talked about his days handling pig iron, weaving colorful stories about the rigors of when he was a young ride man around a railroad carnival called the Olson Shows. Now Floyd and Baxter sent all their worn bumper car motors to old George to be rebuilt.

Trusting my judgment, Glen gave me creative freedom. I found an area in the shop to call my own where I could make patterns, create designs, cut out fancy-shaped sign boards, and make sign plaques of all kinds. I coated the boards and made sure they would be extra durable, but I was especially glad these pieces of art wouldn't get beat up like the road show signs did from being loaded and unloaded so many times in the course of a season.

When the boards and plaques were dry, I decorated them in a specific way for each attraction to give them individual personality. I studied old-time advertising examples to create authentic period-looking signs for the old-time railroad station, the carousel, and all the rides in Kiddieland. I also created a European Alpine-themed sign with snow on the letters and icicles hanging down for the entrance of the Sky Ride. I painted the kinds of signs I wanted to paint; it was like a dream come true.

Mary joined me that spring in Chattanooga. Originally from Maryland, I discovered her father, being an editor at the National Geographic, was connected politically, socially, and affluently. Like me, Mary didn't seem to care about the typical ambitions encouraged by her parents. Although she aspired to be a journalist, she also wanted adventure and fulfillment. We had a plan to live, love, and work together.

Although knowing nothing about horses, she was willing to help with the livestock until the sign work was completed here at the park. After that, we would head to Kansas, and then Michigan, where I would board the horses while we launched another season of our T-shirt painting service on the carnival midway. I enjoyed having her along as we entered into a rhythm of horse care, sign making, and living our lives together.

When my workday concluded one afternoon, I was ready for a beer, but Mary wanted me to teach her how to ride Bingo. In the clearing at the top of the parking area, her riding lessons began. The process of learning to ride a horse involved making lots of corrections before the student started to produce commendable behavior.

There's a certain delicate touch required when teaching. Although I was skilled with paint and in my own riding ability, I wasn't a skilled teacher. I was focused on the goal Mary said she wanted to achieve and what was needed to get there. After listening to me point out flaws, repeat requests for what she deemed the impossible, and offer strict demands, Mary became sullen and retaliatory.

From my viewpoint, those sessions interfered with our getting along, not to mention it delayed our evening beer. I would learn the hard way that my attempt to teach the skills of horsemanship to my love interest was not a good idea, but I suffered from compound ignorance; I didn't know that I didn't know. I lacked the vision required to understand how far encouragement, positivity, and reassurance would have gone to both her seat and my happy home.

Like two mixed-up kids, we drank every day—regular consumption had become a stronghold by this point—but this bump in the road introduced us to a new revelation about our drinking. In the midst of all this tension, we believed our beer consumption interfered with our ability to find harmony, so we agreed to not drink. The only problem was we didn't know how to not drink.

Tension mounted again, this time from a different source. Being irritable, restless, and discontented without alcohol was perhaps an indication of a real problem we had yet to recognize. After several hours with the pressure mounting, I suggested we go get a six pack. The tension melted away immediately as the cool amber beverage did its magic. Beneath the surface, embryonic alcoholism was blossoming while our

relationship was slowly crumbling. If only we'd seen it sooner.

As Memorial Day loomed, the park prepared to open. Mary and I moved the horses from the picnic shelter to an area out back where the public did not venture. I moved the trailer behind the Cannon Ball roller coaster that had been silent all winter and set up my canvas awning to the side to rig up a stable. This also placed the horses near an area filled with the fresh grass that had begun to grow. Because my two animals had bonded, I simply tied one of them up and let the other wander around to graze, thereby keeping them securely in proximity of each other while I worked elsewhere.

As opening time for the park grew near, Jack and the rest of the coaster crew had to get the ride ready to go, which included a practice run or two. The steel track had a thick coat of rust from being dormant all winter. Jack explained when the train went around the track the first time each year, the rust that had settled on the

track slowed it down. Sometimes, the train would be too slow to make it over one of the hills and he would have to climb up with a come-along to winch the train over.

That was a lot of climbing and winching, so every year during the first coaster run, Jack kept his fingers crossed that the train would make it all the way around.

In preparation for the first run of the Cannon Ball, I tied Bingo, the more experienced of the two, along the coaster fence and let Sassy walk free. It was time for some more exposure therapy. The roaring sound of the coaster train going down the first hill terrified them. Bingo strained at his tether and Sassy ran away, only to return a moment later when she realized her companion hadn't followed.

When the sound came from the other side of the wooden structure, Jack was relieved. The train had made it all the way around. With the danger extinct, the horses resumed their grazing. As the days went by, Bingo and Sassy grew more and more accustomed to the noise, gradually able to remain calm during the unusual racket coming from the roller coaster. I counted it as a success. The more they experienced, the more bombproof they became.

As I scrambled to finish up all the sign work, busloads of kids and family cars filled the parking areas on opening weekend. Overnight, Lake Winnie turned into a bustling center of activity. I was proud to witness how my finished work was adding to their fun.

I would return to the amusement park for many years to come, but for now, it was time to go. Mary and I bid adieu to our new friends, loaded up our four-legged family, and headed west.

E.S. Webb Company

Traveling to Kansas each spring allowed for an easy visit with my folks in Arkansas on the way. It was nice bringing Mary along this time, and I knew my folks would be proud to show her around the commune.

"Oh, David!" Mother beamed as we wrapped our arms around each other. "It is so great to see you." Pulling out of our embrace, she glanced at my companion. "And this must be Mary?"

"I'm so glad to be here," Mary responded. "This is a lovely part of the country."

"Son!" dad emerged from the worksite to join in the reunion. After a long hug and meeting Mary, he told me, "You'll be proud of the progress we made."

The construction of their home was making good headway. Wiring, insulation in the walls, and window installation had all preceded the drywall.

While we visited, I watched Dad use my old red VW bus to retrieve materials for his construction project and I suddenly realized it would make a good bus for my T-shirt booth. Luckily, he understood. When we continued our trek west,

Mary drove it to Wichita behind me.

To break up the long journey, Mary and I took a detour to see an under-canvas circus. After the fun diversion, we continued on our way. I boarded the horses at a farm near our destination, and we set up quarters next to Butch Webb's shop. He had more work for me.

Butch had a fleet of root beer and ice cream stands that went up into Canada each summer and on to the big fairs in the central states during the fall. He also had a big pizza kitchen trailer imported from Germany. His route culminated at the State Fair of Texas, where Red had introduced us the year prior. Butch only had so much lettering and decorative work to do, so to provide me with full-time work while I was there, I did other types of painting for him as well.

I learned on-the-job skills of a body man while preparing pieces of his equipment to receive overall paint jobs. I learned to sand and prepare the surface for paint, paper off large areas, and spray an even coat of paint with a big gun. These skills would come in very handy for a blossoming career I had no idea was in the works for me several years down the road.

This was a great place to get some of my own projects underway as well. Butch's large shop was equipped with every kind of power tool imaginable. Sharing my dad's innovative leanings, I loved making things. Across the street was the Harder Brothers' Welding and Machine Shop. They could fabricate almost anything, and I had ideas for my truck bed, the horse trailer, and my T-shirt booth.

Since Mary and I lived in my horse trailer next to the shop where I had all these tools at my disposal, I started on my many personal projects after work. I made improvements to my rig and began fabricating components for our T-shirt stand. I crafted two folding corner columns for flash, and after studying a book with examples of European fairground artwork, I created special scrollwork décor on the base of each. I also built an inventory box and folding jack stands.

Using the bandsaw, I cut out individual letters for two airbrushing signs that featured a gorgeous blonde astride an airbrush. I planned to use these signs on my booth on the Elliott Amusement Company and at the state fairs.

This small, quiet town stuck on the outskirts of Wichita had

an environment consisting of vast flat country, which offered nothing for Mary while I kept busy. She didn't participate in the shop while I worked on Butch's stuff all day. Every evening, I continued to work on my other projects. She did not appreciate this opportunity to get things ready for our upcoming summer tour back in Michigan. She was bored.

I had my first beer at the end of the workday, but while I sipped and continued to work late into the evening, Big Al and the other guys knocked off at quitting time. Mary hung out and drank with the crew. I did not know what to do, so I just continued to work. I felt abandoned and rejected. When I went back to the trailer one night, she was nowhere to be found. I went inside the deserted trailer, locked the door, and prepared to go to bed.

In the middle of the night when she was finally done

drinking, Mary discovered she couldn't get into the trailer. Fury filled her blurred mind. She was mad. I'll show him. She began to kick at the door on the horse trailer. It didn't take much for her foot to go through the flimsy entry door. The ruckus woke me up, but the damage had been done.

In the morning, Butch and the crew looked at the wreckage and concluded what had happened. We sheepishly looked at the kicked-open doorway. That episode was a testimony of how drinking affected our union. We had both contributed to the insanity. We felt bad, but neither of us knew how to fix it. What we did know was that neither of us was happy, so Mary made plans to fly back to Maryland. Maybe some space would help.

Despite this embarrassing episode, working and living at the E.S. Webb Company would become an annual stop. While in this part of the country, I met some of the local businessmen who also wanted sign work. One place repaired farm implements and had sheet metal, a break, and a shear. I painted a large sign for the front of their shop, and in return I could use it to bring the plans for one of my projects to life. I cut and bent a piece of steel to size with ease and accuracy on their metal break.

Being in charge of Butch's paint shop placed me in a good position to get my own overall paint jobs completed also. While there, the old red bus received a two-tone paint job, complete with a new airbrushed Letterfly logo and pinstriping. Eventually the time came for Butch and his fleet to go north and begin their season, which meant it was time for me to depart as well. My mind was already spinning with more ideas I could accomplish at this location. Each time I returned to Maize, Kansas I could make additional improvements to my rig.

Recruiting a driver to follow me in the newly painted T-shirt bus, I headed northeast with mixed feelings. I was grateful to have found a market for my creative inclination with paint, but still bewildered about the turbulence with Mary. I returned to Michigan for the summer carnival circuit. At least I would be among friends there. I boarded the horses near Fowlerville, rehearsed my circus acts, and then returned to the Elliott Amusement Company to paint for my favorite showmen on my expanding list of carnival customers.

Elliott Amusement Company

The creation of Victorian scrollwork had always piqued my interest. While attending a fancy dinner as a child, a paper napkin with delicately embossed elaborate scrolls that graced the entire surface kept me fascinated for hours. Rather than enjoying the social activities going on around me, I became obsessed with studying the rhythm of the spirals that gracefully intersected and sprouted into other shapes. That discovery inspired my early attempts to imitate what I saw. While I recreated my new obsession in a sketchbook, I pondered the intention of the creator. In later years, I would learn that over a hundred years ago heavy circus wagons depicted sculpted goddesses, animals, and clowns, surrounded with hand-carved rococo designs and gilded Victorian scrolls. The brilliant sight wowed the rural masses whenever these show wagons paraded through town. The premise was that no expense had been spared by the show to bring nothing but the best attractions, royal entertainments, and educational features to the town. As building materials evolved, wagon design progressed and the decorations used by traveling showmen streamlined into the use of hand-painted artwork to imitate the grandeur of yesteryear.

Life on the midway provided an endless source of similar fascination. Far from the plain contemporary sign work I did for regular townsfolk, showmen had a relentless appetite for outstanding, stimulating, and entertaining works of art—a proven constant throughout the history of showmanship.

Thanks to Red introducing me to his showmen friends in other parts of the country, I now had a route that kept me busy creating this type of fascinating artwork almost year-round. During the winter in Florida, I worked for Butch Netterfield. Each spring after painting for Lake Winnie, I visited my parents on my way to moving my operation to the E.S. Webb Company in Kansas. Then I hit the road for my summertime pattern in Michigan, where I worked the fairgrounds and joined the Elliott Amusement Company en route as their show painter. I would forever be loyal to Red for his willingness to go the extra mile to help me succeed.

The Elliott Amusement Company was populated by my favorite carnival people, but when an up-and-coming carnival started out, it took a few years to develop a solid route. Some spots required a certain number of attractions before they would even consider a particular carnival company. As the Elliott Amusement Company slowly grew, they were able to secure festivals in affluent areas that generated more income. I was proud to be a part of this growth with my artwork helping to make this show attractive, admired, and successful.

Each year there were new rides, games, and concessions added to the lineup. Having me show up every summer gave them the ability to plan for new decorations. By this time, the show had outgrown the single ticket box I'd decorated that first summer. During the winter this year, Red had built two new identical ticket boxes that unloaded from a flat trailer made just for them. These two pieces would need to get decorated.

My style of sign painting now heavily included the airbrush, enhancing the designs, scenic effects, and animated lettering of my brush and combining the best of both worlds. Plus, thanks to accumulating the skills of a body man at the Webb Company, I could use the big spray guns to my advantage, clear-coating the finished artwork for durability.

After sketching my design for the new ticket boxes, I made

patterns for the festive scrollwork that would frame each of the four sides of both boxes. When the exterior was clean and ready for paint, I utilized the spray gun to apply large areas of brilliant color on the corners where they would receive the most wear and tear. When that paint was dry, I transferred my scroll patterns and began to paint the shapes, using the airbrush to imitate form with highlights and shadows. In memory of my six-pony liberty act, I included an easter egg by immortalizing them on the masthead on the back of each ticket box where six ponies galloped in front of the name Elliott Amusement Co. Brilliant airbrushed flashes of light became the final details that animated my depiction and brought it all to life.

As the concession manager for the Elliott Amusement Company, Tim Bors assumed an even bigger role on the show each year by expanding his fleet one game trailer at a time. With his clear vision for the future including colorful motifs, he wanted me as his show painter. His most recent purchase was a ride called the Rock-O-Plane.

Tim was the only showman who always gave me six months' advance notice of what my next project was going to be, and this was no exception. During the previous winter in Florida, Tim had asked me to meet him one afternoon at Specialty Trailer in Tampa, where his latest game trailer was under construction. That particular day I drove to an industrial park near the airport to a large metal building surrounded by carnival trailers of all types. Tim was already there standing inside the shop. Behind him, I saw a trailer receiving the exterior corrugated aluminum skin. I observed workers on ladders using the old-fashioned manner of buck riveting, using an impact device on the outside to mushroom the end of a rivet shaft against a metal pillow block held on the inside. This was a noisy process as the workers attached skin pieces one at a time, which meant our conversation would have to move outside in order to be productive. Once we were free of the noisy den of the shop, we found an overhang to keep us dry from the Michigan rain.

"I love the clown you painted for my logo inside the Skee-Ball trailer," Tim said, referring to the job I did for him my first summer on the show. "When you get to Michigan this spring, I want you to create a festive scene on this new trailer with that clown in the center. I'm telling you now so you'll have plenty of time to think up a great design."

I smiled. "I can definitely do that."

My mind began to percolate with ideas while Tim introduced me to Paul Gagne, the short, tousle-haired man who owned Specialty Trailer. Paul radiated genuine concern for anyone in his midst, and he was glad to meet me after having already received accolades from Tim about my talents and abilities. Paul revealed that he had grown up in New England and his whole family was in the carnival business. While his wife and kids ran the Elephant Ears trailer at the carnival, he spearheaded the many functions going on at his shop where he built custom concession trailers, ticket boxes, and game trailers for other showmen.

Tim knew I would appreciate the process and encouraged Paul to show us more.

"Sure," he agreed, his accent revealing his New England roots.

Paul walked us through a maze of ladders, cords, hoses, and other devices the workmen used on the multitude of trailers currently under construction. Reaching Tim's newest acquisition, he inspected the features while briefly introducing me to his concept full of bright colors.

The tour of the plant then continued with the large structural table called a frame jig, where the main rails and support gussets were assembled. Between the bays, parts of trailers in various stages of assembly and machines of all kinds peppered the shop floor. These machines provided the ability

to cut, bend, nibble, punch, or roll a sheet, plate, rod, tube, or beam of an assortment of materials. Other devices facilitated welding, riveting, fastening, and attachment of components that were mostly custom-fitted pieces. The exterior of these trailers received a skin of aluminum with a prefinished white coating.

It required great care for the sheeting to go through the shear to be cut into the right sized piece without getting scratched. As I watched another piece of metal go into the shear, a protective strip to prevent marring was carefully laid on top. The powerful ker-chunk accomplished its task, followed by the clang as it dropped to the floor below. Between the regard that accompanied every facet of each part of the process and Paul's consistent demeanor when interacting with the men in his employ and the customers who sought his talents, it was clear that he demonstrated the utmost care and attention to detail with every project.

I was fascinated with making things and enjoyed this opportunity to learn what Paul did. This shop would become another regular stop, where my enthusiasm and curiosity found a new outlet as Paul taught me to use several of the machines. I became able to operate the metal brake to bend crisp angles in sheet metal, the shear to cut these sheets, and the powerful Piranha tool for nibbling thick steel into specific shapes. After my multitude of training sessions, I proudly added tin knocker to my list of skills.

Thanks to Tim's connection with Paul that winter, I would go on to create a plethora of décor on the many custom units produced at Specialty Trailer, with one special unit that premiered at the carnival trade show known as the Extravaganza. Skee-Ball Lightning included many high-tech innovations as well as my custom artwork—a sexy chrome robot lady posed in a fantasy setting as the sky above the futuristic cityscape skyline morphed from bright pink into a progressively darker blue with stars at the highest points. Along with extravagant lighting and sound effects, my extensive science fiction-inspired artwork helped this piece win "Best of Show" at the Extravaganza, making me an award-winning artist.

Knowing what Tim had been busy preparing for me all winter, I should have had my vision ready by the time I returned in the spring. But somehow during the months that passed between my visit at Specialty Trailer and now, Tim's request had slipped my mind. I hadn't given his project any thought whatsoever.

When I arrived on the show that summer, I saw Tim's finished trailer in the game lineup.

The blank area on one side of the opening and the overhead sign marquee slapped a reminder back into my head. Thank goodness Tim was busy as usual. I scrambled to come up with some ideas before chatting with him. When he finally caught

me in passing, he asked what great design I had come up with for his trailer. Rather than admit I wasn't prepared, I began to rattle off a description of the colorful elements I would include. As I spoke, additional ideas came to mind about what would best convey the cheerful, vibrant setting for his logo. Turned out, my creative-oriented mind was in my favor in such tight spots.

"That sounds great," Tim said, nodding affirmatively. "When can you start?"

Phew!

Bird's-Eye View

As I got busy with the projects at hand, I also got familiar with the many families on the show. Stuart had his food and lemonade trailers; he came from a family with joints at fairs all over the state. His crew included Julie and Tim, both of whom I'd met before. There was an endless stream of independent ride owners like Stuart, along with independent game operators who frequently arrived to augment the show's lineup. Every one of these showmen wanted sign work.

Although Paul was busy fabricating trailers, his family was on the show just as he'd said they would be. His wife, Terez,

ran their Elephant Ears trailer that made sweet fry bread, all while watching over their three small kids. One sunny afternoon at a small county fair, I was pleasantly surprised by one of those kids. I was standing on a stepladder in the middle of the midway to letter a sign high on a joint trailer when a small voice interrupted my concentration.

"Hey, mister painter?"

I looked down and saw a little girl about four years old.

"Do you want to go ride the Ferris wheel with me?"

Although dumbfounded at first, it only took a moment for me to assess the value of this opportunity. I caught Terez's eye, and with an approving nod from her, I perked up.

"Sure!" I agreed.

I came down off the ladder, cleaned out my brush, and put it away. My little host waited, hopping with glee and reminding me to be grateful for the simple pleasures in life.

"Let's go," I said.

We headed toward what the showmen called the Eli 16. The boy running the ride recognized both of us and stopped it so we could get on. When an empty tub was in position, he unlatched the lap bar and held it open with an economy of motion. When we were securely latched inside, he pulled the lever and got the ride running again. While we rose to the highpoint of the midway and looked all around, I savored that surprise break in my workday. As my little friend and I chatted, I learned that Terez had told her daughter she couldn't ride anything without an adult. Since her mom was busy and in an effort to comply with the rules, the girl assessed all the available personnel on the midway and knew I was likely the only one with the flexibility to knock off and accompany her to the Ferris wheel. Clever girl.

As our ride revolved us up and down, repeatedly giving us a bird's-eye view of this man-made fantasyland, I savored the moment.

Staring down at all my proud artwork on the grounds below, I was filled with gratitude once again for the triumph that occurred the day I decided to strike out on my own and become a snapper for the carnival.

T. F. BORS
& COMPANY

Chapter 7
The Golden Age

*"Never give up on something
you can't go a day without thinking about."*
—Winston Churchill

The High School Rider

My fascination with upper-level horsemanship and performing for the circus became an obsession that commanded all my spare time and energy. I wanted to become a better rider. Idle time, if it could be called that, was spent taking riding lessons from my dressage instructor. Spending many hours practicing these skills proved valuable as Sassy and I made astounding progress.

By 1985, Sassy's repertoire included the three-step, where

she would take three strides at the walk followed by the extension of one foreleg straight out in front. She could also march, where a leg extension occurred on every stride. The backward double three-step was a variation of this exercise where Sassy moved backward three steps and extended the foreleg twice. Her spectacular breakdown bow, or camel stretch, brought her chest only inches from the dirt.

The lateral trot work consisted of two-tracks, also known as a sidepass, that developed with practice. Other movements exercised were the rear, volte, bow, and of course, her spectacular passage. Our training sessions reviewed these movements in the same sequence each time for two reasons. The use of the same series aided her understanding of what came next, and using a familiar routine was a training device used to ease the addition of a new movement.

Being a hot-blooded horse, Sassy simply did not have the temperament for a slow casual walk. Much of the time I spent in the saddle, she spent anticipating what I would ask for next. To mix it up, I would occasionally take her on a long casual walk without asking for any of the usual routine. These walks introduced her to something new - the idea that there were times when we would simply relax, walk on, and enjoy our time together. All in all, Sassy was becoming a proficient performer and a sublime riding partner.

The next logical step was to get her crowd-broke and at ease in front of a live audience. Coincidentally, the Kelly Miller

Circus planned to play several weeks of one-day stands through Michigan that summer on their way to Canada. I made arrangements with the owner, David Rawls, to join for a few weeks to perform my new act with this spectacular mare.

This would take time away from my duties as the show painter for the Elliott Amusement Company, but performing in the circus with my dancing horse was my passion and I wasn't going to deprioritize it. Besides, this carnival crew knew I wouldn't let them down, even if I did take a short leave of absence.

I loaded both horses and joined the circus as soon as they entered the state. Upon arrival, I met Tina, a performer who wanted a horse of her own one day. She was already a capable animal trainer, so I showed her how to work Bingo. We added a two-ring display of performing horses while I worked Sassy in the other ring. It was nice having a friend along for this maiden voyage with Sassy, and it was especially good to be back on a series of one-day stands.

Quickly resuming the familiar pattern, I rose early each morning with the rest of the troupe to drive to the next town. I appreciated that this three-ring under-canvas circus enjoyed traditional grassy lots, ideal for performing with animals. Arriving early on the next lot each morning provided me with extra down time while the big-top crew unloaded and placed poles in position, the stake driver belting out a metallic rhythm while pounding steel stakes into the ground. As the canvas for the big top was getting spread out, I parked in the backyard, set up my portable stable, and tended to my livestock.

Albert was here for the summer with his wife and daughters, all of whom contributed to the circus. He enjoyed my performance, and we soon formed a friendship. I discovered that as the resident mechanic one of Albert's duties was to keep the fleet in top shape. This often involved retrieving truck parts from town, but driving into town was no simple feat—he had to unhook the camper his girls lived in from the trailer he shared with his wife.

Because my duties were light and I usually unhooked my pickup from the trailer anyway, he didn't have to. We rode together into town quite often during that tour, finding plenty in common. These trips became a time of wonder as he shared stories about times gone past, including how he'd owned a circus with his brother, worked for Glenn and Red at Boblo Island Amusement Park in Ontario, and even presented animals in assembly programs at elementary schools.

On a trek to town together one afternoon, my nervous energy while sitting at a red light translated into my inching forward and relaxing repeatedly while engaging and releasing the clutch ever so slightly. Albert noticed.

"What are you doing?" he blurted through an alarmed twist on his face.

I shrugged and he entered into an accurate and graphic explanation of exactly what took place between the clutch plate and the flywheel of a truck, and how my unnecessary behavior caused premature wear.

"I have enough work," he said half-jokingly. "Don't make me add your truck to my list."

As we resumed our trip into town, Albert began to teach me how to use the clutch in a more skillful manner to minimize the friction. Resulting from his tutelage, I reduced the amount of deterioration each time the clutch was engaged for the sake of promoting a long life for my truck parts. I was grateful for the lesson.

Albert positively influenced my driving skills that day and saved me from unnecessarily early and more frequent repairs. Over the years, many more opportunities occurred where I would refer to my lessons with him as I sought to better understand the mechanical inclinations of my rig.

When Albert asked me to paint his family name next to the door on his travel trailer, I readily agreed. His wife, Anita, and their daughters joined his exuberance while we tossed around several ideas for the design. We agreed on "Vonderheid's Camelot." I suggested the inclusion of a small castle in the design with little flags waving in the breeze.

Albert was excited as I prepped the area and grabbed my yardstick. He wanted to watch the entire process, so he retrieved a folding chair and got comfortable. I sketched the guidelines for the wording and the little depiction, then got my paints ready. Albert called Anita and the girls over to watch as I selected the right brush and the perfect color.

Then he thought to get himself a cold drink so he could really enjoy himself as he watched the show. I began the lettering process while he went on his errand. I played around while making the little cartoon of the castle, eliciting fits of giggles from the young girls. Finally returning, Albert took his seat and popped open his drink just in time to watch me make the final stroke.

"You're done already?" he exclaimed in disbelief and disappointment. "That was fast! I missed the whole show."

At his pouting, his daughters erupted into more giggles.

With plenty of free time before and after the show, I had many opportunities to saddle up my horse and go for a casual ride. The multitude of ponies and children soon noticed my morning pattern of exploring the area on horseback, and the trail ride around the new town quickly became contagious. The next thing I knew, before and between shows, every saddle in the circus was strapped onto every willing critter, and I was the Pied Piper.

At one town, the show set up near Lake Huron. I had an idea. Before I pulled onto our next lot, I scoped out a route from the showgrounds to the water. Like clockwork, upon arrival, my contingency of Tina, Jay, Sasha, and a half-dozen kids all scrambled to saddle up to head out with me. Soon, our single-file parade of livestock left the lot.

As we made our way through the town and over to the beach, we must have made quite a sight. When we neared the lake, I decided to ride Sassy out into the surf to see how she would do. Just for fun and to splash around, I asked her to give me some of the three-step in the knee-deep water. Sassy seemed to enjoy it as much as I did. This excursion introduced me to another admirable facet of this elegant animal. Having found her to be fearless in the water, I formed another goal while preparing for the matinee that afternoon.

After the show, the time came for my enthusiastic group to go out on another trail ride. While they all saddled up, I opted to go bareback with the intention of getting thoroughly wet this time. At the lake, Sassy and I entered the water once more. I coaxed her deeper and deeper until I felt her feet no longer touching the bottom. She began to move her limbs in an animated swimming manner with only our heads out of the water. I was still able to guide her direction with my seat.

After a magical session of gliding through the water as one entity, I turned Sassy back toward the shore. In the shallows, she once again found the sandy bottom with her feet. Elated and dripping wet, my relationship with this wonderful horse expanded.

Airbrushing T-Shirts

With the circus behind me and the summer carnival season getting ready to begin again, my thoughts returned to my T-shirt booth. Thanks to working for elite concessionaires, I had learned how to place effective visual marketing in front of the potential customer. The Netterfield operation was the most attractive and effective in the business. While I worked on his and my other customers' concession trailers, ideas for my own display began to coalesce.

When I got to Butch Webb's shop in Kansas, I knew exactly what I needed to build for my own booth. From two four-by-eight sheets of special sign material, I made two eight-foot columns that would fold face to face. These would become the outside upright corners of my booth to which everything else would attach.

I decorated the bottoms of these columns with elaborate European-style scrolls, and then covered the remainder with artwork to give my customers an idea of my talents and details they could request on their custom airbrushed T-shirts. I also built an inventory box with jack stands for the sales counter and a shirt-painting easel. My booth was ready, but now I needed to return to my commissioned projects.

When I arrived back with the Elliott Amusement Company in Michigan, Tim directed my attention to my first project. His newest game was called Happy Hippos. I became fully immersed in developing a festive cartoon image of hippos enjoying themselves in a tropical beach setting. While I worked, an abundance of other sign work for the show began to accumulate. Near the end of satisfying all these requests, I revealed my ambition for the summer to include my newly renovated T-shirt booth.

The show had some busy spots that would work perfectly, but I still had one problem to resolve—I would need a sales assistant. Fortunately, Mary and I had resumed talking regularly, having patched up our differences over the phone. Knowing she was out of school for the summer, I called her up and she happily agreed to join me on the show and help out.

Mary and I arrived at the first of our fairgrounds while all the rides and midway attractions were still being assembled. Tim showed me our location; like last time, we were sandwiched by two rides. Mary helped me unload and set up the columns I had built. Long two-by-fours attached to the tops of these columns diagonally and were anchored at the bottom with tent stakes. My new "Airbrushing" signs hung between the tops. Three panels mounted laterally overhead between these columns to cover with flash designs. The new inventory box sat on the jack stands in the center beneath the structure.

Once assembled, we stepped back to admire our new display. Our T-shirt operation had evolved since the spur-of-the-moment experiment the summer before. Now we had a nice-looking display and plenty of inventory on hand. Although we were deeply proud of our accomplishment, we didn't dare bask in the satisfaction of our progress for too long—there was still plenty to do before the carnival opened to the public.

I sat down and grabbed several blank felt squares to use as

flash. Getting my airbrush out and the paints ready, I drew a blank.

"What can I paint?" I asked Mary. "I need to get the idea across to the customer that virtually anything is available on a shirt."

"How about 'Custom Designed Shirts'," Mary suggested.

That certainly got the message across. I began to paint while Mary continued to dream up creative ideas to include as flash designs and organized the inventory. With each new design, our booth became an attractive and effective sales tool. I was excited for another successful season. We were ready in the nick of time.

With the opening of the fair, the first of the crowd began to mill about.

"Be on the lookout for customers," I stressed. "And be ready."

Mary laughed and rolled her eyes, continuing to do what she had already been working on. I knew she thought I was being overly anxious, but I had learned from the previous summer that the current shirt sold the next shirt. We needed to get that first shirt sold immediately. I paused to scan our surroundings filled with bright attention-grabbing carnival attractions. I perked up and pointed across the midway.

"See that guy over there wearing the shirt that says 'Boss'? He's our target. When he gets close enough," I stressed, "sell him a shirt."

Although Mary chuckled again, I had to hand it to her—she did her job well and we soon had an audience. The gathered crowd stood around to watch while I painted, and just like last time they started to ask questions. Mary provided an explanation which soon became another sale, and then another. Handing me each shirt with unique instructions, I painted the one-of-a-kind design for each of our customers. Soon, an endless series of painted designs on shirts were being mass produced at our booth yet again. With the string of fairs in front of us, we could really thrive this summer.

After giving our operation a shakedown during the first festival of the season, we discovered there were a few things we needed for the county fairs coming up. Mary requested a chair due to some recent surgery she'd had on her back. I also realized from our initial experience that there must be a way to become even more efficient as a painter. I could get equipped with multiple airbrushes and an abundance of bottles for paint.

"These county fairs are preparing us for an even bigger opportunity," I revealed to Mary that evening. "I met an operator last year in Texas called Wicked Wanda. She has an opening for an airbrush artist on her state fair route and she invited us to join her."

Mary's eyes widened with joy. "Really? Wow!"

Wanda wanted a live artist at each booth to attract attention. When we were done with our circuit in Michigan, we would meet up with her at the Ohio State Fair, and then travel together to Little Rock. Wanda also provided a hole for me at the State Fair of Texas in October. Things were really looking up.

At the end of the Michigan circuit, I stored my booth in the horse trailer, and Mary and I drove the VW bus to the Ohio State Fair. In a big dusty exhibition hall, I set up my easel next to Wicked Wanda's T-shirt booth, where it didn't take long for Mary and me to learn the routine at the state fair—up early every day, long hours, and peak traffic in the evening. Fortunately, we had plenty of help. Each booth had two salesgirls behind the counter, Mary being my personal salesgirl situated outside with me.

After ten days of this rugged routine, Wanda showed up to figure out our portion of the earnings. It was less per shirt than when we worked in our own joint, but we got a lot more traffic due to Wicked Wanda's well-established name and location, plus the extra help from the salesgirls—it all balanced out pretty well. Happy with the results, Mary and I tore down and headed for the next spot.

The State Fair of Texas is about as close to a world's fair as you can get. Wanda had five booths in that massive place. We worked an outdoor booth near the Cotton Bowl where the Texas v.s. Oklahoma game took place the first weekend of the fair. Thanks to my association with the E.S. Webb Company, Mary and I could get as much free pizza from his fancy booth as we wanted. Because food was so expensive at the fair, Mary and I opted to eat pizza morning, noon, and night.

Business was always good in Texas and this fair was no exception. Populated by so many independent operators, I met other carnival contacts for future sign painting projects. With a route of several carnival owners, large-scale concession operations, and airbrushing T-shirts at major fairs, I was entering into an era of abundance that would soon proffer less of a need for free pizza.

When the State Fair of Texas was over, Mary flew home. We had enjoyed another huge success. After finishing up a few sign projects for the Texas showmen, I headed to the Ozarks to see Mom and Dad. They were excited to hear all about my recent successes, and shared the progress on their home. The drywall was finally being installed while Dad worked on the finishing woodwork. They could see the light at the end of the tunnel.

At the conclusion of our visit, it was time for Superdog and me to head back to Michigan. I needed to get the rig, load the horses, and head south for my next gig in Florida where I would paint once again for Butch Netterfield. But with a bit of extra time on my hands and my heart getting a tug, I decided to make a detour, traveling east to see Mary and meet her family.

Maryland

Mary found a place to park my rig near her home that had stalls for Sassy and Bingo. Excited about my visit, she met me there. After parking the horse trailer and getting familiar with the barn, we saddled up the horses and went for a ride with a specific destination in mind. Mary rode Bingo while I rode Sassy, and of course Superdog accompanied us on this adventure. Our little parade left the stable on a perfect Indian summer day, bisecting the elegant Washington, D.C. suburban countryside through trees with leaves of bright orange, russet, and yellow.

Halfway around a bend in the trail, a deer hidden in the woods spooked the horses as it ran across our path and out into the road. I was impressed Mary managed to stay on when Bingo bolted and spun around before collecting himself. Sassy jumped straight up in the air, landing in a wide stance with her legs spread and her feet firmly planted on the ground, blowing her nostrils to signify her disapproval of the whole event. Overall, I was proud of how my horses handled the surprise. Because of my ambition to perform, they were going to have to get used to sudden distractions—a circus career would have plenty of them.

When we reached her parents' elegant home, I met Mary's mom and dad. Mary let her little sister sit on Bingo while I demonstrated Sassy's repertoire on the front lawn. I showed her how to ask Bingo to bow, which she thought was simply amazing. A small crowd had gathered to watch the impromptu performance. After posing for a few photographs and being the sensation of the neighborhood, we rode the horses back to the barn and got them settled in before driving back to visit with Mary's family.

Mary's folks invited Superdog and me into their magnificent home. I was honored to be so warmly welcomed, but in Mary's magazine-worthy lifestyle, I felt like a fish out of water. I had come from a homelife far different from this unfamiliar world. Though my parents tried their absolute best and I did feel a sense of healing in adulthood, things hadn't always been the picture of perfection during my childhood. As a result, I had turned my back on contemporary life right after high school.

These days, I was used to living outdoors and working in an ever-changing backdrop. Part of me resisted what I had rejected from my family of origin. At the same time, I tried my best to be gracious and open-minded about the experience. With every comfort I could possibly imagine at my fingertips in this environment, I was surprised when her siblings revealed a lingering complaint.

"There's nothing to do here," they whined.

I thought the complaint was odd; I had never had the problem of nothing to do, always keeping busy. When the drinks started to flow, I soon understood why they felt so bored while I sipped my beer. I was used to balancing my painting projects that focused my attention and challenged my skills. I wasn't used to simply sitting around, smoking and drinking with no other activity to keep my mind occupied. But here in Maryland, there were only places to go drink and places to go get something to drink. There wasn't anything to actually do, so instead we just drank.

When I went to grab another beer, Mary told me the rule of the house refrigerator.

"Have another, but do not drink the last two beers. Sometimes late at night, Daddy wakes up and wants a couple beers."

Although behaving as graciously as I had been trained to as a child, the nonstop drinking paired with the boredom brought out the enduring tension between us once more. The bickering and fussing that had resulted in our separation earlier that year resumed as alcohol wafted through my head and distorted my perception.

I was disappointed in Mary. Seeing the real her in her childhood home was eye-opening. She wasn't proactive about anything productive. In contrast, I was on all the time, constantly in production mode. Even now, I was frustrated because I wasn't accomplishing anything. To soothe my frustrations, I drank some more.

The several-day stopover included an excursion into D.C. to visit the headquarters of National Geographic, where her father was a senior editor. My head was full of cobwebs from all the excessive drinking, and I was irritable as we traveled on the subway. Although I was not in a pleasant mood, Mary and I rode into town that day to meet him at his office.

When we arrived, she navigated the labyrinth of offices to find her dad. Once inside, Robert knew that as an artist I would appreciate the elaborate painting hanging on his office wall of

Lee's Surrender to Grant at Appomattox.

"Notice how Lee's boots are muddy; he was the working general," Robert pointed out. "In contrast, Grant and the Union staff spit-shined and polished their boots for the occasion."

While I studied the details of the oil painting, I could only guess the amount of time it had taken to paint the massive amount of recognizable facial features, military uniform details, and the elaborate interior of the small parlor where the surrender took place. Despite my overall unpleasant mood, I was in awe of such a wonderful accomplishment.

"This painting was commissioned by the National Geographic to accompany a story about that pivotal occasion of American history," Robert added proudly. "It appeared in our magazine."

"That's amazing," I exclaimed. "And you're the lucky one who got to hang it in your office?"

Robert nodded. "Once completed and scanned for printing purposes, my office was selected due to my immense interest in the Civil War."

Mary smiled at our common appreciation for artwork. He then showed us off to his colleagues before taking us to the cafeteria for an elegant lunch.

After a few days of going to parties, feeling unable to relate to the local jet-setters, and overdoing my consumption, I was ready to get out of Maryland. Plus, the weather had turned cold and my horses were being neglected. But Mary had another party she wanted to go to. Her mom encouraged us to have some fun, even offering to drop us off and watch Superdog for me. I didn't feel I could do anything else but agree to one more party before my departure.

In a warm apartment packed with people I didn't know, the drinks flowed while the rock and roll blared. Dressed for the cold weather outside, I was hot in this cramped environment, which only added to my irritation. I tried eating the finger foods, but my frustration with Mary seemed to accelerate the urge to consume beer instead. I was restless being idle, while she seemed content to keep partying.

Eventually, the blend of what was in my stomach combined with my overheated body to percolate into a mixture that didn't agree with me. I searched for the bathroom with urgency, finding a locked door. In desperation, I knocked.

"We're busy!" a voice shouted in response.

I tried to contain it, but it couldn't wait. I heaved all over the door.

Witnessing this atrocity, Mary was disgusted along with everybody else at the party. She called her mother to come and pick her up. Embarrassed, I tried to follow her out the front door, but I was banished. Remaining behind in a stranger's home in an unfamiliar world, I passed out on the stairs in the hallway, and there I slept until morning.

I awoke at daybreak, eager to make a quiet exit. Hiking out to the highway in the bitter cold, I put my thumb in the air and waited. After a few rides from kind strangers who took pity on me, I somehow, eventually found my way to Mary's elegant home and knocked on the front door.

"You don't look so good," Mary's mother said bluntly upon seeing my disheveled state.

I didn't feel so good. Not to mention, I was ashamed of what had happened. Without another word, Mary's mom opened the door wider so I could come inside. My stomach turned as I gathered my things, and, honestly, I was grateful that Mary was nowhere to be found. I took the opportunity to leave, walking the few miles with Superdog to where my horses and rig awaited our departure.

Eager to get out of Maryland, I headed south to Netterfield's for the winter of 1986. With every hundred miles, the weather warmed up and my head began to clear. I wasn't made for yuppy life; I just didn't fit in there. I decided I'd better leave the partying and bars to the people who knew how to do it.

The growing distance displaced the frustration that had short-circuited my relationship with Mary. Reminiscent of a decision made as a youngster, I firmly believed I was better off figuring out how to do everything by myself. At Netterfield's, I could resume my familiar pattern of sipping while I worked in an environment where I felt accepted.

Opportunity

I unloaded the horses at the nearby stable of Ruth Gimple before heading to Netterfield's. Ruth's specialty was Saddlebred show horses, which she kept in her traditional Saddlebred barn—large and long with big box stalls that flanked the wide aisleway, deep with sawdust used for riding and driving horses up and down the middle rather than using an arena. Her elegant tack room doubled as a showroom, sporting many photos of her clients with their horses and the ribbons they'd won.

Having this diversion after my days spent lettering popcorn and lemonade trailers introduced me to the local demographic of this genre of horsemanship. While Ruth's crew of quiet, steady workers provided a comfortable atmosphere for the horses to enjoy, there was a tendency among a few of her customers to startle their horses so they could see the whites of their eyes and hear them snort. I preferred to let mine remain at peace in their stall; the circus would provide plenty of surprises on its own.

Through Ruth's connections, I received an invitation to

bring my dancing horse to the yacht club in Tampa. They were delighted to learn about the guy who aspired to perform with his Saddlebred and asked me to participate in their annual saddle horse show. I needed to get Sassy ready.

Fortunately, an older gentleman who worked at Ruth's stable took me under his wing and showed me how to get my mare into saddle horse-show shape. He taught me how to trim the hair in and around her ears, leaving a little diamond shape at the tips. Then we removed her excess nose whiskers and shaggy fetlock hair. Thanks to his help, on the day of our debut, Sassy was slick and clean.

Once unloaded, tacked up, and groomed to perfection on the Hillsborough Bay side of South Tampa, I found an interesting combination of a marina and a Saddlebred stable that had been in existence for a long time. Sassy and I performed our established routine in front of a crowd of aficionados of society horses. I was thrilled when we were well received.

Backstage afterward, I interacted with the members and guests as I untacked Sassy. Completely unexpectedly, an interior designer approached me with an opportunity to paint a mural on the ceiling dome of an elegant home in Little Rock. It seemed the more I got out and exposed my talents, both in the painting and the horse worlds, opportunity just seemed to find me. I added it to my lineup and said I'd be in touch.

Back at Netterfield's, I found out about yet another opportunity to perform. The annual Gibsonton Showmen's Club Circus took place in January. This would be the perfect venue to show my peers in show business my newest horse. Two performances took place under a big top set up behind the club, and also served as a networking mecca for the variety of personalities who filled the ranks of this interesting business.

What I didn't realize was that talent scouts from Busch Gardens were in the audience that day also. They found me after the show and extended an invitation to perform during a dress rehearsal in their amusement park venue. If we all liked how things went, the goal would be securing a contract to perform for the summer. I agreed to an orientation excursion at the corporate offices of Busch Gardens to talk this over and see the venue.

On the day of my appointment, I entered the office complex. I found the place seemingly deserted. After waiting for umpteen minutes and not knowing what to do, I began to wander the hallways. Around a corner, I found the entire staff surrounding a television and watching the rerun of the Challenger blastoff. I joined the huddled group and shared in their disbelief that the space shuttle had exploded only minutes before.

After some time to absorb this monumental news, the entertainment personnel welcomed me into a room to proceed with our meeting and plan the dress rehearsal. I would provide the announcement content and my musical accompaniment preferences, including "Star Wars," "New York, New York," and "Runaway." I also wanted to inspect the venue with my own eyes.

All of these requests had to go through the appropriate

channels of this big company. They were able to secure my music of choice from their vast collection, but for whatever reason, I did not get the opportunity to inspect the venue ahead of time.

When the time had come to load my mare in the back of the trailer and head to Busch Gardens, I was disappointed to learn that there was no dirt backstage on which to warm Sassy up. The plan for the future would be to warm her up at the stables where she would have proper footing, but for today, I would just have to warm her up in the parking lot.

My second disappointment came when it was time to rehearse. The show took place in a large round building filled with seats that surrounded a circus ring. I had hoped there would be natural earth in there at least, but I found a painted concrete floor instead. This hard, slick surface created some concern. We went through our rehearsal routine as best we could, and next thing I knew, it was time for the live show.

After the juggling duo that followed the aerial act, I heard the announcement.

"Busch Gardens is proud to introduce Class n Sass, the American Saddlebred dancing horse!"

We entered the ring doing the passage. I sat up straight in the saddle with one hand in the air to acknowledge the crowd. We then demonstrated all the aspects of classic high school horsemanship to the peppy tunes played over their sound system. In that sterile place, we did all of our usual act except for the rears; our performance went well. The audience loved us. The staff loved us. But I still had a concern about the flooring. Although the rough-painted concrete was fine for elephants and jugglers, I wondered about my horse's legs. After the show, I inspected her and noticed wind-puffs, or swollen places, adjacent to her ankles. My heart lurched at this indication of the severe impact that concrete flooring had on her. If I continued performing on such a surface, it could lead to possible future problems for Sassy.

I had to do what was in the best interest of my mare. In spite of the exuberance of the personnel at Busch Gardens who genuinely enjoyed our contribution to the show, I told them I was reluctant to continue performing there. In an effort to keep us, they offered me a six-month contract. As tempting as it was, I loved my horse too much to knowingly cause her harm. For Sassy's sake, I remained firm to not pursue that opportunity. Something else would come along.

Lipizzan Horses

At Christmastime, I took a break from lettering at Netterfield's. My circus friend, Joanne, invited me to join the Wilson family for the holidays. I thought about how fun it would be among such a big family celebration. I accepted her invitation to venture to their home in Gibsonton, where her parents, sisters, and each of their families would all be gathered.

Joanne's niece, Sabrina, was a beaming, bright-eyed girl, approximately my age. Her mom, Joanne's sister, was married to Harry Herrmann, whose family was connected with even more of the circus performers in Gibtown. The Herrmanns came from a circus performing family who'd wandered Europe with a bear, wire act, trapeze, and cowboy act. Like many, they came to this country to escape war-torn Europe. The two brothers, Harry and Otto, thrived on the many under-canvas three-ring circuses in America.

A happy accident occurred during one of their tours in Puerto Rico when the circus they were on folded. In lieu of pay, the employees were offered equipment. The Herrmann brothers took a few horses, among them a highly-trained Lipizzaner that did a specialized act.

A short, stout breed, the Lipizzan horse was ideally suited to support the heavily armored warrior of the sixteenth century. Because of this, the breed had been endangered by the various warfares that swept across Europe, including the War of the First Coalition and World War I. Made famous by the Spanish Riding School of Vienna in Austria, these horses demonstrated the classical movements of dressage that included controlled, stylized poses, jumps, and other movements known as "airs above the ground."

The release of the 1963 Disney movie Miracle of the White Stallions highlighted the rescue of the Lipizzan horses by American troops during WWII, giving this amazing breed worldwide notoriety. It wasn't long after the release of the movie that several touring shows featuring white performing horses would launch themselves out on the road. Creative showmen like Harry and Otto took advantage of the resulting popularity of Lipizzans, capitalizing on the white horse frenzy by acquiring even more and launching a show of their very own.

Harry had already become a sensation as an accomplished horseman riding the capriole on the Sells and Gray Circus. This began with the horse standing on his haunches in a pose known as the levade, similar to a rear but with the haunches sitting deep. From here, the horse would launch himself into the air and kick out with his hind feet to achieve the capriole. Astride their newly acquired and superbly trained Lipizzan horse, Harry now rode the levade, capriole, and even the courbette, or several hops in the levade pose, and their careers only went up from there.

A principal rider with her family's show, Sabrina had seen

my dancing horse perform at the Showmen's Circus. Understandably proud of her own vocation, she wanted to show me her family's horses as well. We began to build a friendship based upon our common interest of performing with horses.

As we grew closer, I wondered whether Sabrina could possibly help me with an idea I'd been tossing around for some time. In those days, the concept of videotaping an act to show circus agents and producers was new. Only large enterprises with vast resources had the equipment to capture such footage. Having a tape would place me at an advantage when I was trying to book my act with various circus tours and independent venues. I decided to take my chances and reveal this ambition to my new friend.

"I'd like to capture some video footage of my horse act," I confided. "Having a demo of my act would allow an agent see my entire performance; it would really help me book more performances…but I don't have a video camera."

"My family has one," she revealed. "Maybe we could help you! Come out to our farm, watch our show, and I'll find out about shooting your act."

As Sabrina gave me directions to the Herrmann ranch on the outskirts of Sarasota, I was thrilled with the opportunity to obtain an invaluable demo tape of my act. It would also be nice to spend more time with my new friend and watch her family of showmen perform on their beautiful Lippizan horses, which they did at their home every Saturday during the off season. I assured Sabrina that I would love to be her guest soon, but for now I needed to return to painting at Netterfield's.

I thanked Joanne for inviting me to their holiday celebrations with her fantastical family, and directed my van through their gate and down the road.

Not-So-Special Guest

When Netterfield's crew began setting up for the state fair, I drove south toward Sarasota to see my newest friend again. I turned east onto a long gravel washboard road that shook my teeth loose while leaving a cloud of brown dust in my wake.

When I arrived at their farm, I took in the view of the vast grassy area split by fenced rows. I found a place near the horse barn to park my van. Superdog knew how to blend right in; after the usual orientation with the farm dogs, he turned his back on them and began his own exploration. I went to where the horses were kept.

Sabrina was inside the long main barn getting the livestock ready for the show. She introduced me to some of the other riders and then took me to a special place where Superdog and I could watch the show. My perch would be adjacent to and over the main entrance of the arena.

I settled into a comfortable couch with my faithful companion at my side. A wonderful feeling came over me while I took in my surroundings. Bleacher seating lined the sides of an exhibition area. Barns filled the background. A few oak hammocks were spotted here and there in the distance. A large shelter housed a variety of trucks and trailers. But the best feature was directly in front of me. Accenting the structure where I waited was a brass sculpture of Pegasus, the winged horse, like a hood ornament on a tall post.

Every Saturday afternoon, the public was invited to see their show, and today was no exception as people poured into the bleachers below me. To retain agricultural status on the property, the family would pass the hat rather than charge admission. I was complimented to be here, receiving royal treatment as Sabrina's guest. Taking a deep breath of pure joy, I relaxed in the glassed-in room that usually housed a performance director, dignitary, or members of the media. This place was perfect.

The preamble for the show began with recorded music reminiscent of the gilded era. Chamber music and orchestra presentations set the mood. Though Harry had passed away by this time, Otto remained the spokesman of the family. Dressed in an Eisenhower jacket decorated with military medals, high-ranking chevron slashes, breeches, boots, and a vintage high-brim general's hat, he took command of the dirt arena and began the introduction to the show.

"Welcome to see our horses," he spoke in broken English with his thick Czechoslovakian accent. "Today you will see the training of the horses exactly as has been taking place for centuries..."

A mustache completely covered his mouth, eliminating any possibility of lip-reading his difficult musings and the microphone shielded any remaining clues. I joined the rest of the audience who strained to understand the rhetoric while Otto went on to describe the almost magical qualities this breed possessed and gave us a hint of what was to come.

After his lavish announcement, eight horses and riders walked single-file around the arena to allow us to make our visual inspection. Each light gray or white horse walked with purpose. Taut reins insured contact with the horse's mouth and the front of the horse's head maintained the ideal vertical. Each footfall was intentional and gentle at this pace, raising little dust.

The riders wore the short midriff jackets with clawhammer tails, white breeches, and black boots with a protective rise in front of the rider's knee. As the horses and riders walked down the front, they lifted one hand up to their hats in slow unison. They then lifted their hats up and off to salute everyone. Next, they slowly returned the hats to their heads and placed their arms back down.

The slow rhythm of the initial movement of eight horses and riders set a pace for the audience, securing a hypnotic grip that would promote the lead-in of successive displays. When the parade encircled the arena, crossed the diagonal, split into two groups, and threaded the needle on the diagonal, the audience was fully prepped with anticipatory wonder.

After the group exited the arena, Otto resumed his broken English appeal to patriotic inclinations and began the first of many thanks to the armed forces. With one more salute to the military veterans in the audience, enough time had lapsed for the riders to change costumes and horses. Two of them returned with one of the horses walking between them on long lines for the next demonstration.

The patter that Otto provided was reminiscent of the sideshow talker in the circus, providing great boasts about many unsurpassed merits of the horses. A plethora of curious details poured forth from his active mustachioed mouth. I was drawn in just as much as the rest of the audience. His description accompanied a solo demonstration from the horse that had been patiently waiting for his signal. The next display involved horses being walked around the arena with trainers behind them, guided with long reins. They demonstrated how handling the lines in a particular manner facilitated having the horses describe a circle around them, and how raising the off-side line over the haunches allowed the trainer to describe a small circle while the horse made a larger circle.

The next demonstration brought in several riders on multiple animated horses. Otto directed the attention of the viewer to the various aspects of both horse and rider as he stressed the point that years and years of relentless training were required to get these magnificent animals to this point of perfection.

During the frequent lulls between acts when costumes and tack were changed, Otto filled the time with captivating patter and storytelling. He shared facts about the Lipizzan's breeding and the training techniques for both horse and rider, anecdotes about life in a performing horse family, and even pivotal tales of bravery that led to the survival of this stunning breed.

With references to patriotism, acknowledging the veterans in attendance, one essay described the Nazi danger that threatened these horses during World War II when they began to penetrate the portion of Austria that produced this magnificent breed. Otto captivated the audience as he weaved a theatrical history of military strategy and relentless bravery about the allied army making a special effort to rescue the horses that would have been destroyed by the Nazi army. While his embellished account was revealed, his description implied that he stood right next to Patton during this miraculous exodus, bringing the story to life.

Between his broken Czechoslovakian accent and the interesting word sequence, I had to pay close attention and invest thought to interpret his tales, but with each story as sensational as the last, it was well worth it. I wasn't the only one who thought this either, every member of the audience was intrigued and hanging on his every word. As the result of Otto's stories, the unified patriotic emotion in the audience was heightened, which segued perfectly into the introduction of the quadrille, a routine that involved eight horses and eight riders.

I enjoyed Sabrina's frequent appearances in the show also. While taking a victory pass around the arena after her solo demonstration of a single movement, her uncle Otto reinforced the family aspect of the show with a light teasing, announcing to the audience that Sabrina was single and looking for a rich husband. This theme was repeated later when she participated with riders in larger groups, gaining more laughs each time.

As I basked in my comfortable seat in the elevated viewing platform, observing the wondrous results in the arena below, I reminisced on the saga of how this horse show came to be. I found the greatest asset for success with the ambition to perform with horses was to provide your horse with a sense of safety. It was clear that these horsemen also savored this holy ground and the miraculous results that occurred while interacting with these noble creatures that seemed to only want to please us.

I looked forward to expanding my connection with the Herrmann family of performers, incredibly humbled and honored to be watching their performance. I eagerly anticipated receiving a big boost in the form of captured video footage of my own horse act and hoped for some guidance and tips from the years of wisdom Otto must contain. My hopes were high and my emotional state reached a new epoch, but after the performance I would get a surprise I wasn't expecting in the least.

When the show concluded, I had plenty of time to visit backstage with the multitude of sisters and cousins who had filled the saddles. The crew was made up almost entirely of family members. The cook was a goofy guy who was intrigued to have a person from outside the family to confide in. I received more information than I wanted as his attention interfered with my purpose for being here.

When Otto finally made it backstage, I managed to excuse myself. This was the moment I'd been waiting for—the opportunity to meet him and compliment him on the show. I had met Harry, Sabrina's father, several years prior. He was the most talented horseman of the family and we related on many levels during our brief evening visit. I expected the same connection with Otto. But upon seeing my highly decorated van, he set right in with a potent interrogation about my career as an artist, his body language informing me that he was not interested in getting to know me.

"So, you think you can draw a Lipizzaner horse?" he chortled in an aggressive and challenging manner.

This affront was very different from his persona during the performance as an altruistic entertainer. I was taken aback as I thought about his challenge. I certainly could draw a Lipizzaner—through careful observation of my subject, I was able to create an accurate rendering of anything, and my favorite thing to draw was horses. But being put on the spot did not reflect principles that promoted a flow of encouragement or safety, both aspects of a healthy environment. In spite of his belittling aggression, I retrieved a sketchbook and a pencil, seeking a specimen to study. I began to draw under fire, forging a feeling reminiscent of the bullying experienced in my childhood. As that feeling rose up to take a firm grasp on my gut, Otto grew more and more impatient with my industry.

"Tanya, show this man how to draw a Lipizzaner horse,"

he commanded his eleven-year-old niece.

There were times, due to the intense hurt experienced as a child, that I found myself incapable of saying a word. With no power to oppose Otto's demanding nature, I surrendered my sketchbook and pencil to Tanya, mystified by this treatment coming from Otto. Up until this point, I had only experienced encouragement and regard from the horse trainers I dealt with. Otto was clearly running a racket—being cordial in front of the public and later taking delight in sadistic abuse. Like pouring salt on a garden slug, an inner part of him achieved a sick satisfaction from my writhing in agony.

I had relied on the encouragement received from Sabrina, assuming the path had been paved for me to bring up the topic of capturing video footage of my horse act. I thought all circus performing horsemen were eternally grateful for their own humble beginnings and would be eager to help their fellows just getting started. As Tanya sketched out a horse, I attempted to use my tied-up tongue to bring up the reason I was here, but my words stumbled out. It didn't matter; Otto had his mind already made up.

"What is the matter with you?" His defiant stature waxed pale compared to his belligerent contempt. "You must be mad!" he shouted, bombarding my unsuspecting nature with cynical laughter. "Do you honestly think we would allow you to use the good Herrmann name for the sake of your puny attempt at a circus horse act? You can't even draw a Lipizzaner correctly!"

Hurt and bewildered by his behavior, I did what I did best—I simply withdrew. I was discovering that self-centered, arrogant, and fearful people took delight in tearing others to shreds. I left that farm brokenhearted and flooded with a mixture of emotions from disbelief to confusion to sorrow.

Blindsided, I had no voice once again.

I attempted to process the data as I drove away. Perhaps it stemmed from fear or jealousy. Maybe Otto perceived me as a threat, both as a possible suitor for Sabrina and as a fellow competitor. Maybe he was attempting to protect his family. Whatever the reasons, the thing that hurt the worst was that this damage occurred in front of Sabrina and the rest of the Herrmann family.

Chapter 8
Society Horses

"We are all apprentices in a craft
where no one ever becomes a master."
—Ernest Hemingway

The New Horizon

The experience of stabling the livestock at the Saddlebred barn north of Tampa introduced me to the world of society horses. Painting concession trailers by day and rehearsing the act in the evening kept me busy from morning till nightfall. This was a big improvement from going through the long winters of training without any income.

Preparations for the upcoming tour included making another new wardrobe—as a showman, the attempt to shine more every year was a never-ending task. I purchased used tuxedo jackets and created designs to enhance them using rhinestones. A sparkly jacket would complement my white riding breeches, cummerbund, and black boots. The wearisome task of sewing these stones on one by one was welcomed by a retired performer whom I had trooped with years ago. Marie Pettus, widow of the elephant man, wintered nearby and needed the income. She sewed many decorations on my wardrobe and enjoyed sharing stories of her interesting life in show business with Bert and the elephants whenever I stopped in to see the progress.

When the new season arrived and Butch and his fleet left their winter quarters, my travels resumed as well. I began to seek other Saddlebred barns along my route. Cathy and Bendy had one near Lake Winnipesauke at Fort Oglethorpe. They welcomed my presence while I served my amusement park clients in Chattanooga.

Before heading west to Wichita, I decided to take the opportunity offered to me during my Busch Gardens performance. It was time to paint a mural on the interior ceiling dome in the foyer of an elegant home. That occasion would take me to the middle of Arkansas, ideal for slipping in a visit with the folks afterward.

When I arrived in Little Rock, I looked for a Saddlebred farm and found a friendly fellow with a small barn. Yes, he had room for me, my horses, and my rig. From his place, I could easily commute to the lavish home site to paint each day.

Tall, wiry, and fair, Lyle had a one-man operation, handling all the aspects of his string of horses early each morning and enjoying training sessions in the evenings after work. I enjoyed living at Lyle's farm, learning from his process for training a show horse. I watched as he attached elastic surgical tubing between the front feet of his horse prior to giving him exercise, explaining that this device would strengthen specific muscles to get the front feet going higher and higher as the horse trotted. Being able to travel and meet a plethora of people, I could learn something new every day, so long as I kept my eyes and mind open.

The mural project started with painting on my back like Michelangelo. While lying on the top of the rickety scaffolding set up in the main entrance of the home, I transferred my design to the ceiling before brushing on colors to depict a round, spoked, Victorian-style scroll design with intertwining lavish ribbons throughout. It was a unique project.

When completed, the interior designer was pleased, and he had something else in mind before I took my leave.

"Let me show you something," he said. Pointing out a problem to the right of the foyer, he explained, "I need something to soften, explain, and enhance that space."

I thought for a moment as I inspected the problem area. A recessed wall hid the stairwell that went down to the ten-car garage. Everywhere else surrounding the foyer—the formal dining room, the sitting room with the library, the distant living room, and the corridor that led to the center of the home—worked perfectly fine, but this one area looked clunky.

"Let's bring the outside in," I suggested. "That will solve the problem."

With his enthusiastic approval, I began to design an Italian countryside vista. A pastel horizon with a row of cypress trees would delineate a vineyard peeking between marble pillars that connected the floor to the ceiling. I would also add large flower pots in the foreground, making it seem as though this were an opening to the landscape outside.

This additional project would require extra time I didn't allocate with my original estimate, which meant I would need to chat with my generous host about extending my stay. When I did, he told me about a big horse show coming up. Wow!

What timing! I was grateful I would still be here. Lyle contacted the committee on my behalf to tell them about my dancing horse, and they welcomed the idea of having me participate.

Lyle had taken a liking to my mare. All I originally planned to do during the upcoming horse show was to perform my high school act, but Lyle encouraged me to enter her into a class, believing she could win. This ambition launched a lively discussion. I didn't know anything about showing a horse in that regard. He revealed the list of categories and explained the typical requirements for each one.

Many of the classes required the horse to have a roached, or shaved, mane. I didn't want to remove the luscious hair from the top of Sassy's neck. I wasn't even in the habit of cutting a bridle path. I didn't like the idea of altering Sassy's natural hair in any way, aside from a basic show trim. We found one class where we wouldn't have to make any drastic changes. She could fit into what was called the model class without any trouble.

The model class was simple; the horse was judged solely on how she looked—no athletic ability would be ascertained and no cosmetic requirements were necessary. So, with his help and this modified plan, I began to get Sassy into show shape after painting each day. I trimmed her facial whiskers just like I'd learned before, trimmed the fur from the interior of her ears and fetlocks, and then groomed her to a nice shine.

On the day of the show, Lyle and I moved our horse operation over to the fairgrounds. We found the large steel arena complex surrounded by a sea of trucks and horse trailers. We found our way to the row of stalls reserved for his string and my mare. Soon, I was immersed in preparing for both our usual act and Sassy's model class alongside the multitudes of fellow horsemen milling around us.

The aisles of the barns were decorated with canvas stable signs, fancy tack racks, and even floral arrangements with portable water fountains and elaborate décor. Horses, men, and women were all groomed into show shape by an army of attendants.

Performing at a horse show proved to be somewhat unfulfilling audience-wise. The seats here were often left vacant, with the entire populace that attended the show being involved with the horses they brought. The only folks standing near the rail were those with a few minutes to spare before their next horse came on. On the other hand, multitudes of horses, riders, trainers, and drivers of four-wheeled buggies poured in and out of the dusty venue to perform in their various classes.

When the time was right, Sassy and I assumed our position at the gate. We would first perform our act for the eerily quiet stands. Our announcement echoed out over the complex and the double gates swung open. The organist played our theme song, signaling the beginning of our grand presentation.

In a circus ring, our routine was confined to a forty-two-foot circle. Here in the vast coliseum there was no reason to perform in a confined area, so I elongated the trajectories traveled during each of our exercises and relied on the changes of direction to assist the mare with recognizing the next portion of our routine.

After the leg extensions, the music changed as we began to present Sassy's spectacular passage. Our routine concluded with canter rears all around the arena floor. Out of the small audience that was able to catch what they could, many had never seen a Saddlebred do any of these movements. In the end, we received an enthusiastic applause and another performance under our belts.

Back at Sassy's stall, I removed the bridle and saddle, walked her to cool down, and carefully toweled the moisture off. I needed to get her appearance top-shelf again for the upcoming model class competition. When the time arrived to return to the arena, Sassy was slick, proud, and wearing only the show bridle Lyle had lent me. This style of tack was brief at best; the idea of using a minimum of bridle was to allow the head of the horse to be prominent with only the slightest distraction.

When the gates opened for our class, I led her into the arena. Our group of about twenty horses walked in parade fashion around the perimeter of the arena. After a few laps, we were instructed to line up where the judges could inspect and scrutinize the features of each contestant. While we stood there with all this activity going on around us, Sassy stood as calm as a cucumber, no doubt because she had grown up in a wilder environment than this mild version. The judges came down the line, inspected her, made notations on their clipboard, and moved on to the next horse.

After all the inspections, the judges returned to their complex in the center. I was in suspense, excited to be here, but not knowing what to expect. Lyle thought we could win, but this was our first attempt at such a show. My breath caught when I heard the announcement ring out.

"Third-place award for the model class goes to Mystic's Command."

Hooting rose from one group of onlookers at the rail.

"Right behind him in second place is Mandy's Seahorse."

Applause came from another group of spectators as my hopes dwindled. Oh well. I guess placing near the top for our first show was a long shot.

"And the winner of this year's Saddlebred model class," the announcer's voice echoed throughout that vast hall, pausing to build the suspense before completing his thought, "is Class n Sass, taking first place!"

My mouth dropped open. I couldn't believe it. Patting my horse on the neck, I told her, "Good girl!"

Motioned by the steward in the ring to take my victory lap, I said, "Come on, Sassy." We burst into a trot, my heart bursting with pride. After our lap, we walked up to the judges to retrieve our ribbon and get our picture taken.

Proud of us and beaming at my accomplishment, Lyle was also having a good day with his own horses. Our triumphant contribution to the horse show world was a success. Many other horse aficionados congratulated us as we navigated through the sea of magnificent horseflesh to return to our stall.

When my mural painting project was completed, I thanked my new friend for hosting me and especially for encouraging me to show my mare. Then I headed west to the Ozarks. I would visit my parents before heading to Kansas to paint for Butch Webb.

I savored the memory of the recent coup as I drove, not only for completing the interior mural painting project in an elegant home, but also for showing and performing in the society horse show world. Little did I know that word was getting around about the circus guy who had a nice act with an even nicer Saddlebred horse.

Surprise in St. Louis

I regularly kept in touch with Evy who now traveled and helped Bobby with his bears. They were en route on a tour of Shrine Circus dates that crisscrossed the country. She told me they would show in St. Louis in May. That was great news! Our paths would cross in the spring, and with Evy's help, I secured a slot for my horse act at the Shrine Circus while there. I valued Evy's knowledge as a horse trainer and looked forward to working with her again.

When I finished sign painting for Butch Webb in Wichita, I eagerly headed east to St. Louis. Finding the huge stadium, I was guided to my parking area inside and settled in. With the animals tethered in an unseen location in the immense labyrinth below the seating of Busch Stadium, my preparations for five days of circus shows began.

Taking myself on a tour of the grounds, I noticed an

unfortunate aspect of performing here—the coliseum officials feared damage to the Astroturf that covered the arena floor and had laid plywood across the area designated for the five circus rings and the aerial rigging. The well-worn and warped flooring, laid like a checkerboard on the ground, would require both caution and compromise as I guided my horse through her paces.

I decided we would not attempt any aggressive speeds during our act and would exclude the rears from our conclusion. We had plenty of other things to do, including trot work, the lateral sidepass, bow, three-step, march, backward double three-step, breakdown bow, and, of course, the waltz. In that vast arena with the audience so far away, we must have looked like ants during our performance. Still, Evy was pleased with Sassy's progress and so was I.

I had noticed on Sassy's registration papers that she had been bred by Marion Brown in nearby Florissant, Missouri. Curiosity piqued, I looked up the number of the stable and called him.

"Is this Marion Brown?" I asked.

"Yes, it is," he answered. "How can I help you?"

"Do you remember a mare you bred by the name of Class n Sass?"

"Yes," he answered slowly, interested in what this was about. "I do."

"Well, she will be performing twice a day for the next five

days with the Shrine Circus at Busch Stadium. I'd be honored if you came to check it out and see what became of that mare."

"I'd love that!" he exclaimed.

Marion was there that very afternoon. He found me, delighted to be included backstage and to get to see this horse perform. While I attended to getting Sassy ready and cooling her off afterward, we bonded as I shared my stories of getting used to Sassy's defiant nature during the circus training and the bonding that had occurred now that she lived with me on the road. Marion also told me many stories about when she was a baby.

"Do you see this little scar?" he asked, pointing at a specific place on her lip.

I had never noticed the little ridge on the outside corner of her upper lip before.

"That happened when she was a newborn foal in the stall with her mother," Marion began. "One day, I was sitting in my office with a client when my groom had stopped in briefly. I asked him to go and check on the baby, and in a few moments, he came back and reported that he couldn't get the sliding door open because the foal was tied to the inside of the door."

Marion shook his head at the memory. "That was strange because we never tie up the babies. So I excused myself and went to investigate. Sure enough, the baby was attached to the inside of the door. I had my groom go into the next stall and climb the wall to drop into the mare and foal's living area." He paused briefly. "Sassy had found a snap hanging from the door latch, and in playing with it had somehow hooked it to the side of her lip."

"Oh, wow! That certainly fits with her personality," I said with a chuckle. It was fun seeing through this window into my mare's past.

Marion laughed too. "Her lip had been punctured, but at least she didn't need any stitches."

After five days of performances, another echelon in Sassy's dancing horse career had been achieved. We collaborated on another season with Bentley Bros. Circus the following year, and then I bid adieu to Evy and headed for Michigan to resume my sign painting service with my carnival clients. My year ahead was full.

Calm Before the Storm

After another productive summer of painting for the Elliott Amusement Company in Michigan, my fall tour once again included airbrushing T-shirts at the State Fair of Texas. Once those gigs were over, I retrieved my horses from Michigan and headed for Florida. Evy and her dogs, horses, and pony wintered there with Bobby and his bears. After painting for

Netterfield's, I moved my operation over to Bill and Cindy's elephant farm in Gibtown—a huge step up from the sad excuse for winter quarters I'd experienced the year prior.

Among the tasks accomplished during that fallow time between seasons was helping Cindy paint the stripes on their elephant trailer, designing and painting a logo for them, and a conversation with the agent who represented Bentley Bros. Circus. Tibor produced contracts for all of us to perform during the upcoming season. There were five weeks in California and then seven weeks in the Midwest. I had never been to California before. Without a big top, the tour would utilize coliseums, grandstands, rodeo arenas, and armories on the west coast. I looked forward to some new sights and hoped the footing would be appropriate for our act.

During negotiations, the agent relayed the owners' request for me to bring both of my horses. Although I planned to perform solely with Sassy, I remembered how much Tommy and Clancy enjoyed using my horses during spec on the previous tour. I assumed that was the purpose of their request, so I easily agreed. With the contract signed, I resumed my work as a traveling artist until the circus tour began, grateful to have found the ability to pursue my passion by having this trade to finance everything.

After providing my sign painting services at Lake Winnipesauke and later in Kansas, it was time at last to meet Evy and Bobby in Texas, where our trio of vehicles began the jump west together as an unusual convoy of horses, dogs, and bears. With the need to tend to the stock, our travel criteria involved regular stops for fuel, water, exercise, and rest. This made the jump to California a several-day ordeal.

I had discovered that during these long jumps Sassy would turn noodle-legged. Because of this, my plan as we headed west was to stop each day to unload and exercise her. While Evy ran her dogs and Bobby tended to his bears, I unloaded the horses and longed my mare to give her some exercise in a vacant area, typically behind a truck stop. That way she would have her legs under her when we arrived, allowing us to go to work immediately.

In the spring of the year, the normally hot states of Texas, Arizona, and New Mexico were quite pleasant. Having been taught in the manner of an old-school truck driver, I used the engine to control the downhill speed by staying in low gear when we found the mountains.

Despite the beauty that California had to offer, this state was incredibly strict compared to others. Reaching the state boundary, officers at the agricultural checkpoint inspected my load, the horse's papers, and for some mysterious reason, confiscated the good Michigan hay I had on the roof.

Welcome to California.

Upon arrival at the first building, we discovered the other acts that would be working with the show included the twelve-horse liberty act of Rex Peterson, Bucky Steele's Elephants, the Zerbini Bros. bareback horse act, Josip Marcan and his tigers, along with an impressive array of talented dogs, flying aerialists, jugglers, wire walkers, rola-bola acts, a bevy of clowns, and Captain David Smith: The Human Cannonball. Holy moly! This was a serious cast of performers.

The show owners demonstrated an appreciation for the performing arts due to the impressive lineup, and I was complimented to be included. One display of this lavish production consisted of three rings of high school horses, including Rex and his sister-in-law on two horses in the center ring, Evy in one end, and me in the other. I could hardly believe it; the time had arrived for me to shine as part of an impressive exhibition of accomplished horsemen. I had come full circle with this horse, landed on top, and was back on the same show where it all began.

The trend of many circuses had become to use fewer and fewer animals in their performances due to the accusations of animal neglect and abuse by activists who only knew half the story. Bentley Bros. Circus was one of the few circuses left with an impressive lineup of animal acts. I had received validation from Tommy Bentley the last time I was here for the amount of time, dedication, and relentless practice it took to achieve a level of perfection with my high school horse. Complimented to be here again and recognizing this as a rare opportunity, my intention was to devote all of my energy to do my absolute best and prove my value. I was confident Tommy would appreciate the result of all my hard work in the off season with Sassy.

Dysfunction Junction

"This is Chad," Tommy said prior to the first show on opening day. He motioned to a pockmarked and disinterested teenage boy standing next to him. "I want both of your horses in the ring performing together."

I cocked my head to the side, not fully grasping what Tommy wanted. He obliged with clarification.

"I want Chad to do the act with you on your other horse."

I stood aghast as I looked at this awkward kid with a severe complexion problem who clearly didn't want to be here any more than I wanted him here. I couldn't believe it. I had worked so hard with Sassy preparing for this tour, and Tommy knew the amount of practice required to prepare an act to perform, yet he seemed satisfied with this unrealistic wrench-in-the-works request.

But Tommy had made his decision; there would be no reasoning with him. As he walked away fully satisfied with his bizarre demand, I realized I was finally seeing the side of Tommy Bentley that the others had warned me about. I looked at the kid who was still standing there waiting for my direction and wondered how our act would ever succeed with an incompetent amateur flogging hopelessly around the ring in this highly regarded art form.

I did my best to be optimistic, saying, "So, you want to learn the art of performing on a high school horse, huh?"

Chad let out a snide scoff, never meeting my eyes as he answered, "Not really. My parents used to have a chimp act, but now they just sell popcorn. Guess they wanted to find something to keep me busy."

My heart sank further. That kid definitely did not want to be here. Not only that, but he didn't even like horses. He longed to be back in Kansas rather than being forced against his will to perform on horseback. Unable to speak, I stood in disbelief. I could already tell this kid and my horse were not going to be a good combination.

My aspiration to succeed would be derailed by this quirk. A tightening grip in the pit of my stomach rendered me voiceless as I searched for a way out of this sticky situation. A moment later, it came to me and I searched for Tommy to make it known.

"I have no saddle for Chad to use," I said, hoping that would be the end of it.

Unfortunately, his mother, Millie, was nearby and a little too quick to tell me she knew someone with a saddle I could buy. She would have it shipped to the show right away.

Tommy shrugged and walked away.

Without the luxury of time with which to prepare a strategy for teaching Chad or the necessary equipment to do so, I should have been suspicious of what was coming my way, but my mind had been short-circuited by this whole debacle. Sure enough, a few days later, an old flat saddle arrived in a box.

Although it was shiny thanks to a coat of spray paint, I would later discover it had a broken tree.

Like putting lipstick on a pig.

The art form of riding a high school horse demanded a high degree of awareness, personal control, and the utmost attention to detail. Because this wondrous animal was sensitive to how we felt, a compassionate, proactive emotion was also required. On a short time frame, I could have made progress with someone who was genuinely interested in horsemanship. But Chad did not want to be on my horse or even in the show at all.

With his closed-off attitude, I had no chance to get even a smattering of understanding across to this unwilling kid. I had no time to create and prepare a pleasant and sensible routine for two men on horses in the ring together.

Still, I was under contract. I tried my best to work with Chad. Referencing the method in which Bob Grubb first introduced me to how to work Bingo, I started the orientation. During the first session, I attempted to teach Chad the basics of the sidepass, march, and bow—all things Bingo already knew—but it was an utter disaster. As I explained the proper use of legs, hands, and seat, I received only annoyed eyerolls in exchange. Chad sat sloppily in the saddle, scoffed at the idea of using alternating aids to get the march, and talked back to me instead of demonstrating a desire to understand. That turbulence alternated with periods of remaining stubbornly silent. None of this was helpful or progressive.

Under Chad's seat, Bingo became jumpy, irritated, and uncomfortable. I didn't blame him one bit; horses were often a good judge of character and Bingo resented having this uncaring lump on his back. The slouch in Chad's posture and the whine in his voice informed me that he suffered from his family situation, turned sour, and had resigned. Any command from me went unacknowledged due to the complete lack of interest he had for the task at hand. My hope to shine in the ring dropped to a depth with no precedent.

I was growing increasingly bitter about my situation. This wasn't what I had intended to sign up for. Riding solo, I could have enjoyed quiet solitude and devoted all of my attention to remaining calm, fluid, precise, and deliberate. Instead, twice a day I was forced into the ring with this untrainable, unwelcomed, pizza-faced kid knocking needlessly on my poor horse. Chad's belligerence rocketed any semblance of peace into orbit as my last remaining hope was dashed on the rocks by the evil that had blindsided me.

Sassy felt it, Bingo certainly felt it, and the resulting mish-mosh of boggled and misguided intentions, infectious fears, curdled frustrations, and putrid attitudes combined to make this pas de deux the worst disaster in the history of circus horsemanship. Not only was the circus ring clogged with an awkward, resentful obstacle—a bitter teenager on a horse—Chad also had a gift for getting and staying right in my way, messing with my own ability to perform at my best. Rancid energy combined with contempt radiated from his soul to feed my angst. It was no wonder that the animal activists found fodder for their fire at the circus.

As I popped open a beer that evening, I thought about my previous experiences with the circus. I had enjoyed several wonderful tours with other circuses. The environment that promoted those memorable tours started with the attitude at the top. The owners of those shows savored the intention of everyone having fun, making money, and generating goodwill.

During those exceptional seasons, everyone pulled together as a team. Their admirable attitude was contagious, and we experienced outstanding camaraderie and togetherness while we got the show up and down day after day. We overcame the natural challenges that occurred together and had regular cookouts after the show when our big family of performers and workers mixed and had fun together.

In contrast, this environment with the Bentley Bros. Circus was downright miserable. I now fully understood all the warnings I had received two years ago about avoiding getting on Tommy's radar. Oh, how I wished I had adhered to them.

As Tommy marched around making sadistic demands, unrealistic requests, and treating us all inconsiderately, the overall experience on this tour was of frustration and agony. The dynamic this cruel man created among his staff made the consideration of driving a nail into one's foot seem appealing in comparison. And it wasn't just about his unreasonable demands; even basic standards were tossed out the window.

All those negative attitudes trickled down through the ranks. Others followed suit. The guy at the bottom of the pecking order kicked his dog. I simply withdrew.

Also contrary was the typical efficiency a rolling show was famous for. Usually, parking privileges were assigned to acts in a reasonable manner to facilitate productivity. Those who had the most equipment to set up in the arena and those who made the most turns in the show received priority parking. That wasn't the case with the Bentley Bros. Circus where the standard practice was every man for himself.

As each vehicle staked out it's territory near the building, the fleet that brought miles of smiles and loads of fun to children of all ages took on the appearance of an exceptionally tense log jam that surrounded the building. Fortunately for me, with just a couple of high school horses, I had no props to worry about. I could easily ride a block to the building when the need arose. My single criterion for parking was simply to find a comfortable place for the horses to reside. But others weren't so lucky.

Rex Peterson was a movie horse trainer, the protégé of horse training legend Glenn H. Randall, Sr. His medium-height stature was animated by his brisk gait, a Snidely Whiplash mustache, and high-top cowboy boots with pants tucked inside. This was his first stint on a traveling circus during his horse training career, and after this, it would be his only—and for good reason.

The two horse acts he provided—a twelve-horse liberty act

and two dancing horses—were all carried in a semitrailer. A large aluminum box ring curb was necessary for his liberty act in the center ring. This was also carried on the back of his semi. The ring curb involved manual labor and a cart to carry each piece in and out of the performing area in every town. For these reasons, Rex would normally qualify for a reserved parking spot adjacent to the door of the building where equipment and animals went in and out. Sadly for him, this circus had no such parking strategy.

Rex's frustration at having to park some distance away was further irritated by Bucky and his elephants. They moved in a semi that supported a massive awning to provide afternoon shade for the pachyderms. As a result, Bucky's entourage had a big footprint, using ample and valuable space in each lot.

In addition, he did only one turn in the show and had no massive props to move at teardown. Because of this, Bucky had the ability to leave the building immediately after his act and head to the next town while the others had to wait until the show was over to even begin teardown. By the time the fleet of circus transport trucks, travel trailers, and support vehicles all made it to the next town, they found Bucky already set up as close to the building door as he could get.

Appeals by Rex to the show owners for help to secure convenient parking instead of the remote spot in the back forty fell on deaf ears. No consideration would be awarded for his legitimate concerns about getting equipment in and out of the show area. Rex was nearing his boiling point.

Tommy wasn't the only negative effect on this show. The rumor mill constantly churned out ugly attacks at virtually everyone on the show, no doubt perpetuated to the delight of the show owners. Not one person was immune to this treatment. Tempers flared, fights broke out, and the big ego of performers dependent on large amounts of approval from others had to find new outlets because of their twisted misbehavior. The resentment made some people retaliate with schemes of their own, while others simply resigned and waited for the eventual death of the season. I was among the latter.

Coming from many generations of bareback-riding performers, the Zerbini brothers were split down the middle. Several seasons prior, they traveled with Mama and Papa who kept them in line and encouraged them in broken English to "pracktick, pracktick, pracktick." The result of extensive rehearsals included an amazing somersault from horse to horse, leaps through hoops, and many other admirable feats unique to the art form of being graceful on the back of a cantering Belgian horse.

This season was different—Mama and Papa were not on the show, so the Zerbini boys were on their own. Roberto was here with his wife and son, maintaining a respectable position in the community with their modest behavior in the backyard. But his brother, Mario, was single and preferred the wild life. Without Mama and Papa, Mario ran amok. An egotistical showoff, he'd often parade his revolving door of women around the backyard. Wine consumption was also part of his demeanor, the liquid lubricant driving his behavior. The regular routine of practice to keep his abilities sharpened had been discarded.

Since horses didn't especially enjoy the constant snorting of the elephants or the smell of exotic cats, the horse people tended to congregate together. Because of this, the Zerbini rig was often my neighbor, though I sometimes wondered whether Bucky and his elephants would make for better company. Mario proved my theory correct, not once, but twice.

One evening after the show, I heard a knock on my door and opened it to find a very drunk Mario. He was ranting and raving in his heavy foreign accent, yelling a litany of obscenities at the top of his lungs. I could barely understand his claim that he was going to kick my ass, making no sense as to his reasons. Rather than take him up on his offer to step outside, I remained indoors and let his unexpected anger slowly subside.

Another time in an especially tight parking lot in downtown Berkeley, my rig was parallel to the concrete curbing of the sidewalk that led to the access ramp on the back of the building. Mario had parked his truck next to mine, precariously close to the curb. After he crosstied his horses to the side of the truck and bedded them down for the night, one of his horses lay down. Unfortunately, the hocks of his back legs grazed the curb, which skinned them raw. This only added fuel to the fire for the animal rights activists who believed all circus animals were mistreated.

To escape the bitter negativity of the show, Evy and I adopted the habit of finding interesting tack shops at every opportunity along the tour. During these outings, we found many wonderful items. At a saddle repair shop in Monterey, I found an interesting cavalry officer's saddle in good shape. Upon my invitation to trade the flat saddle with peeling spray paint, the saddle maker inspected it and threw it in the corner in disgust. His gesture affirmed my suspicion both as to the caliber of the saddle and of Millie's crooked nature. Even without the trade, the officer's saddle became a welcome upgrade and an appropriate addition to my dancing horse operation.

Despite the beautiful scenery, my five weeks in California were not over soon enough. With the first part of the tour completed, I drove east for the interim before the next part occurred, trying to think of a way out of my predicament with Bingo being tormented by Chad. I couldn't wait to get back to the carnival in Michigan where I had a safe place to thrive as a welcome commodity.

A Lesson in Integrity

Red had become perhaps my favorite person of all time. Jokingly claiming to be an amateur psychologist, he was always searching for an ennobling way to motivate the people who worked for him. A clever man, he also demonstrated how to make something out of nothing.

Back at his winter quarters, he was giving a major rebuild to a new ride and asked me to join the crew. He had found a Himalaya-like ride that was mostly intact, although four of the tubs that looked like swans were missing.

"My idea," he began while directing my attention to where tubs were supposed to be, "is to have you make four interesting panels to mount in the openings between the sweeps."

Upon seeing my quizzical expression, Red laughed.

"I'm not worried, Davee. You'll think of something."

He was right. I came up with the idea of dragons chasing the swans. I cut out the shape of a dragon's head from a sheet of plywood and drew a dragon's arm with fierce-looking talons to fill the other gap left by the missing tubs. With this visual, the logical theme for the ride became Conan the Barbarian.

The tops of the building poles where the roof would normally attach were also empty, and Red had another idea for this area. He wanted me to draw a pattern for a shield-like shape to span between poles that he could have his crew cut out of plywood. After they were coated with paint, I could decorate them with barbarian-style weapons and motifs. The ring of shields around the perimeter of the ride would be the finishing touch.

As I began to airbrush the scenery on all the exterior panels,

I recognized a feeling of comfort and security. I took advantage of this feeling and confided in Red about my quandary.

"I still have eight more weeks on my contract with the circus from hell," I disclosed to my kind friend. "I want to work Sassy

in the show, but I don't want to expose my quarter horse to any more misuse by that resentful kid." I sighed. "I just don't know what to do."

Red thought for a moment and said, "You have a responsibility to do the right thing in spite of the behavior of others."

Even though he would have preferred my remaining on his show to enhance the midway with painted imagery and sign work, he appreciated my ambition to perform with my dancing horse in the circus. His gentle reminder about my role with integrity did not offer any obvious advice or answers, instead leaving me to make the right choice, whatever that may look like for me.

While airbrushing images of sexy barbarian men and

women, I pondered Red's words, and soon I made my decision. In an effort to take advantage of the opportunity to perform with Sassy without breaching contract, I would return to the circus as agreed. But in the best interest of my other horse, I would leave Bingo safely behind.

In true show business fashion, the finished pieces were rapidly made, painted, decorated, and loaded in the trailer while still wet. They could dry during the trip to their first county fair.

My friend, Albert the mechanic, visited our winter quarters while Red was using the forklift to load the platforms. In the middle of our conversation Red interrupted us.

"Hey fellows," he said, maneuvering close to a stack of ride parts, "step up there and stand on the edge of that stack of platforms."

Without thinking anything about it, we both stepped up onto the stack. That was when Red began to lift the stack and move it toward the trailer. As Albert and I stood on this moving platform we became simultaneously alarmed.

"Holy shit!" I yelled out. What did I get myself into this time?

Red just laughed while he used us as human counterbalances. Albert and I realized we couldn't do anything but stand there. If one of us tried to jump off, the whole stack would fall down and the other guy would be injured. Fortunately, with Red's expertise, the load was soon safely on the trailer. We had to climb back down to get on the ground, but I was grateful to feel that solid footing beneath my feet. What a frightful bonding experience.

At the fairgrounds, the crew began to set up the cobbled-together and freshly-painted ride of swans and dragons. It looked good. I was proud of its appearance on the midway. The

Elliott Amusement Company now had its first major ride on the show.

Wishing I could stay for the carnival season rather than return to the Bentley hellhole, I knew it was time for me to go. I thanked Red for the work, the friendship, and the advice, and then Sassy and I headed out with Bingo safely boarded at the stable. Driving east to Johnstown, Pennsylvania, I mentally prepared to begin the second and final portion of the Bentley Bros. Circus tour.

Building Tensions

When I arrived at the same fairgrounds where I'd met Evy two years prior, Tommy noticed I had only one horse with me but he didn't say a word. I hoped that meant everything was good. Later in the week, the agent who was supposed to represent the performers came to see me with a document to sign. In spite of what I told Tibor about the unrealistic demands that Tommy had made and how inappropriate it was for a rank amateur to work a horse, he continued to extend the amended contract out to me. Tibor did not do his job; instead of acting on behalf of the artiste, he focused on whatever was easiest—and that was to make Tommy happy. The replacement contract had a compromised amount of pay that would provide me with less than the cost of fuel for the remaining part of the tour. I was truly between a rock and a hard place, but Tibor didn't care.

With a shrug, he said, "Either sign this amended contract or breach the previous contract. It's your call."

We both knew I didn't really have a choice. I reluctantly signed the document, grateful I had earnings from my other trade to finance this lesson in life. I continued to meet my obligations that tour, but I had no further direct dealings with either Tommy or Tibor.

At least there was one good outcome—I was left alone in the ring to concentrate all my energy and devotion on my wonderful horse. I used my newfound spare time to keep her in top shape and we performed our act in peace. Sassy and I developed a stronger bond on that part of the tour due to her having no other companion besides me. I kept busy providing outstanding care for my mare, grooming her to perfection, and remaining deliberately professional in the limelight.

Although Tommy's slimeball tactics bubbled beneath the surface, my performance with Sassy shined. Twice a day, Class n Sass commanded the attention of appreciative audiences. In our downtime, I found a quiet place to reside in solitude with my animal. But even as I maintained my distance, the insanity infecting the personnel caused tempers to flare in an erratic rhythm and with different intensities. The bickering and dysfunction perpetuated by the boss continued all around me as the wars raged among the performers.

The two Anastasini brothers did a Risley act, a diablo act, and a juggling act, and boy, did they love stirring the pot. Their dad, who always kept one foot in the front yard, trotted to the backyard one day during teardown to announce that the animal acts were not to move to the next town for two days. That caused an uproar.

From a distance, I watched these negative conversations unfold, validating my decision to remain reclusive. With no valid reasoning for the delay, the animal men disregarded this warning and went to the next town anyway. Upon arrival, we found the staff lounging around, smugly pretending to be unaware of any legitimate concern about our so-called early presence in their festering clump.

News of an exceptionally tight parking lot at another stop behind an armory heightened the already brittle tension between the warring factions in the backyard. True to form, once the bulk of the fleet pulled into proximity of the building, we found Bucky parked with his awning up and elephants gently swaying in the center of the only flat parking spot by the doors.

Rex had been chewing on a resentment about the parking all season and was later than usual on this particular jump. When he pulled onto the street adjacent to the building and saw the elephant rig sitting sweetly in the perfect spot that blocked the rest of the cast from easily getting their stuff in and out of the building, he'd had enough. In a fit of anger, he abruptly hit the brakes on his truck. The sudden stop for his horses caused a few of them to topple, thrown down from the force of the unexpected cessation. A horse on its side was vulnerable and would frantically scramble to get up. In tight quarters such as a trailer, the wild scrambling would take out the supporting legs from under the next horse, causing an awful domino effect. Just so, a horrible scrambling sound came from inside Rex's semi.

His anger subsided as worry for his equines set in. He had to get to his horses fast to relieve the explosive situation he had created. The ramp was hastily placed in position, and the first horse led out. As the terrorized horses lying on the floor were provided a place to get up, some relief from the self-inflicted hell began to occur.

Once the entire herd had been unloaded, the damage tally was made. Cuts and bruises required doctoring, swollen legs had to be held in buckets of icy water, and bandages needed wrapping over antiseptic spray. Per his contract, the liberty act went on as usual. If there was a victory as the result of this debacle, the trophy would go to the incompetent, apathetic choreographers of tension who fueled this stupid showdown in the first place.

When the season was finally over, Bobby and his bears headed south to Texas. Evy and I went west. Though to different destinations, the start of our trip was the same. As we drove through the night, one of the tires on my trailer burst and went flat. The bottom edge of the spring shackle dragged the pavement, creating a rooster tail of sparks behind me until I found a place to pull over and mount my spare tire.

When the tire man investigated what had punctured the tire, he pulled out the culprit, handing me a souvenir from my final days in the hell known as the Bentley Bros. Circus. I took the triangular piece of carefully broken-off hacksaw blade, my cautiously restrained anger and hatred now coming to the surface.

"Looks like someone left you a parting gift," the tire guy said.

It had been deliberately placed in the groove between the tread patterns. The teeth of that metal rogue acted like barbs and made it travel deeper and deeper through the rubber as I moved down the highway. The repeated contact with the road beneath my tires drove the sharp instrument of sabotage toward its goal, ultimately leading to a delay in my travels.

Although I had a place to shine in the spotlight with my talented mare during the tour, the combined dysfunction and exposure to the destructive, twisted intentions of the owners of that circus made my consideration of future performing opportunities understandably reluctant. The little piece of shrapnel remained as a monument to the insanity encountered and a tragic testimony to my horrible experience during that circus tour. I would never again perform for the Bentley Bros. Circus.

Chapter 9
Big D

"The best and most beautiful things in the world
cannot be seen or even touched—
they must be felt with the heart."
—Helen Keller

The Excursion

Back in Michigan, I was relieved the circus tour was over. Sassy resumed her life at the Saddlebred stable near Fowlerville, and I returned to my place creating visual wonders with both brush and airbrush on the friendly carnival midway. I enjoyed the contrast of the healthy altruistic environment as peace returned to my life.

The circus tour from hell caused me to hesitate with future performance opportunities, but my happy place remained with my horses, and I was hopeful that a better experience would present itself at some point. For now, I would spend my downtime at the barn becoming acquainted with the horse folks who shared my equine passion while participating with riding lessons, horse boarding, training, and care.

I was developing a refined taste for horses. Observing the beehive of activity at the barn fortified my preference for hot-blooded horses and what they could do. With a finished horse ready to perform, I began to consider how having another one in training would be a sound strategy—a second dancing horse would mean I was ready no matter what happened.

While going through the learning curve of making Sassy into a proficient performer, I further realized the limitations of the quarter horse. Although I loved Bingo, he simply wasn't suited for my preference. As I developed the idea of finding another Saddlebred, I faced the fact that the first step toward my new goal would be to find Bingo a good home. I would have to advertise him for sale.

I placed an ad in the Western Horseman magazine that mentioned his background as a performing circus horse and received an inquiry from a lady in Kansas. When she told me her previous horse had also been a retired circus horse, I knew instinctively that Bingo would have a good home with her. The following spring, en route to my client in Wichita, I stopped by to meet this woman and our transaction took place. I showed her Bingo's many tricks and she took to him like a duck to water. I left knowing Bingo would have a good home. I could now begin my search for another horse.

In the fall of that year, I was invited by the couple who ran the Saddlebred farm in Michigan to attend the Tattersalls Horse Auction in Lexington, Kentucky. They were also in the market for a school horse. I could ride along with them in their pickup that would pull an empty horse trailer.

The road trip began when we got on the interstate and consumed the greatest part of the day. When we arrived in Lexington, we met a friend of theirs at a fancy restaurant. Our conversation orbited around the excitement we all shared for horses and wondering what we might see at the auction. I learned Aggie lived close to Jackson, Michigan and happened to own the piece of property that had at one time been the winter quarters of the small, tented Lewis Bros. Circus back in the forties. I was amazed to meet her, having visited that same place with my friend, Hayes, years prior.

The Tattersalls sale barn was a grand old facility surrounded by giant sycamore trees that had provided shade for many years. After parking the rig and making our way toward the entrance, our excitement began as we navigated through traffic plump with magnificent horseflesh. We entered a labyrinth of wooden stalls and horse care facilities into viewing areas where we received our catalogue that described all the horses that would pass in front of the auctioneer's gavel.

I perused the entries based on my criteria and made my top choices. Then I navigated the interior of that facility and found the stalls where my selections awaited. I'd learned the skill of making a good visual assessment from Evy, and this was the litmus test. I found excitement as I explored the hallways, peeking into each stall. I compared the visual qualities with my search criteria and quickly narrowed the field down further.

As I made my way through the crowd to look into the next stall, I found a surprise I hadn't counted on. An old friend was standing with his horse prepared for the sale, answering questions from the parade of people milling in and out.

"Hello, John," I blurted out to my busy friend.

I had met John Wallen at the horse show in Little Rock two years prior. He came from a large family of talented horse trainers, including his dad. John's uncle had a performing horse called Mister Rhythm who had worked many circus dates. After my performance at the society horse show in Little Rock, John had made it a point to find and commend me.

"Dave!" He was just as surprised to see me. "Good to see you. How are you doing?"

"Excellent," I responded. "Sassy is working great. I'm here searching for another horse."

"You'll find one here," he predicted. "That's for sure."

Here in his professional role, he represented horses being offered by his clients, but he was also on the lookout for additional horses to take home for other clients.

"Stop by the farm one day," he requested. "I'd love to talk with you when I'm not so busy."

I was complimented. "I'd like that, John."

I rejoined my friends in the auction area and sat down. The sale had already begun. As each animal was brought into the sawdust-covered area in front of us, I scanned them up and down, practicing my new keen eye. When each attendant trotted his horse, I studied the footfalls, the action of the hocks, and the attitude of the topline.

When the horses I had selected came through the auction, I discovered something about myself. I have been blessed with expensive taste in horseflesh. Every horse I had chosen was a highly desirable, top-shelf equine that ended up selling for an incredible amount of money. I couldn't compete. While my money remained in my pocket, my hosts bought two inexpensive horses to add to their string of lesson horses back in Michigan. Their idea was to speculate and have a horse available to sell to a client.

By late afternoon the auction was over and the activity at the sale barn became solely administrative and logistical as the animals changed hands and found their way to new homes. My hosts' new horses could stay in their stalls overnight, which allowed us to stay for an extra-special treat in Lexington the following day.

Sunday was the final day of our excursion, and it just so happened the Select Sale at Castle Hills Farms was taking place.

After breakfast, we checked out of our hotel, loaded our gear, and returned to Tattersalls to load the new horses. Then we headed over to this impressive estate. From the road, I saw the large turreted mansion that looked like a castle surrounded by acres and acres of horse facility. We joined the throngs parking trucks and horse trailers in the grassy field and made our way to the equally impressive stable.

We were greeted by formally dressed waiters holding trays filled with champagne in plastic stemware. We took our drinks and walked through the foyer into the luxurious indoor riding arena that had been transformed into the sale area teeming with people. We walked across the two-tone sawdust design that had been carefully arranged on the floor—green to designate the ample seating area and tan down the sale runway where fine horses would soon be racking right in front of us.

There was no doubt that this was an exclusive sale with only high-priced show horses going under the gavel. Before the auction began, we explored the stalls to see the horses being readied. I saw John again, this time with another incredible horse, and had a chance for yet another brief conversation.

"Hey again, John," I said with a chuckle. "Fancy meeting you here."

John knew I was on a different level than the affluent who provided him with his living, yet he appreciated the grassroots understanding we shared for horse training. For me, he allowed access to the real trainer.

When our conversation ended, ever cordial, John reminded me, "Make sure to visit me at my barn in Springfield, Missouri."

I promised I would right as the loudspeaker announcement urged us to find our seats in the arena. Waving farewell, I went to find a chair. Once everyone was settled on the sales floor, the wonderful parade of stunning horseflesh began. The syllabic song of the auctioneer filled the air. The spotters chirped at every gesture to buy. And once again I discovered the horses that caught my eye were the ones that sold for big bucks. I couldn't afford any of them, but at least I was developing a good eye.

When the sale was over, we had to scramble. The recently purchased horses were already loaded in the trailer. By early afternoon, the trek back to Michigan began. During the long drive, we chatted about all that we had seen as I maintained my excitement about a future that included another incredible Saddlebred horse.

It was well after dark when we arrived at our digs where my rig waited at my hosts' farm. Despite not yet finding a second horse, the fantasy excursion became a cherished memory as I drifted off to sleep that night.

Man's Best Friend

My dog never played with a toy, retrieved a ball, or chased a stick. He didn't have to. Superdog grew up on the best possible playground there was for a dog—the circus. During our lives together, he stuck pretty close to my ever-active heels. Only when he realized I would be busy with a project for a while would he enlarge his territory for exploration, always with his ears on me.

On both the circus and the carnival, there were plenty of things to see, activities to engage in, and personnel to interact with. But when I evolved into a sign painter for downtown Jackson, the urban sprawl, traffic on the streets and the ominous glassed-in businesses did not have the same warm reception Superdog was used to. Downtown life had a different flow for him.

As the years went by, we had several occurrences where he became lost for a period of time. Often, it was because he was so friendly that he'd jumped into someone's car. This tested my faith. Fortunately, I thought to refer to something learned back when I was training ponies. While studying Zen practices for the mind, I learned to use my imagination to visualize Superdog coming back to me and refused to let the idea of him being lost forever enter my mind.

During our vast excursions in the circus through the mountains, coastal cities, urban sprawls, and the expanse of western Canada, any such disappearance became merely a hiccup in our relationship. But as our years together mounted, teeth, bones, and eyesight grew tired. Superdog's condition slowly deteriorated until I noticed a sullenness begin to permeate his usual exuberance for what we were doing next. Here in Jackson, the day would finally come when I would have to face that which I previously refused to entertain.

During one of my big wall jobs at Kelly Imports in the autumn of the year, he stealthily wandered off. When the end of the day came, I noticed he was nowhere to be found. I entered into the usual confidence about his return, but something about this time was different. When days went by with no sign of Superdog, my visualization recalled the reluctance in his attitude, the anemia in his step, and his loss of appetite. I began to embrace the worst. The mystery of Superdog's disappearance deepened to the point of grief that would have no relief.

My loving, dedicated friend had gone off somewhere to die.

The idea of having my constant companion who'd acted as my personal wellspring of encouragement for many years had been replaced with a truth I did not want to acknowledge. My best friend was gone. The worst part was that I never had the opportunity to say goodbye.

As weeks turned into months, I would be vexed again when some well-meaning person would ask about my dog, reopening the wound that had been trying to heal. I would weep again. It would take a long time for me to get over the thought of not seeing Superdog's friendly smile, his curled-up tail, or his exuberant wiggle when I started up the engine in preparation for another trip. Still, as I looked back I found plenty to be grateful for. I had been blessed with a wonderful animal for the duration of his lifetime and his presence had made an indelible impression on my heart that continues to this day.

Beanie's sister knew how much I missed Superdog. With plans to jump to Escanaba to work the fair in the upper peninsula, Susie asked me to babysit her dog while she was gone. That was my introduction to Nick, an interesting dog who shared characteristics of a German shepherd, elkhound, and Keeshond. With a slightly smaller blend of those breeds, some remarked that Nick looked like he had some gray wolf in him.

Nick took quickly to being my constant companion on the fairgrounds and everywhere else I went. I noticed that he shrank away from loud, stern voices. That told me that he may have been abused as a puppy. Just as I had done in response to Sassy's defiance, I vowed to radiate constant love whenever he became reluctant. Nick's confidence grew when he realized there was nothing to be afraid of when it came to me.

When Susie returned from the upper peninsula to discover our growing attachment, she couldn't bring herself to take him from me.

"You'd better keep him," she said. "It'd be a shame to separate the two of you with a bond like that."

It was true. During that short time, Nick had filled the void left in my heart by the loss of Superdog, and our connection had deepened in that short time more than I'd anticipated.

"I'd love to," I said with a smile.

My heart began to heal.

I never had to tell Nick what to do. He just figured out the best way to get along, bless the most people, and have fun. Soon, he developed a mini route everywhere we went to visit the new friends he was constantly making.

At the State Fair of Texas in October, I went to see one of my regular customers. We walked up the steps of Newport's office in a semitrailer and Nick ignored the big dogs guarding the place, threading his way through the legs of the people standing around and making it behind the desk.

In spite of having large dogs of her own at the fair, Carolyn Newport fell in love with Nick, and their friendship blossomed. She began taking him with her to the bank, appreciating how well behaved he was. While standing in line with her bags of money for deposit, Nick sat alert by her feet. When she moved up in line, he inched forward, staying right beside her every moment.

"Not one of my own dogs is as wise as Nick," she exclaimed after one such trip.

During African Appreciation Day at the fair, all dogs were supposed to be tied up. Since I was in the midst of people all day and Nick's presence might be considered disruptive to the guests, I reluctantly tied him up as required to keep him out of the way.

Fifteen minutes later, Carolyn drove up on her golf cart where I was painting.

"Where's Nick?" she asked.

"I tied him up."

"Don't you ever tie up that dog!" she scolded me. "Let that dog free."

"If the boss says so," I said, laughing as I turned him loose.

Friend or Foe

By the mid-eighties, I began to feel the crunch of the computer-generated sign makers. This new breed began to interfere with the bread and butter of my hand-painted sign business in downtown Jackson, including what I called informational signs—Leave All Parcels at the Side Door, No Parking by the Dock, Regulations Prohibit Consumption on Premises, Anna's All-Day Thursday Specials, All Violators Will Be Towed, Do Not Knock, etc. These signs used a quick-brush letter stye and were easy to jam into the schedule. Although painting those kinds of signs was boring at best, it filled the gaps and paid the bills.

The computer era ushered in a regime who never would have become sign painters except for the newfound efficiency in making such signs with perfect letters spit out by a machine. The output was admirable and I couldn't compete with their pricing. In Jackson, I could still get the wall-dog jobs—lettering a big "Mufflers Installed Here" or "No Appointment Needed" down the side of a large block building—but even those jobs were limited.

I guess I might have been a bit relieved, seeing as that wasn't where my passion lay. What I really wanted to paint were signs with fancy hand-designed multi-dimensional soda-script letters with triple-hue shadows, pinstripe outlines, and highlights.

An even better job was when they wanted me to add a pictorial, some animated pinstriping, or scrollwork to enhance the overall design. That's why I enjoyed painting for the showmen—they always wanted their stuff to be elaborate, interesting, and attention-grabbing. The showmen provided a place for me to develop the skills I needed to become a fine sign and pictorial painter.

Sadly, those jobs were few and far between, and I could feel the crunch in my budget from the loss of those basic jobs the computers had taken over. Fortunately, I could do something those computer guys couldn't do—I could airbrush a one-of-a-kind design on a T-shirt.

The following summer back with the Elliott Amusement Company, Tim Bors was especially excited to have secured the Gerber Baby Food Festival in Fremont, Michigan. Prior to the show moving to this street festival, he encouraged me to get my T-shirt stand ready for that busy spot.

I hadn't spoken to Mary since my embarrassment of the previous year. I would need to find someone new to help me with my T-shirt booth this year. Although I posted a "Help Wanted" sign on my booth, I still had no help by opening day. I went to the popper trailer and mentioned my predicament to Red's wife, Sandy. I guess I expected her to provide a solution to my dilemma, but I was disappointed.

"Yeah, I know how you feel," she said as she busily

prepared another batch of caramel corn. "We don't have enough help in here or in the drink stands either."

Feeling alone in finding a solution for my predicament, I left the popper and headed back to my booth wondering what to do. Two customers were already waiting, ready to order shirts. I went behind the counter and greeted them. Once I took their order, I found the properly sized shirts and collected the money. I then moved from behind the counter to stand at my shirt-painting easel, placing the first blank shirt on the platen and beginning to paint. Of course, this drew a crowd.

Knowing I had to handle all the aspects of my operation myself, I became very careful with handling all the new shirts; I knew I didn't dare get any paint on my fingers. By using utmost care, I adopted the pace of painting a shirt or two and then ducking behind the counter to wait on customers. Most of them figured they would have to wait with how busy I was. I paced myself this way for the entire weekend.

When the festival was over, I added it all up. I'd had a huge weekend without any help. Feeling encouraged, I added the Jackson County Fair to my T-shirt route. Although Red and Glenn didn't take their show there anymore, it was fun having the population of my town see what I could do.

After teardown from the successful Jackson County Fair, I then made an overnight jump to the Lenawee County Fair—

what the carnies call a circus jump. In the morning, I set back up on the new fairgrounds. My joint didn't take long to set up, and in no time I was back at my easel painting shirt after shirt, though tired from lack of sleep. As my weary mind transformed the latest customer's request into another stunning design, someone interrupted my rhythm.

"Hey, I'm a sign guy, too."

I looked up from the shirt I was working on to see an overweight guy of about medium height. He held a box of popcorn and had a toothpick stuck in the beaming grin on his face. Normally, I would have regard for one of my fellow sign guys, but thanks to the new regime that had infected the scene, I learned to observe before saying too much. Noticing this man didn't have any paint on his pants, I figured he might be one of the computer "painters." I had better be on guard. I nodded noncommittally and went back to the task before me. Between munches from his big box of popcorn, he blurted, "I make vinyl letters with my Gerber machine."

Of all the times to get caught not wearing a necklace made out of garlic. With his disclosure, I knew I was in the proximity of the enemy, but despite my cold reception, he wouldn't leave. He remained friendly, watching me paint shirts and asking innocent questions about my process. He truly seemed to be enjoying himself. As time passed with no reason to feel under attack, my demeanor changed slightly. He actually didn't seem like a bad guy.

Later that week, he stopped by again after the tractor pulling was over in the grandstand. While he watched me whip out another airbrushed name on a shirt, he shared news about technical advances taking place in the sign industry, new products being developed to make our jobs easier, and how he was going to attend the upcoming sign industry show in Detroit. Eventually, I let my guard down completely and began to respond to his casual inquiries, learning his apt carnie nickname was Toothpick Tom. He responded by opening up even more, providing me with useful information about products I could possibly use to assist me in the rapidly changing industry from what was once the exclusive realm of the hand painter. As I warmed up to this enthusiastic fan of signs, I found out that Toothpick Tom was a genuinely nice guy.

Expanding the Quest

My route as a traveling artist took me to many locations. Using the leads accumulated at horse shows, stables, and now from my recent sales barn experiences, I knew where a multitude of horses resided at farms all across the country. The time available between painting projects allowed for exploration of these likely places.

The judge from the Little Rock horse show who'd awarded

Sassy her ribbon two years prior had invited me to his farm in Iowa to see the horses he had for sale. When I finished things up in Michigan, I headed west to visit his huge farm outside of Des Moines.

The stallion barn was a mile away from the foaling barn. As his guest, I stood at the edge of a grand field and looked at a herd of horses grazing quietly. My eye had become quite capable of making an accurate visual assessment of the ideal conformation of the horse I sought, and my gaze went right to the best of the best. I was happy I could trust my eye, but I still couldn't afford it.

In the autumn of the year, my routine included travel to the State Fair of Texas to become a T-shirt artist for the nineteen-day run. That task, including travel, consumed an entire month. After the fair was over, I reunited with Sassy in Michigan and the time had come to travel to Florida. My departure was hastened by impending flurries.

After a thousand-mile jump into the southern climate, my sign painting business resumed at Netterfield's Popcorn & Lemonade winter quarters near Tampa. Sassy was again boarded nearby at Ruth's Saddlebred barn. I would connect with my circus friends nearby to cautiously and optimistically pursue aspirations to perform. I was fortunate that my successful sign painting trade financially allowed for such opportunities.

Lexington, Kentucky became a favorite destination in the midst of these travels. The attraction was partly due to my connection with horses and the discovery of the American Saddlebred Association headquarters at Kentucky Horse Park. The association headquarters had a modern museum facility over the offices on the lower floor.

Inside the luxurious building, I saw many stunning bronze-cast statues of Saddlebred horses on ornate stands. One especially grand piece had four greyhound dogs in playful poses at each corner of a grand multiple-layer piece with cartouches, turned hardwood turrets, and bevel-edged marble components, all combining to support an anatomically accurate Saddlebred stallion.

While here, I also became friends with Lynn Weatherman, the editor of American Saddlebred Magazine. He was especially competent with the bloodline aspect of the breed and was interested in my performing career using these majestic horses. Through this friendship, I made contacts with other association personalities.

One spring while I traveled north, I stopped in to say hello to my editor friend. My timing was perfect to see a major show. Lynn invited me to sit in the association's reserved box seats during the Junior League Horse Show that took place that weekend. Intrigued with such an opportunity, I sat in the front row at the Red Mile Race Track and marveled at the large groups of show horses that traveled the long oval shape below.

During this wonderful experience, I reflected on the strategy of thriving and continuing to develop as a performing horseman connected to this wonderful community.

The Big D

Through society horse contacts across the country, conversations occurred for performing opportunities in that demographic. A producer in Chicago explored options for a performance show at the annual four-day Big D Saddle Horse Show in Dallas. The Big D included Saddlebreds, Morgans, hackney ponies, and Tennessee walking horses with plenty of categories for each breed, and the reason for the special program of acts was to add entertainment as an attempt to appeal to an outside audience, sell tickets, and fill the seats.

I was honored to receive a phone call with an invitation to perform at that major horse show and even more thrilled when they wanted my act as the feature performance. Class n Sass received top billing among the other performing acts that included Paso Finos, Roman riders, rope spinners, a cowboy square-dance team on horses, and a girl who had a trick horse.

The advance publicity efforts designed to generate excitement in Texas did the same for me—I enjoyed hearing the news of the approaching show and seeing ads with Class n Sass billed as an equine ballerina. I recognized this show as a major opportunity in my career as a dancing horse trainer and intended to do everything I could to do an especially good job. With plenty of time to prepare before the autumn show, training sessions with my horse took on a new dimension. I had extra energy and motivation with this big opportunity in sight.

But by this point, I had long developed the pattern of drinking every day. An awareness grew in regard to how it might interfere with this professional aspiration. With my desire to do the best possible job, I opted to quit all beer intake three weeks prior to the event.

When I arrived in Dallas, I admired the grand ambience. The horse show coliseum was surrounded by metal-roofed buildings that contained a labyrinth of concrete walls, a web of metal plumbing, and a network of commercial lighting and electrical fixtures. Rolling wooden doors and barred dividers made up row after row of equine housing in a maze of stalls. Dirt throughways covered with sawdust allowed for horses and their companions to pass through these areas. On many of the main intersections of these sawdust arteries were extensive displays brought in by the major stables that included water fountains, floral arrangements, potted plants, and stunning horse sculptures. Mounted photos of exotic features of the faraway stabling facilities and their featured stallions also inspired awe.

Some of the stalls were completely canvassed off and used as dressing rooms while the rest were reserved for the equines taking part in the big show. Some had entire aisles devoted to a single enterprise, but because I was a much smaller operation, just two stalls were provided for my needs. For those larger companies, color-coordinated canvas valances with the barn names were affixed high on top of the entire length of the stall row that each group occupied and fancy signs were mounted at both ends of this arrangement with a main display in the center. Tack trunks and color-coordinated folding director's chairs peppered the aisles between stalls along with tables covered with veggie snack trays, small sandwiches, plastic stemware, coolers full of drinks, and the occasional coffee pot.

Once Sassy was settled into her stall, I collaborated with the announcer and the music and lighting fellows. With this team, we came up with the agenda for presenting my act. I was further excited when I heard they would have videographers on site. Since I had not succeeded in obtaining a video of my act with Sabrina's help, I arranged for the cameramen here to capture footage of my routine each day. I could already tell that this was truly going to be a fantastic experience.

At this massive horse show, I took notice of a vast demographic I was not familiar with. These were society horses, referred to as such because these equine status symbols were historically considered an appropriate pastime for royalty. In this case, they remained for the very rich.

While some equestrians were relaxing near their block of stalls, others were busy grooming their elegant show horses, and still others were in the practice ring. I noticed a stark contrast in behavior, ability, and attitude between the professional horse trainers and workers who knew their way around a horse and were here to make a living, and those who were obviously inept with incredible horses. I wasn't the only one who saw this.

"Did you see the way that girl bobbed around like a rag doll at the trot?" I overheard a pristinely dressed woman say to her friend.

"Oh my gawd! Did you see when that guy went to dismount and his foot stuck in the stirrup?" She made a motion as though she were about to fall over, mimicking the scene she was describing.

I couldn't help but snicker as I walked past. Although they weren't talking to me, I had also witnessed both of those things and I secretly shared in their amusement.

Equine Ballerina

With the circus, I had learned the discipline of being ready at the start of the act prior to mine. This habit was necessary for a smooth and uninterrupted show, especially when the occasional emergency occurred that could cause a last-minute change in the lineup. That was a little harder here at the horse show—my slot to perform was after a different class each day. In addition, the length of time a class took was influenced by how many horses were in the class and how long the judges took to select a winner.

I determined to simply have Sassy under saddle, warmed up from a session in the outdoor ring, and waiting by the rail when the specific class I was due to follow was underway. In this manner, I would be prepared for whenever our time to shine arose.

I had also learned long ago to attend to my animals

immediately upon waking. During the early morning hours of the first day, the grooms, handlers, and individual private horse owners were apparently of the same discipline, stirring along with me. While I went about my routine with feeding and mucking, other stalls were also being cleaned and picked out among the peaceful sounds of chewing, nuzzling the bottom of a bucket, and the occasional snort. For the humans, percolators bubbled and added a refreshing fragrance to the mix.

As the morning grew, the wealthy participants arrived from their hotel rooms and joined us in a myriad of activities. During the frenzy before the horse show, participants of all kinds were primped into impeccable condition by the many attendants who, like devoted servants, combined their efforts to get horse and rider and all the leather, metal, and fabric accouterments in pristine show shape.

Many of the horses had matching wig pieces woven into the tail to add pure luxury. Specially tailored saddle suits were donned, boots were polished, and hair arranged in buns. Tack was shined and muzzle whiskers and ear hairs trimmed while the horse shoer quickly nailed lead weights onto soles of horse feet as needed. The skin surrounding the horses' eyes was rubbed with oil to produce a deep shine, and a special spray sprinkled a slight metal-flake sparkle on the slick, curried finish of the fur.

I was busy with the grooming practices I'd learned in the circus. With careful short strokes of a comb going against the grain in the slick hair on Sassy's haunches, I created a checkerboard pattern on her rump. Next, I glued small mirrors in alternating squares of the pattern for an extra special effect. White leg wraps were securely and accurately wrapped onto each leg between the knee and ankle to accent the visual effect of her actions from a greater distance. Then, a special white saddle pad with gold tube edging went onto her back before I laid my dressage saddle with straight flaps down onto her back. The martingale, or breast collar, went over her head and onto her neck next, and finally, the whole affair was lovingly secured.

Sassy's tail didn't need any of my help to look stunning. Under saddle, the traditional Saddlebred modification caused the tail to assume an elevated position. The massive augmented feathery appendage undulated while the horse ran through her gaits. It added dramatic flair to the Saddlebred's appearance in a beautiful manner, especially in the breeze caused when the order was given to rack on, the most rapid of the five gaits.

With my mare pristine, it became my turn to dress as I channeled my perfectionist, sharp-dressing dad. His neatly arranged closet was his testimony—I remembered special cuff-clamp hangers that held his pants inverted to keep the crease sharp. Padded hangers for his suit jackets were arranged in an orderly row, and when he would tuck his shirttail in, an even overlap occurred in precisely the same location on either side of his girth, a technique he'd learned in the military.

Carrying on this family tradition in the form of my performance wardrobe, I first put on a ruffled-front formal shirt, tucked smartly into white breeches. I covered my waist with a cummerbund and added a bowtie up top. Then I pulled on my black Dehner boots and strapped on my spurs. After that, I reached for my peach-colored tuxedo jacket with glass jewels and gold piping sewed onto the lapels, cuffs, and tails, and slipped on this heavy jacket. Snapping into the proper posture, the costume assumed its position. I finished off my look with a matching Mississippi riverboat gambler's hat.

Once I was finished dressing myself, I introduced Sassy to the double bits of the full bridle. Slipping the headstall over her ears, I guided the bits into her mouth and attached the throat latch. After hooking the delicate curb chain, I circled her one last time to make my final inspection of every last detail.

When the time came to lead her into the aisle, I asked her to bow on one knee as I placed my foot in the stirrup. Well accustomed to this, Sassy easily held this pose as I swung my leg over before rising back onto all four feet. My posture settled straight into the classic seat developed under the tutelage of my many mentors. At last, we were ready to make our way to the warm-up ring to prepare both mentally and physically for the performance ahead.

Prior to my entrance, the building went dark by killing all the house lights. I was poised in the entrance chute as our announcement came over the speakers.

"Ladies and gentlemen, calling your attention to a special presentation," the ring announcer's voice echoed throughout the cavernous building. "The one and only equine ballerina, Class n Sass, the beautiful American Saddlebred dancing horse, brought to you here for the very first time for your entertainment pleasure, trained and presented by Dave Knoderer! Please welcome this dancing duo to the ring."

Synchronized to start at the end of the introduction, the organist played the theme music from Star Wars. Two spotlights came on at precisely the same time, illuminating one specific area in the pitch blackness and revealing horse and rider as we entered the arena floor in the spectacular elevated trot known as the passage.

I noticed the mare was acting funny. After a quick assessment while running through our paces, I discovered she was being spooked by one front leg wrap that had come loose and was now flapping around. I jumped to the ground and removed the rest of the wrap. With this dangerous situation handled swiftly, it was time to resume the act. As usual, I had her bow and put my foot in the stirrup iron. With the graceful remount that followed, I received an unexpected applause, realizing this way of getting on a horse was novel to these people.

Now that the minor setback was resolved, we began to cover ground in the cavernous arena with a path that included several voltes, or small circles, along the way. In perfect time with the music, Sassy's gait showcased just one of many abilities she was proficient with. This manner of starting the act also allowed me to acknowledge the entire crowd while we moved in front of the seating to eventually arrive front and center and begin our unusual routine.

At the circus, I used every bit of the forty-two-foot circle called the ring. Here, the vast expanse had an obstacle in the middle—an extensively decorated arbor-like latticework area for the officials, their attendants, a photographer, the organist, and even the trophies. I modified the path of my routine to present all the features of the act in front of as much of the audience as possible. As the loopy path of alternating voltes yielded to the lateral sidepasses, the announcer made his running comments about the haute école training of the high school horse.

After the final sidepass, the leg extensions began. The first movement was the triple three-step—three strikes with the same leg followed by two forward steps. The movement followed a predictable pattern: left, left, left, walk, walk, then right, right, right, walk, walk, and repeat. This introductory extension exercise created an established forward momentum that was continued as we changed to the other variations, including the three-step.

The three-step encircled the entire arena so everyone could see, following a similar pattern of left, walk, walk, right, walk, walk, and repeat. When we once again arrived at the front side, the three-step changed into the march, during which Sassy did a leg extension on every stride up the front straightaway. We marched forward and eventually reached the place where we changed direction from a stop.

Our backward-extension movements were next. The backward double-three-step appeared as such: strike, strike, back, back, repeat. We backed across the arena in this fashion before performing the spectacular breakdown bow. I gave Sassy the cue to plant her front feet and she leaned backward until they were well out in front of her with her chest just inches off the ground. As Sassy held this position, the organist played a long chord, and I made my sweeping style gesture that promoted applause.

The organist did a teaser with the staccato opening notes of the popular show tune "New York, New York" as we rose up and came out of this pose. In time with the music, Sassy began her favorite elevated hesitation-trot gait known as the passage. She could do this movement all day long. The stunning animation of this exercise was the strongest feature of our presentation, and the horse aficionados in the audience sat up to take notice. The focus of their training was typically elsewhere as they focused on rapid animation and speed. Still, they certainly seemed to appreciate our abilities.

After the passage around the entire arena floor, we took a bow. Sassy raised one foreleg and curled it underneath her, leaning back until her knee rested in the sawdust. Again, I styled to the crowd as she held this position. When we came up out of this pose, the organist struck up the lively tune "Runaway". This tune fit perfectly with Sassy exploding into a canter depart.

We galloped across the front area and around the north end. This animated gait stood in contrast to the graceful and elegant demonstration of the recently completed passage. When we were halfway down the back side, the time came to begin the canter rears. On cue, Sassy stopped in her tracks, reared straight up, and struck out with her front legs as I leaned back in the saddle to assist with weight distribution. Upon landing on all fours, another canter depart transitioned her back into the gallop, but only for a few strides before it was time to stop and rear again.

Several canter rears took place across the back of the venue, and then several more across the front. Racing around the north end, we cantered the last leg of our routine up to a location adjacent to the announcer's stand where we came to a halt. Sassy bowed again, and when she was down on one knee, I asked her to curl the other leg to kneel on both knees for our conclusion.

When the final announcement was made, we rose from our pose and began to make our way to the exit gate at the passage. At the last moment, we turned to face the interior of the arena to make one last acknowledgement to the crowd. I bowed my head in gratitude with my hat in my hand, extending my right arm in the fashion of a formal dressage rider. In this frozen pose, the spotlights went off and I exited in the darkness to massive applause.

Beyond thrilled with the outcome of our performance, I reflected on the details as I cooled Sassy off and then led her back to her stall. Everyone involved did great job learning and doing their part during rehearsal, and as a result, the presentation of our act had gone perfectly smoothly. The acceptance, applause, and approval that came from this community pumped a new elixir into my bloodstream, overwriting any lingering damaged esteem issues that had accompanied me through life and giving me an image of myself that I approved of. I became a handsome prince on a beautiful and talented steed.

Just as I latched Sassy's stall door, a couple approached with a special request. They wanted me to perform that evening at a Saddlebred stable north of Dallas. Prior to the horse show each year, Milligan Stables had their annual open house and fish fry. Their event was scheduled to take advantage of the visiting horse folks who'd arrived to participate at the Big D Horse Show and to allow these aficionados to see their farm and livestock. I recognized this request to perform in front of their guests as an endorsement of sorts, accepting the invitation. Instead of relaxing, I had to get ready.

Equestrian Enthusiasts

A few miles north of town, I found Milligan Stables in the affluent suburb of Plano. Although the horse and I were dressed to a T, this would be a high-grass presentation that took place on the lawn. I would show my act to the crowd while they stood in line for the meal provided, the only time they would be assembled. In sharp contrast to the high-tech rehearsal for the Big D, the demonstration I provided here would have no announcement, no music, and no special lighting. But, as always, I took every performance seriously.

We performed the sidepass, three-step, passage, and all the other elements of our routine and received applause from the patient yet hungry crowd. Once Sassy was cooled out and crosstied to the side of my horse trailer, I had an opportunity to get some grub and meet the other folks who were here to enjoy the festivities. By the end of the evening, I was back at the stable at the fairgrounds and settled in for a long-anticipated night of rest.

As each day morphed into evening, all sorts of lavish parties took place around the activities of the Big D Saddle Horse Show. The variety of age groups in attendance combined their enthusiasm and were regarded as an important contribution to showmanship. A jovial atmosphere permeated the long days filled with animal care, grooming the horse and rider to impeccable condition, and handling the pipeline of various personal incidentals and necessities consumed by this cross section of humanity.

I enjoyed it, but nonetheless found myself along the edge of it all, as usual. That is, until I met another small operation in attendance.

Billy and Joanne had the same number of stalls I had, and therefore, also had all day to primp a single horse. Their talented Morgan stallion named Southerly Piper participated in several classes. They hoped to meet other horsemen interested in breeding with him. Plus, their stallion had been selected to do a freestyle liberty class all by himself. This would be a prime time for their horse to run free, frolic, play, respond to the cheering from the crowd, and delight the audience with spontaneous antics.

Joanne had no idea how it would go because they'd never done anything like this before, but Piper proved to be the perfect equine personality for such a class. Once she turned him loose, he really put on a show. As the crowd responded with their loud approval to his horseplay, he took his cue and pulled out all the stops. His spontaneous escapades delighted everyone in attendance for an allotted amount of time.

"Time's up." the announcer said.

"Gather your horse."

Joanne did not know what to do. As Piper raced past her one more time, she let out a "Whoop, ho," and he magically stopped. Relieved, she was then able to snap a lead onto his bridle and lead him out. The crowd went wild one more time, and as if he knew it was all for him, he became animated in hand at the walk with his proud handler. Their success got the attention of some of the high-stakes Saddlebred folks who insisted that their stallions should also participate in this manner for the show, but all their performances waxed pale in the shadow of Piper's exuberance.

With lots of time during the day to visit, Joanne and Billy exuded comfort and warmth to all they encountered. Their home-spun manner of handling the related tasks at the show combined with their appreciation of peers who became their friends. Their particular interest for what I did with my horse prompted much conversation, building a friendly rapport between us. Joanne even began joining me in Sassy's stall to help checker her rump and glue on the mirror jewels.

In this strange new world, Billy and Joanne made me feel welcomed, accepted, and significant. I was careful to make a good impression as the genuine regard apparent in both their demeanors acted as the perfect segue for a shy guy at a new threshold. After the show, they extended an invitation to visit their farm nearby called Chesspiece Morgans so I could see their operation, the other horses in their barn, and camp out for a while.

In the meantime, they went out of their way to include me in their ever-growing circle of acquaintances, and it didn't take long for us to become friends. The topic we all loved, horses, sparked many stories from all around as we each sat on trunks, bales of hay, chairs, or leaned against a stall door. I learned much about this facet of horsemanship simply by listening, but they were curious about my passion too and encouraged me to share my own anecdotes.

In the midst of all this conviviality, I continued to refrain from the ongoing offers to have a beer or glass of champagne to maintain my sober promise to myself for the duration of this show. In lieu of drink, I thoroughly enjoyed the food and the lively rapport as the nuances of our training experiences or the personality quirks of our equine companions inspired further stories. The flowing conversation heightened the feeling of being accepted and part of this genre.

It certainly didn't hurt matters when a nice redhead friend of Billy and Joanne became a regular part of these daily get-togethers. She piqued my interest, so I created a welcomed excursion for just the two of us, walking through the many thoroughfares of stalls and acknowledging the many parties underway throughout the facility. We paused at each stall to inspect the magnificent horseflesh within. Together, we enjoyed the wonder of the moment, the magnificence all around, and especially the sparkle in each other's eyes. I embraced her presence each day as I prepared for my act. Her interest in watching me perform while I found my place in this fascinating industry opened up an avenue of hope in my heart.

Eye-Opening

With my first performance concluded, I was eager to get my hands on the footage. My new friend and I made our way to the commercial booths in the foyer section of the building adjacent to the main seating area. There we found booths filled with horse-related products and information about all kinds of equine services, including brand-new tack and saddles, tailored wardrobes, boots, hats, custom barn-builder displays, breeding lineage information services, plaque makers, portrait painters, equine books and magazines, truck and trailer brokers, wagons and carts, harness and buggy makers, and every horse trinket and clever device to make life easier at the barn from the top of your wheelbarrow to the soles of your feet.

As we threaded our way through these hawkers and merchants galore, we eventually found the video booth of the crew who filmed all the horses and riders. My perfectionistic desire to be the best horseman I could possibly be would be aided with the footage I soon pored over obsessively.

In reviewing the first session, I discovered the bow had occurred in a place hidden by the central latticed obstacle in the middle of the floor. I was able to calculate the angle they shot from and plan accordingly. During the next performance, I made a special effort to play to the camera so as to include all the features of my act. The resulting footage of each of my subsequent performances became a visual record, a valuable training aid, and an all-inclusive memento for this highlight of my life.

I hadn't seen my cousin, Phillis, since we were kids at the annual family Thanksgiving get-together back in Ohio. My cousin and her husband lived in the area and planned to attend one of the shows, reuniting us after umpteen years. I was delighted to see their presence in the seats on the third day. After the show, they invited me to come to their home for dinner.

When I drove over that evening, Fliss had no way of knowing about my personal non-drinking experiment.

After turning down her initial offer of a cold beer, she said, "C'mon, Dave. One won't hurt."

She didn't mean any harm. She was unaware that my drinking was a growing problem. But, with her encouragement, I went ahead and enjoyed a green bottle full of the wondrously soothing liquid. But one always led to another, and back at the coliseum later that night, I found a party still going on and decided to have even more.

When reviewing my performance during the subsequent show, the resulting compromise to my physical and mental prowess was apparent in the video footage. Seemingly caught in a time lapse, I lagged a moment behind Sassy throughout our performance. I had lost my sensitivity and the adept ability developed as the result of relentless practice and sobriety. Taken by surprise by this unpleasant revelation, I watched in horror as I bounced ungracefully in my seat during the canter rears. This was just one consequence of the fog that impaired my brain thanks to alcohol. I began to consider whether I should quit the bottle permanently.

True to form at the horse show, much pomp occurred at the end of the final act. In spite of my sloppy last performance, Sassy and I were awarded a blue championship ribbon and a silver tray for our unique contribution to the show.

My promise to myself to quit drinking was quickly forgotten amid the celebrations. Besides, with the performance contract honored and having received accolades from legions of horse folks, there was no reason to refrain from the consumption of this accepted and widely available beverage. I deserved to celebrate our achievements.

And so, while the mare enjoyed one final night in her stall, I took a sip of another ice-cold bottled brew.

Chapter 10
The Turning Point

"Perfect reason flees all extremity,
and leads one to be wise with sobriety."
—Molière

The Big Change

Before I headed back to Michigan, I enjoyed an excursion to the farm of Joanne and Billy as a welcomed respite from the recent rigors of show business. I found the long driveway to their abundant horse farm known as Chesspiece Morgans, and they welcomed Sassy into their barn. We had another opportunity to enjoy a quiet afternoon among friends.

While watching the training processes going on with their young horses, Joanne begged me to ride their stallion, Piper. She knew he had talent and recognized the opportunity to test her theory with a rider of my background and training. Once he was saddled up with her Aussie saddle, I began our session with a relaxed walk around the arena to get acquainted with my new friend.

"Hey," I called out, wiggling lightly in the saddle. "I like the way this saddle puts my legs in the right place!"

"Yeah, Aussie saddles are wonderful!" Joanne shouted.

Once warmed up, I found Piper's demeanor to be quite responsive. We began with some trot work along the rail with several simple circles. I bent him first into the travers, and then into the renvers, receiving admirable responses to this lateral work. When I collected him, he gave me a nice elevated and slow two-beat gait.

"All right, big guy. Give me everything you've got," I said, patting Piper's neck.

I asked him to extend and he became so light it was as if we were flying around the arena. The canter work was pure pleasure and Piper was an absolute gentleman as he contained all his energy within and paid close attention to my cues. As a mentor would later teach me, the most powerful horse was not the one who was wildly bucking about, but the one who practiced self-restraint despite his magnitude. I had plenty to admire about this polite stallion who had a good work ethic.

Later that evening, Joanne and Billy quizzed me on my training specialty as we sat at the dinner table. The hospitality of my new friends was a wonderful way to break up my journey back to Michigan. As far-fetched as it seemed at that time, their quaint operation planted a seed for my future and a model to hope for.

"I'm sober now," Mary said over the phone.

Her unexpected call surprised me. Even more shocking was her news. We hadn't spoken since that embarrassing incident years prior. When we had been together, we suspected that our drinking interfered with our ability to get along, but even when we tried to quit together, it hadn't lasted long.

"I stopped drinking for a few weeks before the big show I

just did in Dallas," I revealed, trying to relate.

"That's great, Dave! Are you sober too?"

Mary seemed truly thrilled to hear this, so I was embarrassed to reveal my slip-up at the end.

"No. I had a few drinks before the final show," I admitted. "The footage of our performances showed a big difference, but after the last show, I didn't think there was any harm in having a few more beers with my friends to celebrate."

Even as I spoke the truth, I was developing a desire for life without alcohol. Unfortunately, I wasn't sure how to go about committing to it. Maybe Mary had the answer.

"You should go to an Alcoholics Anonymous meeting," Mary encouraged. "It's really been helping me gain clarity."

Our phone call left me in good spirits. It was great to hear from Mary again and to be on good terms once more. Even if we weren't fit as romantic partners, I would forever have a place in my heart for Mary.

I contemplated Mary's words during my trek back to Michigan. Once settled, I found out where the AA meetings were held. I drove to a rundown house on the edge of town and found the yard filled with cars and an unassuming cross section of society standing around smoking. I sliced through them and headed toward the door, feeling like a little kid who was scared on his first day of class.

Through the doorway, I found a room full of chairs and people sitting around long tables, chatting and laughing while they drank coffee and smoked cigarettes. Choosing a chair near the back, I hoped I would be safe there.

At the top of the hour, the spokesman quieted everyone down, introduced himself as an alcoholic and began with the criteria of the meeting. Several readings followed, containing information about alcoholism that became a blur. My mind spun from information overload, and then the meeting opened up for everyone to contribute.

I listened to stories about how alcohol had kicked their butts, cost jail time, ruined their marriages, wrecked their cars, lost their jobs, and contributed to poor health. Feeling a bit like I didn't belong, I could barely relate to any of it. After all, I'd never been hospitalized, jailed, or even received a DWI. I was here purely because I thought I drank too much.

Yet, these people who had experienced far worse than I had something that I didn't have—the power to quit drinking. As they talked about being sober, I figured there must be some trick I was missing. I kept listening to the opinions shared as they went around the room, some of which encouraged asking for help. Red flag! I had decided as a child that I was better off figuring out how to do everything myself. I discounted the idea of asking for help immediately.

Another topic encouraged finding and relying on a power greater than yourself alongside the program's suggested steps. Double red flag! The repeated references to God caused the hair on the back of my neck to cringe. I didn't want anything to do with God. In church, they used mysterious words such as exalt, repent, and transgressions. These words didn't come with an explanation that made any sense to me. I didn't want to be called a sinner, and the judging from those church-going people didn't work for me. I had been clever enough to come up with my own analogy, and mine had me at the center of the universe. I liked it that way.

In similar fashion, I decided I would pick and choose the tidbits that worked for me from this meeting. After it concluded, I reviewed the list hanging on the wall. I could have come up with a better list than that. All I needed was the gimmick to quit drinking. As soon as I got that, I would wash my hands of this place and be on my way. After all, I had plans. I was too busy to repeatedly sit around these meetings full of useless information.

At an opportune location west of town near the airport sat a business called Jackson Glass. The large blank wall that faced the traffic headed their way was ripe for a mural and a sign. While conferring with my client, we decided that an image of a happy workman handling a windshield in front of a car along with the name Jackson Glass emblazoned across the building would be a great way to take advantage of that space.

Thanks to my apprenticeship back in the seventies, I knew how to brush paint onto a rough block surface. The stiff bristle fitches in my kit were perfect for this job. While I prepared my scale drawing for the customer, the words I'd heard in the AA meeting swirled around in my head. It made me mad to hear what distinguished an alcoholic or that I could have gotten this condition hereditarily from my ancestors. That made me feel like I had no control over it. It also made me mad to find out that I could have gotten what they called an allergy to alcohol from my environment in show biz.

Mentioned at the meeting was the suggestion to try some controlled drinking to determine whether you were an alcoholic or not.

"Go somewhere and have just one," they'd said.

In the interest of research, I decided to give it a try. I'd always bought beer a case at a time. While preparing for my experiment, I discovered that buying a single beer cost eighty-five cents. Holy moly! That was way too much and didn't seem very economical when I could buy twelve for three dollars, so that was what I did. Just because I bought a whole pack didn't mean I couldn't still try the experiment.

I sat down and had one. That went well. I felt relaxed and

content, certain I could stop after the single beer. But when it was empty, I discovered the other eleven bottles were screaming at me through the refrigerator door.

"Drink me! Drink me! Drink me!"

I stood and opened the fridge. So much for that test.

Years ago, Hayes's son-in-law at the time bought the bar on the same downtown block as Kelly Imports. Bill welcomed me and my skills as a sign painter whenever I was in town, believing that having a resident artist to create signs for special events like Saint Patrick's Day or a party would be an intriguing commodity. For now, he had me paint the illuminated sign face for the front with the name Office Bar surrounded by a border of what was supposed to look like the nostalgic brass rails you put your feet on.

With bottomless beer and a kitchen that served hot meals daily in lieu of payment, I spent plenty of time in that place even after my work for the day was completed. I was quickly finding out that this exchange also had its disadvantages. When I had completed a sizable amount of work, the only way I could get paid was to remain there, seated in his bar.

I was never a bar drinker; I found it boring. There was nothing to do but lift the glass or your cigarette up to your mouth, sip, smoke, repeat. Although I got a taste of the fun side when the place would fill up with exuberant people who included me in their antics, I didn't sit still very well. For the most part, I wasn't inclined to mix with others and would much prefer my own company in the privacy of my van or trailer.

I also couldn't help but think about the many other things I could be doing, creating a trapped feeling. Watching a single-file line of bubbles coming up from the inside of my glass only served to mix toxically with the echoes from the AA meetings, fortifying this so-called activity as a waste of time.

Between learning episodes, I returned to those smoky AA gatherings, always sitting in the back and just listening. One thing I heard while sitting there was that some people could not stop. I did not understand the concept of powerlessness and addiction. These new ideas infected my thinking during the day while I continued to paint for my customers around Jackson. Out of curiosity, I began to monitor my consumption.

In those days, it was normal to bring beer to work with you. As an apprentice sign painter, I had found an acceptable way to settle my nerves with beer, and my pattern had become to drink the same amount every day while I worked. Now while doing so, I reflected on what I heard at the meetings about gradually losing the ability to stop.

These days, I tended to reach for a beer without much thought and oblivion occasionally took over. With cobwebs in my head the next day, I would return to the meeting to hear some more in an attempt to gain clarity. I spent several months doing this cyclic behavior of getting nowhere, running like a mouse on a wheel, as I alternated sipping on a beer and wondering why I was doing it.

Something grew inside, but not before I found resentment, anger, and frustration for what I'd discovered about the disease. I became especially infuriated at the concept of personal powerlessness. I had always been proud of the fact that I could accomplish anything I put my mind to, believing I had the Midas touch.

Yet the AA members kept talking about how I had to admit complete defeat in order to begin the process that resulted in sobriety. It would require that I admit my inability to stop drinking and the unmanageability of my life. What? That can't be right!

Four months passed with me in denial of the problem. I

would go drink for a while and then return to attending meetings. My world was spinning. Eventually, I had to admit I was getting frustrated with my inability to leave the stuff alone for any length of time.

Before heading to see my folks in northwest Arkansas, I had a stop to make along the way. John Wallen had invited me to visit him in Missouri when I had run into him at the horse auction. I still hoped to obtain a new horse as a valid strategy for my performing career. Maybe he'd know of one. I loaded Sassy and headed out of the Great White North.

After the long drive, I got my mare bedded down in a comfortable stall at John's barn outside of Springfield. My dog, Nick, knew to stay by her in the barn, so John and I headed out to a few places to talk to girls and drink beer. While we chatted, I shared my ambition of finding another dancing horse. John was also considering the purchase of new horse, though he wanted an all-around lesson horse that he would have the option of selling.

With a similar mission and John's knowledge of where the horses were, we headed in a different direction each day. We saddled up many of the animals we found for sale by day, and by night we found another beer joint to pass the time.

Although we inspected and rode much horseflesh, nothing seemed to fit the bill. However, I did see a horse trailer for sale at one barn that was much nicer than the one I had. I asked the owner about it and learned the trailer held too many memories of the grand times he and his wife had enjoyed together as he now grieved her loss.

"I'm sorry to hear that," I said, despite the fact that I couldn't relate to such a relationship.

I inspected the trailer closer. It was an eight-foot-wide three-horse slant-load gooseneck with living quarters in the front that represented a big improvement over the narrow two-horse version I had currently. This unit was priced right, but I didn't have it in my budget.

"I'd love to have this trailer," I told him. "I'll be in touch if I can come up with the money."

One evening at another bar, John was engaged in a conversation with a love interest, leaving me alone and lost in my thoughts of grandeur. There wasn't much to do but drink while I waited for the evening to be through, just killing time.

On the ride back to John's stable, he told me, "You don't drink like most people."

His words were simple, yet heavy. John's observation echoed in my mind and mixed with what I had heard at the meetings back in Michigan. Leaving a tremendous impact on my soul, he unknowingly pushed me another step toward seeking sobriety.

The Obsession Is Lifted

My parents waved as I pulled up their driveway. After parking the rig in the grass, I followed my usual routine of caring for my livestock first. I put up an awning and prepared Sassy's bedding underneath. She would graze in the pasture by day and be crosstied under the awning at night. When that was done, my parents and I enjoyed a meal and the fellowship in Shiloh.

They wanted to get caught up on all that had been happening in my interesting career. When I told them about the horse trailer I'd found, they were eager to help.

"Call that man up and tell him you're coming back to buy it," my dad insisted while my mom nodded approvingly.

I was in awe of their willingness to support me. That purchase would boost my quest to perform as a horseman and provide a rolling home while working as an itinerate sign painter. I contacted the owner right away, beyond excited when we came to an agreement.

"I'll be there tomorrow to pay for it," I said.

"See you then," the man acknowledged.

Dad went with me the next day to see my purchase, agreeing it would make a nice upgrade. But because my truck had a generator and an air compressor mounted behind the cab, it would have to be modified before I could haul the trailer away. My host generously offered to drop it off at a welding shop where they would stretch the hitch, welding new steel to place it out in front.

When that was finished, I returned to hook it onto my truck. Standing back to admire my new acquisition, I thought it sure looked handsome. I drove the trailer to my parents' place and parked it next to my old one. I now had a new project—modifying this unit to suit my unique purposes.

I was familiar with the daily routine at the Shiloh commune from my multitude of previous visits. As always, I accompanied Dad for the early morning spirituality lessons. After a hearty breakfast, we returned to his homesite where I began the tasks of converting the new trailer while Dad continued finishing his home.

I soaked the floorboards with wood preservative. Then I covered them with marine plywood. That would ensure a long life in spite of the rigors of tolerating manure and urine. Next, I rearranged the horse compartment from the existing three-horse slant-load to two side-by-side stalls. I built removeable dividers that attached between the floor and ceiling and installed two hip-height boards laterally on the inside walls to keep the horses erect and comfortable. While I only had one horse at the moment, I planned to get another someday.

Once I found my second dancing horse, this setup would place the horses in the middle of the spaciousness and allow me to enter the trailer with access to both of them and the ability to attend to every need while the horses remained loaded. I could hang a hay bag in front of each horse, throw a blanket over them when needed, groom and inspect them, and even have a specific place behind them for the manure to accumulate. In the meantime, I had the ability to remove the dividers and give Sassy the whole space.

Pleased with these upgrades, I moved my attention to the living quarters. There was never enough closet space for the costumes used for performing. In addition to making closets, I built cabinets along either side of the bedroom, moved a bulkhead in the saddle closet, and created storage for the props used on the road. These modifications transformed this trailer into an efficient and portable self-contained horse care and dressing facility.

My dad was glad I was home again. He had the framing of the house completed and needed an extra hand with some of the innovative features planned. Having been disappointed with the original contractor, he'd opted to take over the task himself with the help of two carpenters. Although the pace of construction was slower, Dad was better able to control the installation of his innovative ideas for energy efficiency, including super insulation, solar baseboard heating, extended eaves, and triple-pane windows.

While completely immersed in all these activities, I had a sudden thought that had never before popped up in my mind. Hey, I don't have to drink. Just like that, on an otherwise uneventful day, the compulsion to drink was lifted from me with no effort on my part. I had been struggling for months to find the gimmick to stop drinking, frustrated in my inability to stop. But on this day, I simply received.

As I look back and wonder how this release and freedom occurred, I can only fathom this occurrence in one way. My sobriety was a gift, and I had to give all the credit to God. Although I'd pushed Him away up until that point, God had truly come through for me in that transition of my life.

All of this was new territory. I'd better proceed with caution.

In the Fog

The experience of early sobriety seemed to be disorientation as my brain cleared. While I learned skills in the past, my synapses had grown in a plasma of alcohol. I tried to use my brain the same way I was used to, but now in sobriety it was different. Everything was different. My progress felt painfully slow as I remembered hearing the AA slogan from the meetings: Time takes time. Patience takes patience. You can't think your way into a new way of living…you have to live your way into a new way of thinking.

Those same brain synapses formed in alcohol had to regrow as my body went through the motions in this new state. On one level, I was grateful for the change. But on another, I felt as if I was stuck in frustratingly slow motion. My mindset made this new experience wrong. I focused on how foggy my brain was and that my thinking was slower. As I went through familiar routines, I believed myself to be inefficient.

The time spent fashioning the cabinets inside the new trailer took far too long. I attempted to communicate this blend of slow-motion confusion to my dad, but he was focused in the midst of his own industry and had no experience with my condition or the withdrawal from alcohol. Unable to relate, he did not know what was going on inside my mind while these noticeable changes were taking place. In an effort to be helpful, he encouraged, reassured, and commended me for the great job I was doing, but I didn't find that helpful. Though I was thankful for his attempts to uplift me, I was overwhelmingly confused and alone. I took baby steps. I kept up what seemed to me as a snail's pace. In this new lost feeling, everything seemingly came to a stop. I was cautious about moving forward an inch at a time.

At the local meetings, I met men who reached out and wanted to coach me, but I just wanted my old-fashioned comfort of staying home and sticking to myself. I was grateful for the distraction and safe haven of my parents' home, the nutrition each morning, and for keeping busy. I would push ahead on my own, just like I was accustomed to doing with everything else.

When Christmas was over, the rig was also completed. My dad encouraged me to move along. Leaving was not something I wanted to do yet. I was reluctant, preferring to stay here with Nick and Sassy where it was safe. In my cautious state with this newfound sobriety, I really wanted to stay a while longer, but I was getting a different message from my dad. In response to his strong urging, I hesitantly began my trip to Florida.

In hindsight, a lengthy fallow time to allow the fog to clear and attend meetings would have been paramount in my journey. I did not realize it at the time, but the mental processes taking place while finding balance with my fresh sobriety had run amok amid old beliefs adopted as a child that interfered with this new paradigm. My strong independent and self-reliant nature found the AA-suggested procedure for recovery to be flawed and I resisted the principles being taught.

Creating a self-inflicted separation from the sober members who could have helped me, I compared myself to them instead of attempting to relate. The thought remained that I wasn't that bad while listening to the others testify about what they'd lost to alcohol. I was not drinking, but I was still lost in a self-induced quandary. While completely unaware, I had become stark-raving sober.

I have no idea why I gravitated toward Mel when I landed in Florida. I had met him several years ago at the Michigan carnival headquarters for Red and Glenn's show. When he arrived in his homemade motorhome, the men of the show flocked around him. Red had been instrumental with the concept of trailer-mounted rides and Mel had a huge fabricating facility in York, Pennsylvania. Mel tackled Red's innovative projects with gusto.

I was encouraged by Red to meet this man considered a legend in the carnival culture, knowing he would also be interested in some of my creative artwork. Unfortunately arrogant, self-righteous, and feisty, Mel considered only his ideas to be correct and was quick with hasty judgments. He wandered over to look at my two-horse trailer I'd used back then, disgust already written on face.

"Stupid," he snarled. "Such a waste of space."

He referred to how the horse industry engineered the best way to provide a safe area for a horse to ride in a trailer. Instead of the trailer body taking every bit of allowable width, my trailer had floor space only between the tires. Wrapped up in his own familiar thoughts, Mel was oblivious to the fact that this standard was perfect for this particular type of cargo. Hurt by his cursory declaration, I would soon learn that this contempt for anything outside of himself was part of his peculiar persona.

Even so, Red was right about him wanting artwork. Mel built his motorhome out of an old milk truck van by splitting it and adding metal down the middle to make it extra wide. Admittedly a clever machinist, he had taken three rear ends to make one that was wide enough for his needs. The interior had railroad car features including a hinged sink that went up against the wall, ornate cabinets, bunk beds, and lighting.

Mel wanted Native American motifs painted on the sides. This transaction gave me an idea. It could prove mutually beneficial if I could only overlook his negativity. He wanted artwork and I wanted a custom rack over the cab of my one-ton truck, on which I would carry ladders. In lieu of payment, Mel said he could build that for me. We engineered a swap.

When I visited his shop in Pennsylvania later that summer, I saw many innovative trailer-mounted rides underway, all made with Red's guidance. I began painting the requested motifs on his camper while he measured, cut, welded, and bent metal into a custom ladder rack. The whole experience was confusing at best, but at least I came away from our exchange with a nice overhead rack that I would use for years to come.

Now in my confused state, I gravitated toward Mel yet again despite his awful attitude. I was not happy with the rear of my new horse trailer. Without a ramp, if I parked in an unlevel location Sassy would have to step up really high to get in. I wanted a fold-down ramp to assist her.

Being around Mel's turbulent personality was perhaps not appropriate for me in my fragile condition. From my last encounter with him, I knew Mel was difficult to deal with—driven by cunning contempt, his agitated state prevented him from being a good listener or having regard for others' ideas. Yet, I also knew he was a capable machinist if I could just get him to hear my idea.

I attempted to communicate what I knew would work for my specific purposes, but unknown issues continued to drive his demeanor. Mel waved his hand in the air to dismiss me, his nose wrinkled.

"No, that's a dumb idea. I will make it better."

In my brain fog, something had taken my voice. I was unable respond to his aggressive behavior. As he began building his own concept of what I needed, creating two metal pans on hinges that utilized slick galvanized metal, I already knew this would be inappropriate for a horse ramp. Between the slippery composition and simply being too small, I knew I should voice my concerns, but, intimidated by Mel's manner, I was unable to do so.

Powerless to insist on what I wanted that I knew would work, I felt as if I were in The Twilight Zone; this episode would have been called "A Town With No Syllables." The scattered mental syndrome that accompanied my newfound sobriety was a normal condition that would eventually pass, but in that moment I hadn't yet learned to use the AA fellowship as a safe place to sound off with the vagaries of life and get helpful advice. Displeased, I simply withdrew, resigning myself to the wasted effort and resources as I remained unable to find my voice while Mel progressed with his useless vision.

As expected, the exchange concluded with an unsatisfactory product. I left Mel's shop with my impractical contraption and headed south to a farm belonging to some friends. When the reality of this wasted effort sank in, I became pissed. In a fit of blinding white-hot anger, I cursed as I dismantled the useless pieces Mel had made. Discarding them in a dumpster, I dusted myself off and resisted the urge to reach for a beer.

A Love Story

"You just gotta come check out these mules," Gee Gee insisted over the phone.

Gee Gee had a colorful history that started with the Cole Bros. Circus in the forties, where she rode a Roman team of sixteen horses in spec. She'd long ago adopted the gruff demeanor that brought about success in this tough industry. Gee Gee had recently retired her husky dog act that caused a sensation everywhere she performed while dressed in a revealing furry Eskimo outfit and making an entrance on a dog sled pulled by a team of huskies.

A savvy operator, she still had three elephants that toured the show circuit with her handler while she stayed home and ran the office. From her desk surrounded by eight-by-ten black-and-white photographs of circus performers, Gee Gee coordinated acts with engagements and served as an agent from the comfort of a solitary and steadfast location lacking in the rigors of travel.

Currently, Gee Gee was inviting me to come to her elephant farm to see a couple of mules she'd provided a temporary home to for her friend. Although I enjoyed visiting my friend, I was apprehensive of her offer that clearly came with a catch. I was looking for another Saddlebred, not a mule. I had no idea what she thought I could possibly do with such an animal.

"Dammit, Dave!" she shouted over the phone when I hesitated. "You just got to come see them."

At her continued insistence, I agreed to drive over to her farm and take a peek, though I had no intention of going home with a mule. To solidify my point, I decided to drive my VW bus over and leave the horse trailer behind.

My lack of horse trailer upon arrival didn't phase Gee Gee as she launched into her introduction to the mules.

"Jody was making a black-and-white tuxedo act with these two mules," she confided as I leaned on the fence and looked at them indifferently.

The white one was pink-skinned with a juggy looking head that did not impress me one bit.

"But one night when Bucky was drunk"—she paused to snicker—"Jody'd had enough of his shit. She beat him up, then she had to move out."

Just then, the baby jet-black mule began an animated trot, catching my eye while she bounced joyously around the pasture. I perked up at the sight of her pretty face. Despite my obstinance, I had to admit it was love at first sight. As I studied this black mule, I came up with justification for having her around—it was taking longer than expected to find another Saddlebred and that mule would make a wonderful companion for Sassy in the meantime. Besides, what's one more mouth to feed?

Noticing my sudden interest, Gee Gee continued, "I got Jody a job handling elephants at the Miami Zoo, but she can't have any animals of her own. That's why she has to sell these two." She paused, taking note of the particular mule I was eyeing. "Plus, she is going to need a car…"

Her voice drifted off as though hinting at something.

"Huh?"

Gee Gee pointed at my bus. "Do you have an extra one of those?"

I smiled as understanding dawned on me. Since I now had the orange bus, I could spare the red one for Jody. With Gee Gee's help, we engineered a deal and Betty the jet-black mule soon became part of my family. I told her I'd return with the trailer to pick her up as soon as I could.

Change of Direction

The engine in my truck had been getting tired. Before I could pick up my new mule, I would need to give it a rebuild.

While wintering at the Morris family winter quarters, Bobby hoisted the engine out and dismantled it for me. He put new bearings and rings into the engine block, and before reassembly he had the valves ground to allow for a tight seal.

When the engine was almost finished, Bobby had an errand to run—he needed sawdust to bed down the cages of his bears. Since I had only one horse with me, Sassy got the entire width of the back of the new trailer, approximately an eight-by-twelve stall. She enjoyed the room all to herself and I thought sawdust would be a luxurious addition. I joined Bobby on his trip to the cabinet shop.

While we shoveled the dusty stuff into leaf sacks, he became satisfied with the coup. Once the bears were bedded down and Sassy was enjoying her newly enhanced digs, we resumed the engine rebuild. The engine project progressed nicely, but with rain on the way and no available pasture, the Morris family didn't have the ability for me to stay at their farm for the entire winter. Once the engine was completed, I would have to go.

I didn't have a good place secured for the winter, so I moved temporarily to Billy's trailer park nearby to wait out the wet weather. With no yard for the horse, this place was not ideal either, but I didn't have many other options. The parking location was on terrain that left the rear of the trailer elevated. While in this situation and still without a ramp, unloading would have been difficult due to the acute angle. Satisfied with the comfort I had created inside with the sawdust, I opted to

leave Sassy loaded while I continued my search for a better parking place.

I was due to pick up the mule soon anyway, so I thought to contact Gee Gee. She had room for the rig, plus a stall and pasture for the horse. She warmly invited my company and I made plans to move out there immediately.

I was eager to let Sassy out where she'd have more space to roam. While backing the mare out of the trailer, I was horrified by what I saw. Sassy walked gingerly, obviously in pain. She positioned her front feet way out in front of her to take the weight off them. Gee Gee called the vet who arrived in a hurry. Unfortunately, he didn't know what he was looking at, what could have caused that condition, or what could be done to provide immediate relief.

With unenthusiastic resignation, he shrugged and said, "Let's give it a few days and see what happens."

Not knowing any better, I proceeded to care for Sassy as best I could in her new stall. Without any experience or knowledge with this mysterious condition, I was left at a disadvantage that would rapidly lead to larger problems.

Even through delicate and constant care, Sassy did not improve. Gradually, I came to learn about a disorder called founder where the tissue inside the hoof wall becomes inflamed due to a variety of reasons. The most common cause was from overeating highly nutritious food. Even though the ailment seemed to match Sassy's symptoms, this notorious cause didn't seem to fit, and I remained at loss as to the reason my horse was foundering.

In an effort to get off her painful feet, she began to lie down a lot. Wrenched with an emotional pain of my own, I took every effort to provide comfort to this wonderful mare who represented an important part of my future ambitions. I refused to embrace the truth, beginning the relentless pursuit of finding anything I could do to eliminate this condition and restore Sassy to health.

A follow-up conference with the first veterinarian further established him as incompetent. Another doctor informed me an immediate introduction of an antihistamine could have reversed the inflammation, but only during the introductory stages. That brief window had long since slipped by.

As I learned more from this vet, I discovered the wood shavings traditionally used for horse bedding included pine or other softwood due to the fact that several hardwoods were poisonous. I now knew the cause for her founder—the sawdust Bobby and I had retrieved contained certain hardwoods that had promoted a fever in Sassy's feet. Stuck in the trailer before we were able to come to Gee Gee's farm, Sassy couldn't escape it as the temperature in her feet went up and the laminae in her hoofs became inflamed.

The resulting inflammation in her feet caused the tissue contained in the hoof to expand. Since the hoof wall acted as a container for this tissue, it could only expand downward like toothpaste coming out of a tube, making contact with the ground incredibly painful. This was why Sassy rocked back on her heels in an effort to get off the uncomfortable tender sole. At this stage in the illness, her prognosis wasn't good.

When the vet left, I was once again alone with my horse. I knelt down in the sawdust of Sassy's stall and gently stroked her neck. Her kind eyes yearned to understand what was going on.

"Everything is going to be okay," I whispered.

Though I tried to be brave for Sassy, I was afraid. She had filled the void in my heart scoured by the frustrations of my childhood. I found approval from all walks of life with my horse by my side. As Sassy transformed from a fiery rogue into my gentle traveling companion willing to go anywhere I asked of her, she had transformed me, too. From timid and insecure, I had grown into a confident new man.

I basked in her beauty, responding to her gentle nudges by stroking her neck. Sassy reached with her nose to breathe on my face, filling me with appreciation for this magnificent mare. She had been in my life as a conduit for growth. While learning the nuances of communication through my seat and hands, that same sensitivity showed up in my creative efforts with paint. Small considerations resulted in breakthroughs that grew into dedication for even the slightest details that became an everyday part of my creative life.

As I reminisced on our time together, sadness mixed with appreciation for how far we had both come. I gently caressed her neck, tears filling my eyes and blurring my vision. Letting go of my emotions, I felt myself revert into the sobbing, blubbering, fearful boy of my past. I was afraid of what was next. Would Sassy be okay? Would I ever be able to ride her again? Would I be forced to put her down? Where would that leave me without my beloved horse?

A militant part of me took over in that moment, refusing to entertain this grief. I wiped my tears away and swore an oath. In spite of what was going on I would grapple with the idea that there had to be something I could do to heal this horse. I would apply myself to this just like I had with anything else important in the past. After all, I had succeeded with accomplishing the impossible before. I would do it again.

I found new motivation in spending time with Sassy, tending to her every need. Her condition was grave, but that didn't stop me from bedding her every day in an attempt to make her as comfortable as possible. I also provided her with a regimen of pain relief via supplements. As Sassy's condition worsened, I merely increased the level of her care.

Time seemed to slow down. In the first few months of my sobriety, I was oblivious to the truth. This life was a dichotomy—neither good nor bad, but rather a blend of good and bad. I wasn't ready to say goodbye. Instead, I focused on keeping Sassy comfortable and training my new mule.

A Light in the Darkness

Thank goodness I was blessed with another to love. In the midst of devastation, Betty the mule found her way into my life and proved to be a great distraction from seeing the pain in Sassy's eyes. Gee Gee had a ring set up for practice along one side of the drive. During idle time at the farm, I began training Betty to work at liberty like my palomino ponies—the style of responding to my positions and gestures in the round pen while free of restraints.

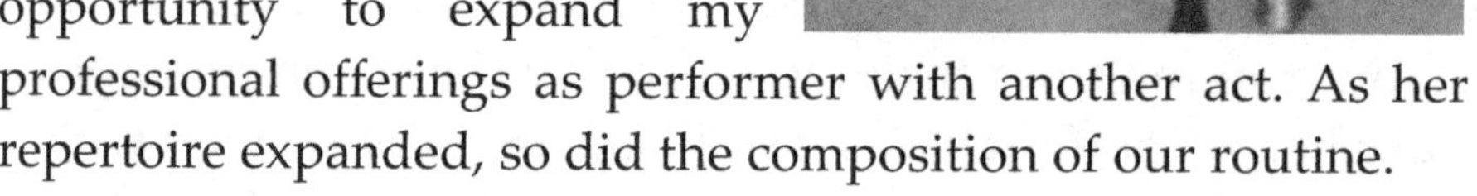

I started by teaching Betty to bow, immediately taking notice of her bright willingness to learn and the deep understanding in her eyes. Oh, you want this? Betty seemed to say as she folded one foreleg back. When I patted her on the neck, she absolutely melted under my affection. Oh, I get a pat on the neck? she asked with her loving gaze.

Betty represented an opportunity to expand my professional offerings as performer with another act. As her repertoire expanded, so did the composition of our routine.

My love affair with Betty the mule had officially begun. Over the years, I would discover that this ever-willing animal would allow me to train her to do more than any of my horses ever did.

My days were filled with horse care and sign work for carnival folks in the area with various results—some wholesome, some not. Distracted by the dilemma with Sassy and my unfamiliar sobriety, my head still seemed to be filled with cobwebs. But with Betty, I had hope for a brighter future.

In the midst of all this confusion, I became a regular at the local AA club. I was still driven by intense independence. Although hungry for relief, an internal rigid streak mixed with a demand resistance that continued to prevent me from fully entering the method for recovery. The process described in the curriculum was achieved by following simple instructions, but like the shiny metal ball in a pinball machine, my direction was

erratic, aimless, and driven by self-delusion, misguided intentions, and scattered fears.

What I didn't realize was that rock bottom was just around the corner.

With the winter season over, the time came to travel to Wichita to paint for Butch Webb and his large concession operation. I loaded up the livestock and headed west. The trek had to be an excruciating experience for my mare who did not have the ability to lie down during the entire trip. Sadly, I didn't have a choice; I had to bring her with me in order to continue her special care.

Nick perked up in the seat beside me as we arrived at the tree-lined farm situated in the midst of vast flatland where I always boarded my horse. I fixed Sassy a stall with extra-deep sand and fluffy shavings. It was fun being reunited with my horsemen friends

I had known from years of coming to this place. I hoped that they could help or offer advice for Sassy's healing journey, but I was disheartened to learn that not one of them was familiar with founder. As a group, we only had experience with using our horses in health.

I supposed that was a good thing, but it meant I was alone in my battle. My friends watched as I provided Sassy with as much comfort as I could. Instead of practicing my dancing horse routine like I would normally be doing during this time, I was monitoring Sassy's sore feet, giving her supplements for nutrition and pain, and nurturing her each day.

While painting for Butch, I had the urge to confide that I was newly sober.

"I have to hand it to you," he responded, "I have respect for someone who realizes they have a problem and does something about it."

The thought popped up that I needed to acknowledge the problem with my horse in this same manner. Several people had attempted to reach me with the truth in regard to the gravity of Sassy's situation. The irreversible condition in her feet had progressed into the chronic phase by this point. There was no reversing it. Still, I just wasn't ready to consider what they were suggesting.

Blinded by self-delusion, I continually wanted to try just one more thing. I refused to believe that Sassy's dancing career was over or that our companionship was coming to an end. I continued to seek information from every source I could. I talked to veterinarian schools about their willingness to use her as a case study to facilitate a breakthrough discovery. I was hoping for a miracle cure.

After multiple conversations, I was slowly educated to the reality of this plight. But instead of embracing the truth, I continued stubbornly searching for a cure. In the midst of all this misery, I received a single thread of hope. A farrier college in Oklahoma City made the claim of being able to reverse the effects of laminitis. I gave them a call.

"Yes, we have experienced remarkable success with reversing the effects of founder," the spokesperson announced over the phone. "Bring her in and we'll take a look."

I clung to that tiny thread of hope for dear life, but before I could head to Oklahoma City I had to finish my obligations here.

At the shop, Butch used the usual pressure to get sign work tasks done on his fleet prior to the beginning of his season. My work ethic had changed now that attending meetings and caring for Sassy had become my priorities. I no longer worked late whenever he asked and this promoted a resentment in my host, even though he assured me that he understood. My focus elsewhere interfered with his ambitions, though I did manage to get his fleet on its way on time.

A Miracle Cure

At last, the time had come that I could take Sassy to Oklahoma City and try the corrective shoeing procedure they claimed could heal her. When I arrived, I found a large metal building with a simple sign bolted to the side that read "Farrier College." The campus consisted of two long barns and was surrounded by pickups and horse trailers. The rhythmic, piercing sound of hammer against steel greeted me as I went through the rear roll-up door. Inside the dark building, a dozen students were learning how to make shoes with a forge and anvil.

I asked around and found the man who'd made the claim over the phone that they could help. He had me bring Sassy inside where he inspected her, lifting one foot and holding it between his knees. While looking at her feet, he gathered the class around to see her condition firsthand.

Directing everyone's attention to her foot between his legs, he announced, "See the coffin bone protruding through the sole? This is a highly advanced state of laminitis."

The students leaned in for a closer look and asked their questions. As I listened, it became evident that I could no longer deny the truth—Sassy's condition was grave.

"She can stay in there," he said, pointing toward the row of stalls. "We'll see what we can do, but I've got to be honest, Dave. It doesn't look very promising."

All my expectant hopes were dashed to the ground as I walked her over to one of the empty stalls. They were crude and musty, with old oat hay for bedding. It was below her usual standards, but I was out of options. I had nowhere else to go and no other methods to try. This was my last chance to save Sassy.

When I returned in the morning, I was saddened to see Sassy had developed open bed sores from lying on such coarse bedding. As I worried about her new wounds, I received the inevitable prognosis of what I had been in denial of in the form of a demand. "

Her condition is too advanced," the man who'd welcomed us here practically shouted at me. "There's nothing we can do.

You'll have to put her down!"

Having my hopes peak during the trip only to shatter upon arrival had me believing the day prior that things couldn't possibly get any worse, but I'd been wrong—this was a new low. The mandate from this less-than-sensitive service provider left me in tears as he walked away. Though he was ready to wash his hands of the matter, my entire world had just been rocked to the core.

I stepped outside to call Evy, hoping for some understanding and guidance. I was ashamed to report to her what had happened to the magnificent horse she'd helped me acquire and train. I feared Evy would blame me for my ignorance and was certain she would be disappointed. Instead, she was a source of comfort and helpful advice. When I'd said all there was to say, she took a deep breath before offering her thoughts.

"David, I know you love her," Evy said, "but it's time to end her suffering."

I sobbed while I gave my consent to the vet, but I couldn't bear to witness the euthanizing and discarding of my beloved once-proud dancing horse. Filled with fear, I left that place on a dreary day in a blowing rain, my vision blurred by tears.

As I returned to the shop in Wichita, I sank into the most emotionally devastating depression of my life. With just my dog and Betty by my side, Sassy's absence left a gaping hole in my heart. I felt alone and completely depleted. Sassy had been my companion and partner, something I had felt was missing from my childhood. She kept me motivated to make it through another day, always seeking to improve and grow. She even showed me the depth of my alcoholism and helped me determine to rise above it. Sassy had given me a whole new perspective on life.

In her honor, instead of reaching for the bottle in the depths of my despair, I sought relief at the AA fellowship. I listened to the usual angst about withdrawal and reports of progress, mixed with confusion and dilemmas. When it became my turn to talk, I shared the tragic loss of my mare, and, perhaps for the first time, I really opened up and attempted to describe the depth of sorrow I was feeling. My crude testimony deteriorated into sobbing. Even though none in attendance could relate to my equine partnership, the entire fellowship rose to wrap their arms around me.

With my emotional resources tapped, I returned again to the next meeting. When it became my turn to speak, this scenario repeated. At the third meeting, I began to look at my fellows with relatedness and found comfort in encouraging others in their own plights. The following days gradually turned into weeks, and about all I could bring myself to do was go to these meetings.

I slowly learned about my condition of untreated alcoholism and how delusional thinking was compounded by my grief for Sassy's loss and withdrawal from something else. Though I did not understand it at the time, I had developed a codependency on my mare who provided me with an image of myself that I approved of. I used her as an antidote for my damaged self-esteem while being a handsome prince on a stunning horse. Without Sassy, I was left with a brokenhearted void in my soul and the lingering question of whether I would ever be worthy again.

Days later, I woke to discover Nick lying paralyzed, quivering, and struggling to breathe. I laid him in the back of the van and raced to see the vet only to be turned away. They were too busy. The only option I had was to put him down myself.

I returned to Maize and went over to the welding shop to ask the two Harder brothers to help me with this task. They had a gun, but also had some strain with the sheriff. They couldn't consider shooting inside the city limits. Instead, they loaned me their .22 rifle.

While tears flowed freely, I carried Nick's convulsing body to the grass north of the shop. Through my obscured vision, I had to feel my way to lay the end of the barrel on his forehead. One loud crack, and he lay at peace. I dug a hole and placed my friend at the bottom.

"You were a good boy, Nick," I whispered while replacing the dirt.

Then I paused to say a prayer. Betty was now all I had left.

From the Depths

I was stranded and broke. The time away from the pursuit of my livelihood to care for Sassy had depleted my cash reserves. This combined with having no current direction for my life. Without a plan, I quickly sank into the deepest emotional devastation I'd ever experienced. At least I was attending meetings. Most of the time, I even went to two a day. In this phase of my sobriety, I finally met the admission requirements—I'd hit bottom. From the depths of that lowly place, I began to hear the message coming from others who had found a new life of happiness, purpose, and productivity. They described experiencing a shift in perception and how they began to see things through fresh eyes that had been opened for the first time.

Sobriety was about more than simply not drinking. Although I hadn't had a drink in six months, I also hadn't truly joined the fellowship until now. I'd been hovering near the outskirts. My real recovery started when I finally took my hat in my hand, reached out to another man, and said, "I need help."

I began to concentrate on going to meetings and asking for help. I even participated as a meeting leader so I could suggest topics I was curious about for discussion. One guy in the group made sense every time he spoke. Dwight was a gaunt man about my age. I had heard his story about getting shot up in Vietnam and how he had been knocked around in life as a drunk and a drug addict ever since he returned.

When the meeting was over, I asked Dwight to be my sponsor.

"Are you an alcoholic?" he asked.

"Yes," I replied.

"Do you want to get well?"

"Yes."

"I would be happy to be your sponsor." He smiled. "Now, let the real work begin."

Dwight and I connected between meetings and talked on a regular basis. He pointed out the first word of the first step was "we." We are in this together. We will get better together. Alone and away from the herd, we remain vulnerable. When I joined the rest of the group, I entered into the solution. We must admit we are powerless.

He explained what was in the big book, the AA manual for recovery. One page at a time, he walked me through those simple words and discussed how they applied to my situation, how they had value in that particular sequence, and what exactly they meant. He clarified that the problem was that I was self-centered, and the solution was for me to enter into relationships with others, especially with a power greater than myself.

From that humble beginning, I sought a practical way to

find, enter, keep, and expand my relationships with others. By becoming willing, open-minded, and honest with the fellowship, they helped me uncover what had previously kept me separated from them. After uncovering the cause of my isolation, I could discard the condition and find hope for a new direction for my life.

"In Vietnam, I adopted ways of coping in an effort to survive," Dwight confided. "There were gooks out there who wanted to kill me, and drugs and alcohol were available to calm the jitters. But when I got shot up pretty good and returned stateside, instead of appreciation for what I went through, I received scorn from the country I had fought with my life to protect. It didn't make any sense. I didn't know what to do, so I just continued to seek oblivion."

Dwight revealed similar beliefs and behaviors that had kept him stuck in the past and how his repeated hospitalizations had kept one foot in the drugs. Like me, he had to lose everything in order to hit bottom. But from that bottom, he found others who introduced him to hope. He told me what he found as the result of working the steps and that he had to carry the message forward as part of his ongoing treatment.

As Dwight poured out his tale of alcoholism and recovery with AA, it hit me that Dwight was introducing me to myself. I began to understand the value of feeling connected and understood. My dad had been unable to grasp it due to his lack of personal connection to the illness, but in the fellowship my plight was deeply and empathetically understood. I had a whole new outlook and a guide to help me move forward—someone who had been in this exact same place.

One, two, three...Dwight guided me through the first of the twelve steps, each one providing a little more relief. So far, I had admitted I was powerless over alcohol, began believing in a power greater than myself who could restore my sanity, and made the decision to turn my will and life over to God. I was now ready for the next step in the process.

Step four suggested an inventory of my behaviors, resentments, and moral conduct—my greatest handicaps. I was entirely willing to begin, or so I thought. When I sat in front of an empty notebook with the intention of starting my list, I simply stared at the page, unable to think of one thing to put down. I gave up and went to bed.

At the meeting the following day, I shared the story of what happened, or rather what hadn't happened. Using humor to deflect, I made light of my frustrations.

"I guess since I couldn't think of anything, I must not be such a bad guy after all."

To my delight, everyone laughed. But after the meeting, my sponsor brought me back down to earth.

"Dave, why are you here?"

"Oh, yeah," I sheepishly responded.

Dwight suggested that we take a step back and ask God for the willingness and clarity to uncover whatever it was that interfered with my ability to begin step four. Together, we knelt and repeated the third-step prayer.

"God, I offer myself to Thee—to build with me and to do with me as Thou wilt. Relieve me of the bondage of self, that I may better do Thy will. Take away my difficulties, that victory over them may bear witness to those I would help of Thy power, Thy love, and Thy way of life. May I do Thy will always!"

With the fresh reminder of the prayer, Dwight offered further assistance.

"Keep it simple," he offered. "Start an easy list: Mom, Dad, sister, brother, girlfriend, boss. Just put down the names first, and then wait for clarity in regard to the offending incident."

With his help, I moved forward and became willing as I made my list later that evening.

The biggest offender was my brother-in-law. I poured out a rage while immersed in the memories of incidents that had caused so much frustration, embarrassment, and anger. Dad was on my list too. Though we'd since created a new bond, his unfair judgments in childhood, perfectionistic demands, and impossible expectations had taken their toll, adding to the emotional turbulence that required something anesthetic to soothe. I was finding my rhythm and my list started coming together.

While we pored over what I had written, Dwight made me understand that the source of my troubles was not something anyone else had done to me, but rather something I had done to myself. I didn't know what he was talking about. He explained that my perception of the behavior of others influenced what I believed and drove the decisions I made as a child. It would take some time before I fully understood this.

"A thousand forms of fear have driven your behavior," Dwight explained.

He continued to uncover this potpourri of kaka, pointing out how it affected my relations with others. Those dynamics affected my security and esteem, combining with the biggest culprit of all—my pride. Having the written evidence staring me in the face, I could only admit that every bit was, in fact, my fault, as step five suggested. Every morsel of pain, fear, anger, and suffering had been self-inflicted.

As I steeped in this putrid realization, my sponsor continued to radiate nothing but an abiding love toward me. This complete deflation became the perfect segue for him to explain how these decisions, behaviors, and beliefs contributed to the obsession I had developed with myself, promoting grandiose desires, perfectionism, warped perceptions and, in an effort to survive, withdrawal from others.

I began to understand how fear, shame, regret, and resentment drove my perceptions and behaviors. Fortunately, Dwight introduced me to an upgrade - spiritually driven responses that would also promote a healed perception of my surroundings, a greater truth. Through this recovery process, I found a design for living that started with a shift in perception called the turnaround. The turnaround was like taking off my tainted glasses and seeing all of my surroundings as beautiful for the very first time.

Dwight relished this dramatic shift in me, explaining that I will need to do this same healing work with others.

"You must remain diligent," Dwight stressed. "God needs you to cooperate."

Like the phoenix, we have been empowered through the gift of devastation to heal others afflicted with our obsession. As I considered this purpose for my life, I began more and more to feel the presence of a loving and all-knowing higher power. I let go of my attachments to what had kept me separated all these years and I began to feel a strange yet comforting presence. I admitted my faults, embraced my humanity, entered into humility, and allowed connectedness to take place with my flawed fellows, and for the first time in my life I truly felt the presence of God.

By working through the steps and listening to others at the meetings, I became related, connected, and part of the group. The concepts that had once kept me separate from those around me now became our very reason for connection. Having recovered from these things, I could now share my experience with others.

From this low point in my life, I found perhaps the greatest gift of all - freedom. Freedom from a prison of my own making. Freedom from self-inflicted wounds. Freedom from myself.

For the rest of the summer, I attended three meetings a day, fully immersed in the recovery process. I gradually healed, and when the time was right I received inspiration for a logical destination to begin the next chapter of my life.

Exodus

Butch Webb loved things. While stranded in Kansas due to my lack of funds after Sassy's elaborate care, Butch provided me with several restoration projects to work on at the shop, some for his personal collection at his home. One endeavor was a prototype coin-operated roulette wheel that he acquired from a curiosities dealer. Although this prototype had never made it into production, he wanted it to look as if it had by giving it a handsome paint job, elaborate gold-leaf lettering, and extensive scrollwork designs.

Also among the jobs to complete were several antique wooden merry-go-round horses. These hand-carved relics had actually seen service on carnivals during an era long ago. Part of the challenge of this sort of work was the removal of multiple layers of paint, repairing the broken corners on ears, and making new legs. With his well-equipped shop and plenty of time during the summer months, I began the slow process of restoration.

Butch noticed a change in me. Although he had previously

told me he respected a man who realized he had a problem, he secretly held resentment toward the new sober me. He used to be able to get me obsessed with working day and night, but now recovery came first. In sobriety, I prioritized my recovery by attending meetings and working through the twelve steps, but this meant that Butch's projects didn't get finished as quickly as they had during my drinking days—a detail which he did not appreciate.

My mind was really starting to clear by the time Butch's fleet returned to the shop between the tour through western Canada and heading to Texas. Through the fog, an idea for my future began to materialize. At age thirty-four, I had the idea that perhaps I should get a degree, and through some research I discovered Southern Illinois University had the best graphic arts program in the country.

While perusing a sign trade magazine called Signs of the Times, I found a sign shop in southern Illinois advertising for a sign painter. I couldn't stay in Kansas forever, and Butch wasn't happy with me anyway. As I made my plans to head out, he employed the shifty manner for which he was famous, engineering a plan to shortchange me for the restoration work I had completed over the summer.

One day without a word, he stealthily left on a plane for Vegas. I went to his secretary for my pay and she only gave me a fraction of what I had coming. It wasn't her fault; she was simply doing what she'd been told. This was when I realized what Butch had done.

Drawing on my past experience with holding some of my work ransom until I received what was due, I took one of the wooden merry-go-round horses and transported it to a safe location in Wichita before attending an AA meeting. When he found out I'd hidden one of the horses, Butch called his foreman and instructed him to park trucks around my rig and box me in.

He did as told, but, fortunately for me, this foreman had plans for the weekend and didn't want to play babysitter. After encircling my rig with trucks, he left the shop confident that his efforts to thwart my travel plans were effective, but he was wrong.

With the foreman out of the way, I had time to figure out a solution. I had developed a friendship with the Harder brothers who owned the nearby welding shop. Over the weekend, they helped me drop a drive shaft out of one tractor and pull a truck out of the way so I could leave. With my rig freed up, I thanked my true friends and left town with Betty and the ransomed merry-go-round horse.

The long flat trip across Kansas gradually yielded to rolling hills as I passed into Missouri. When I entered the rugged coal country of Southern Illinois to assume my new role at the sign shop, I was just in time for the first semester of school. My plan was to take full advantage of everything in Carbondale.

I checked in at the sign company and found he had room for my rig near the shop. He also knew someone who had pasture for Betty. I settled into a new routine of accomplishing sign work each day at the shop.

During the first lull on a quiet afternoon, I headed over to the campus to get acquainted with the dean at the university. While he looked at a portfolio of my work, I revealed my ambition to him.

"I've been thinking I should earn a graphic arts degree," I said.

He looked up from the work, paused for a moment to collect his thoughts, and said, "I have students with a degree in airbrushing who can't do this stuff." He motioned to my portfolio. "You don't need a degree. Just keep doing what you are doing."

With the dean's words echoing in my mind, I wasn't sure whether to feel frustrated or honored by his admiration of my work. After all, this degree was the whole reason I had come here.

Exploring what else was available on campus, I signed up for an English grammar class. My teacher scrutinized each paper for proper capitalization, punctuation, and sentence structure, and I eagerly drank up every piece of knowledge he bestowed upon me.

"You seem to be the only one in here who's interested in what I am teaching," he told me one day.

I was flattered. I guess in my state of recovery, my mind was more open to learning than most.

Searching for other opportunities in the area, I became familiar with the nearby riding farm. Even without a horse, I was eager to develop my skills and stay in shape riding horses. I began taking riding lessons that provided access to a number of the school horses.

During my time at the barn, I reviewed the dream I had not so long ago about getting another dancing horse. I considered the ideal criteria to train a horse into a circus performer. He'd have to be young, but not too young—a five-year old would be ideal. A horse who never had any training meant there weren't any bad habits to overcome. He'd also need to be tall, hot-blooded, kind, and flashy—all good traits for showmanship.

The focus of this particular barn was dressage. Their string of horses needed to be bombproof and easygoing for the novice students. Always interested in learning something new and seeing how I could apply it to my personal goals, I became familiar with the procedure for dressage riding and practiced for upcoming tests. A formal horse show was scheduled for a few weeks out. I joined the rest of the students in getting ready.

When the time to prove ourselves finally arrived, we would ride proper tests in front of a judge and an audience. Like most specialties, the student would ride through a series of maneuvers and transitions to earn acclaim as the aspects of each level were completed in succession according to strict guidelines. This situation was not unlike performing, as the seasoned school animals already knew the routine.

But not knowing that the school horse I rode was crowd-wise to this situation, I soon found out Cramer knew he could cheat when an audience was present. Just like on a circus, when the animal knew the audience was gone, they knew they'd better act right. But the opposite was also true. Cramer knew that he could get away with ignoring commands and cutting corners without being reprimanded in front of the judge.

Some of the students who knew this horse and that I was new to this type of performance had been anticipating an entertaining scene. They would be disappointed; I didn't let my horses get away with misbehavior.

When my turn came to ride my test pattern, I sat straight and proper and waited for the call. After riding into the center of the arena, I acknowledged the judge with a tip of my hat. I then began to ride the sequence of that particular test. As I entered into the beginning of a ten-meter circle on one side of the arena, my horse began to veer back to cut off a significant amount of the shape I intended to ride. He'd never done that during our practices. Using my whole leg, I gave him a swift thump to drive him back out onto the path. That got his attention, and he paid better attention to me for the next circle.

"You got a pretty good ride from Cramer today," one of them said as I made my way back to the paddocks.

It had been a nice ride, but participating as a riding student just wasn't the same as riding in a ring in front of a circus audience. My dream remained to obtain another horse to augment my passion for performing. Although I did have Betty, this gap in my career seemed an unsurmountable hurdle that made no sense.

I had no idea how long I would stay in Illinois. Since I wouldn't be pursuing a degree as originally planned, I was up in the air about exactly what to do. I wasn't familiar with the feeling of being somewhat planted in one place and I missed the road.

Even so, being part of a community in Illinois was an integral part of my sobriety. Being planted in one place made me feel a part of the group in Carbondale—connected, inspired, and hopeful. Learning to live one day at a time without any long-range plans was a new concept to me, but this daily reprieve and my newfound responsibilities to myself and others filled me with gratitude. I was learning to trust, use my faith, fill my mind with positivity, and seek to uncover my purpose.

As I generated honorable behavior, I had the feeling of accomplishment. I was learning to trust my higher power and be on the lookout for His purpose for my day. Plus, I had plenty to give at my fellowship. I was listening, sharing, and finding ways to be helpful to others. I had discovered a new sense of motivation and a new direction for my life simply by learning to stay in the moment.

Chapter 11
To Walk with Purpose

*"The road to freedom must be uphill,
even if it is arduous and frustrating."*
—Andrew Goodman

The Sign Shop

Larry was the most unlikely person on the planet to have a sign shop, and yet he was my new boss. Not gifted with any visual prowess, design sense, or artistic ability, Larry made odd choices as he trudged forward—his Midas touch didn't turn anything into gold. When I had worked as a T-shirt artist for Wicked Wanda, I learned the slang for a reject was a Larry; I now fully understood why. It seemed this Larry had achieved a semblance of momentum simply by being a fan of the industry.

An admirer of industry great Mike Jackson from Oklahoma City, Larry hired a young man who had once worked at Mike's shop, assuming he would have access to greatness through him. But the laborer only proved to be a good laborer. Larry did have some employees with artistic sense, but whenever he tried to participate, the project got bogged down. This frustrated the capable among us.

When an airbrush mural opportunity for an interior of a restaurant came along, I thought for sure he'd utilize my proven ability with that specialty. Instead, he brought in a man from a printing company to tackle the project, a decision neither the printing guy nor I understood. Such was life at Larry's sign shop—deflating enthusiasm and promoting apathy.

I decided it was best to simply show up for the paycheck and concentrate my energy on my other ambitions.

"I'm working in Missouri," Evy told me over the phone.

"Where?" I asked, intrigued. That was just the next state over.

"I'm at Dave Hale's exotic animal farm in Cape Girardeau."

"I'll come see you this weekend," I promised.

I didn't have high hopes for the location, given what I'd learned Evy found acceptable in Texas. But with the loss of Sassy, I longed to be in the proximity of someone who would understand.

When I arrived at the farm that weekend, I was pleasantly surprised as she gave me the tour. This amazing place was filled with many species of animals from all over the world. Looking out over the vast pastureland that rolled out from the main complex, a large herd of camels could be seen walking single file, the dominant male trailing behind.

During my visit with this master trainer, I shared that I was still riding despite my setback with the loss of Sassy. Evy was pleased to hear that and encouraged my efforts. While chatting with her, I refreshed my understanding of the criteria to look for in another horse as my soul healed just a little more.

As one month after another went by, I realized this sign painting situation wasn't going to take me anywhere—it was a dead end. Though I remained in the area, I left Larry's shop to resume freelance sign work in the region, renewing my role as a snapper and yielding greater results and happiness. The money made went to further my primary focus—my passion with horses and healing through the recovery process. I would soon discover something even greater was in the works.

Searching for Home

The move to Carbondale occurred at a time when I was ready for change and had developed momentum in my recovery. The devastation, emotional bankruptcy, and finally hitting bottom in Kansas had made me willing to go to any length to seek improvement in all aspects—sobriety, clarity, and success. In Carbondale, I began to attend meetings regularly.

"My name is Joe. I'm an alcoholic."

Normally the group responded by saying, "Hello, Joe." But not Rocky. The guru of the community had a unique deviation.

"How's it going, Joe?" he said, adverse to the rest of the group.

Although small, this deviation from the accepted format promoted resistance in me. Hey, he's doing it wrong! My observation of what I considered a deliberate fault short circuited my flow of gratitude, distracting me from reaping the benefits of the meetings and secretly agitating me in what I perceived to be Rocky's intentional annoyance. My anger blocked my focus on healing.

Although away from the security network I had found with my original group back in Wichita, I realized I had better also get connected here if I hoped to continue on the upward path I had found. I ignored Rocky and focused on the others, mustering up courage to share in the meetings. As a participating member of the group, I revealed my internal thoughts about feeling valued less than others, being bombarded by an inner critic who was never satisfied, and the belief that it was impossible to ever measure up.

I was introduced to the concept of having fear in many forms; fear of what others thought about me, fear of not being good enough, fear of never being understood. I also confided that the swirling cycle of obsessing about these concerns seemed to have no end. Instead, they accumulated, multiplied, and grew ever more putrid.

I even went so far as to share my deepest secret—thoughts that I would be better off dead. This was the first time I had ever admitted this out loud. Although I was safe here, admitting that I had gone so deep in my misery and felt so desperate to find peace, even if it meant death, was terrifying. The outward revelation and emotional validation accompanied by tears produced an even greater bond with my group, including with Rocky.

This intimacy ushered in a new connectedness with the group that I hadn't yet felt here in Carbondale. Plus, I was becoming an example to the newcomer, just like Dwight had urged me to do back in Wichita. Thankfully, purging this toxic secret created a gradual change within.

In another group discussion, I revealed more about my predicament—I had decided as a teenager that my family was the problem, so I rejected my origin. I had chosen to be on the road without roots and attempted to get this abstract idea across to my peers, but this was a foreign concept to these non-showmen.

Although they couldn't fully empathize with my lifestyle, these towners wanted to be helpful. They had ideas logical for those who lived in set communities, but theirs was a vastly different world than the one I had chosen.

"Why don't you just go home?" a female member offered.

Go home? That idea opened up a floodgate of emotions. This suggestion seemed simple to most, but for me, it had struck a nerve. Years of dammed up feelings about the frustration left behind erupted into a tsunami of epic proportions. I started to weep.

As a child, I had perceptions of a cruel world that surrounded me. School and church were full of bullies and I became a target for their taunting. As a preacher's kid, I could never measure up. Attempts to communicate did not make any sense or headway. In order to survive, I found it necessary to withdraw, become self-sufficient, and learn how to figure things out myself. I didn't feel a place of comfort and security like most people felt about their home. Once old enough, I turned my back on my home and family and launched myself out on the road.

Years later, I now enjoyed visiting my parents and the

healing had begun with my dad, but their home could never be my home. Home was meant to be a safe space, and I did not have that.

"I don't have a home," I admitted through tears.

The group was stunned. After a moment, another member gently proceeded.

"If you had a home, where would you want it to be?"

Now, that was something I hadn't thought of before. The invitation to consider this open-ended idea gradually softened the depth of my frustration and started a new cycle of thinking. I had been to hundreds of towns during my wandering career. I began to review what I liked about many of those places and realized that I enjoyed one place more than all the rest—Clarklake, Michigan.

My career as a sign painter started there, for one thing. I had a talented and willing mentor to keep my skills growing. I established friends who lived in Clarklake. And most of all, I felt safe there. This realization gave me hope, an answer for my fellow AA member's question, and a starting place. Maybe I could call Clarklake my new home.

As I thought about a move to Clarklake, outside Jackson, I reminisced about one of my groups of friends, recalling how we would gather every evening after work at the back door of Kelly Imports to imbibe in an amber beverage. As the years went by, one at a time, each of them quit drinking. By the mid-eighties, I was the only one with a beer in my hand. During a lull in our conversation one day, Kelly said something that made no sense to me at the time, but now held great meaning, and maybe even offered a segue for a chance at some much-needed support.

"If a man came to me and asked me for my help," he began while eyeing me, "and he was still drinking, I believe I would tell him to go get off the stuff, and then come ask me for help."

I decided to write Kelly a letter, letting him know I was now a sober member of AA with the ambition of becoming the best sign painter in Jackson, Michigan. I needed a soft place to land, and I hoped he would be willing to provide that for me. I held onto my faith as I awaited his straight-to-the-point response, which did not take long to arrive.

> *Dave,*
> *You are welcome to set up your sign business in the back of my shop. See you soon.*
> *Kelly*

Hope for a brighter future swelled in my chest as I thought about a new beginning. I began mentally making preparations for the upcoming journey. For the first time since turning my back on my home as a teenager, I would have a place to call home.

The Purge

"Are you ready for your fifth step?" one of my fellow AA members asked while greeting me at the door.

The twelve-step process as was outlined in the AA manual promised peace, purpose, and a path for finding a pure connection with others. The fifth step worked toward a better future through the admittance of past wrongs and mistakes. It was the doorway from confusion to freedom. Today's work would utilize the worn spiral-bound notebook I held under my arm.

As part of step four, I had written an inventory of my resentments, fears, and grosser moral defects. With the help of my sponsor, we began to identify how my perception of other people's behavior affected my security, relations, and self-esteem. This work also helped to uncover the biggest obstacles to a peaceful life—pride and fear.

The inventory was the first tangible evidence of willingness to clean up the accumulated self-inflicted vicissitudes that kept me separated from others my entire life. But the fifth step was a scary proposition—I now had to admit those identified defects to God, myself, and another human being. Because the human psyche warped the true perception as a way to protect the fragile ego, an outside perspective was required to properly assess those defects.

This step would also help me develop the voice I had decided was futile as a child. Identifying my behaviors and bringing them out into the light was only the beginning of the cathartic purging process that brought about healing. Despite that, I had fears about being so vulnerable, fears that took root as a child. Revealing the grosser episodes of my past to the wrong person could affect my status and possibly promote rejection, shame, and humiliation—the very things I had spent my whole life avoiding.

But that was also what made this the prime time to do this; I was planning my departure from Carbondale soon. It was fitting to continue to make advances toward a brighter future prior to my fresh start in Clarklake, and then leave any shame behind in Illinois. With all that in mind on this quiet afternoon in Illinois, I answered his question to the affirmative.

"I am ready."

He nodded his approval. "We can talk after the meeting."

"You are not alone," my understanding host pointed out to help me feel safe. "If the deed has a name, it's likely others have done it, too."

With a deep breath, I began to disclose the hatred I had as a child for my brother John who produced the odd behavior that frustrated the whole family. My mentor silently validated each emotive gesture as I elaborated about the cruelty received from the bullies at school and church.

"And all because I was the little brother of a weirdo," I said. "It made me withdraw from boyhood society entirely."

When I was completely spent about that topic, I showed my mentor the next item on my list. I was still angry about the treatment received from Frank, the new carnival owner of the Wade Shows. When he threatened me while I painted the most beautiful Victorian scrollwork of my career, it had stopped me in my tracks and killed all inspiration.

"It just wasn't fair. I wasn't being appreciated for doing the exact thing I was hired to do for that jerk!" I slammed my fist onto my thigh.

I went on to explain how Frank's belligerence made me white hot with rage and how I drank to extinguish the burning emotion. Every time I thought about that episode, I got angry all over again. Even now, I could feel my chest tighten and my face grow red.

Throughout my verbal rampage, my host simply listened while remaining calm, loving, and accepting.

When I eventually paused, he seemed to know I wasn't through. Without any pressure, he offered gentle encouragement.

"Is there anything else?"

I clenched my jaw. There had been an embarrassing event that occurred in my teens. Something that I had vowed to never tell anyone about. I planned to take this terrible occurrence to my grave. I realized in that moment it hadn't made it on my list, and I wasn't sure I was ready to disclose it just yet.

I nodded once. "That's all."

My mentor began sharing some of his own story. He revealed many similar episodes to mine, and I was surprised to discover that what had happened to me was not unique. Seemingly for the first time, I found commonality with another. Through our link as imperfect people, I found the path to healing lay just beyond what had previously only produced agony and separation in my mind.

For the first time in my life, I felt a presence that was much larger than all of what I had been paying attention to in my stuck self-centered condition. I was recognizing this expanding connection as the presence of God, and in releasing those defects I was empowered through grace to embrace my capacity to grow beyond all that had limited me for so long.

With this new sense of empowerment, my time in southern Illinois was over. Just as I would leave this place behind, so would I leave my guilt and anger. The time came to travel to a fresh start in my new home.

A New Beginning

With Betty the mule loaded in the back, I headed to Michigan. Tom let me park my rig behind the Beach Bar where

the campground used to be. Betty would enjoy the summer on pasture nearby. I set up a simple easel in the back of Kelly Imports and got to work, quickly becoming reacquainted with the countryside and the people in this state I loved.

I missed my friend Hayes who had passed away a year earlier, but I regularly stopped in to see Ken, Clarence, and all the other influential men I had met over the years. A little at a time, I found work to do, trucks to letter, signs to design and paint, and storefronts to embellish.

Every day before noon, I walked the two blocks from Kelly Imports to Michigan Avenue. At the side door of the Economy Art Supply store, I went up the long flight of stairs that led to the massive second floor. The upstairs, although divided into many rooms, was primarily empty. The large windows of the front room looked out over the busy main street of Jackson, and it was in here that a small AA meeting took place every day.

Ruth, an elderly Black lady, usually had the tables, coffee, and chairs ready for the handful who gathered here. This was where I met another Larry, one who proved not all men with this name were rejects. As I contributed what I had previously learned to become part of the bunch, the noon meeting gradually became my "home" group. The recovery process resumed around my new friends and quickly gathered momentum.

"What kind of cake do you want?" Ruth asked.

After being in my new home for a few months, my one-year sobriety birthday drew near. Because every passing year was another victory in sobriety, this was a date worthy of celebration among the AA fellowship.

"I want a chocolate cake with chocolate icing," I blurted out. After a brief pause, I added, "With chocolate sprinkles on top."

A few days later on the sixth of June, 1988, we had my sober-birthday party after the noon meeting.

"Congratulations, friend!" Larry said, producing a great big smile. He initially reached out to shake my hand, but instead gave me a warm embrace.

Ruth cut the cake and placed the pieces on paper plates while others also gathered around to hug me. Two guys were in their first thirty days and one girl only had a few days. I guess I was a hero to them. Still others had multiple years of sobriety, and they were my heroes.

As I savored a bite of my chocolate cake, I looked around in a moment of reflection. All these people were here to celebrate my achievement and completely understood what I've been through to get to this place. We had all found the circle of support and connection that helped each of us accomplish what individually we could never do. Like survivors in a lifeboat, we shared a special joviality that day as our sense of community grew along with our acceptance, laughter, and hope. Together, we can do this.

I beamed at the irony of me being part of a group. Staying put for the first time in my life provided the ability to develop connections and the stability needed for the process of recovery to blossom. This consistency brought about real change—something that did not exist in the whirlwind life of a showman.

Through the example and encouragement of others, I learned how to feel and express what I was feeling. I became familiar with the instinctual parts of me that had been denied due to my previous attitudes and habit of consumption. Through my security network, new intimacy came to the surface. While finding alignment with the contemporary way of living, I accumulated a spiritual manner of thinking and became hopeful about the future.

At an AA men's retreat on the Olivet College campus two years later, I listened to one of the guest speakers while he shared his experience, strength, and hope in front of the group assembled in the auditorium. His enlightening talk had me frozen in my seat, fully locked into the details that hit so close to home.

In front of the entire group, he revealed the story of his youthful innocence being taken by force at the hands of an older man. This was something that he had never told anyone prior to his sobriety. He explained how that painful episode set up a fierce resentment within his core, describing the white-hot anger and the obsessive cycle of blaming himself for what happened. I couldn't believe it. This guy was telling my story.

Having yet to break the barrier to this old hidden wound of mine, I steeled myself and took a chance. While the rest of the group began filing out after the meeting, I went up to him to thank him for his message.

"The same thing happened to me," I blurted out before I could change my mind.

He recognized an opening for healing and invited me to sit down.

"You are not alone, but you're going to have to get it all out in order to find healing." He repeated the same things his own sponsor had confirmed years ago. "I'm glad you're coming forward with the truth. Would you like to talk about it?"

This was an incident I had never shared with anyone, even when my mentor in Illinois knew I was holding something back. I had never said it out loud because I feared that would make it real, and I didn't want it to be real. This was something I was so ashamed of, I intended to take it to my grave. And for that reason, this item had not shown up on my inventory list during the fourth step.

But as this man looked at me with deep, kind eyes, I recognized in this moment that I was in the safest space possible to find healing for this old wound. I nodded as tears began to sting my eyes.

"First, let's pray," he suggested. We bowed our heads together. "Thank You, God, for preparing the way for healing and for providing the courage to take this next step. Thank You for using us to be a blessing to each other as we seek an even greater connection with You. Amen."

When I opened my eyes, he said, "Take your time."

I glanced at the ground and took a deep shaky breath, preparing myself for what I was about to reveal.

"Right after graduating from high school," I began, "I helped with marionette puppet shows in the Chicago school system assembly programs. After that, it was time to join the circus in winter quarters in advance of launching the new season." I looked up from the floor to meet my friend's eyes. "My boss, Melvin, dropped me off at the family winter quarters late one night. He told me to go sleep in the vacant bedroom in the house next to the main building. I was tired and didn't have any trouble going to sleep."

My voice drifted off and I felt like my teenage self back in that bedroom once more. I didn't hear myself speak even though I knew I was still talking, sharing my story for the first time, revealing the deepest scar I'd kept hidden from the world for so long.

"In the middle of the night, I halfway noticed someone crawling into bed with me. While dazed and half-asleep, he told me to relax and not to worry."

A lump caught in my throat as I remembered the sudden piercing pain in my backside. "In my compromised state of half slumber, I was barely aware of what had happened in that moment. Finally, after several minutes, he left me alone and went away. I lay there in silence, frozen in a realm of shock, confusion, and deep shame. In the morning as the fog cleared from my mind, I was mad at myself for not putting up any resistance and for falling for such an underhanded trick, but I never spoke a word about it to anyone until now. Even so, that occurrence set up an unending cycle of anger, an inner resentment, and homophobia that started eating away at my stomach lining."

I wept into my hands as my friend comforted me, accepting me regardless of my disclosure and demonstrating unconditional love. After a respectful silence, he had some questions.

"Did you have any power over this other man? Did you influence or promote his actions in any way? At that young age, did you even know about that sort of activity?"

His inquiry promoted a silent wondering that resulted in a new clarity.

"You see?" he confirmed. "You didn't have anything to do with what happened. Perhaps it was some sort of sick initiation trick the circus people devised. Perhaps this one man just victimized innocent youngsters. Whatever it was, you cannot blame yourself for what happened simply because you were in the wrong place at the wrong time."

His words pierced my soul. I didn't realize how desperately I needed to hear them.

"We are not the only ones who suffer from tainted perceptions of the world due to the cruel behavior by others," he added. "Rather than hate yourself for what happened, can you forgive? Can you forgive him, them, and yourself?"

I was stunned at this revelation, this new perspective, this release from the self-guilt and anger that I had been carrying with me for years. Instantly, I was released from the stronghold in my heart. That introduction to myself gave me the courage to accept that part of my experience, dig deeper, and disclose the whole truth for the sake of possibly helping others. I was becoming willing to do anything.

As my heart softened to include others on a similar plight, I also noticed an emerging feeling of the presence of a loving God. I savored this new connection more than ever. I was part of the herd, a man who could lift his head up and walk confidently among men in union with my newly discovered higher power. I could use my talents, the love in my heart, and this discovery to bless my surroundings as they blessed me.

That day forever changed my future.

Unceasing Progression

My journey through AA continued with the healing effects of step six, where I became willing to have all my defects of character removed. Becoming aware of what interfered with my maximum use to others was first. Then, as I entered into alignment with this functional plan for improving my life and having tasted the payoff, the willingness came easily. Experiencing a shift in my relationship with my past was freeing enough, but I was only halfway through the steps. The promises introduced me to the idea of receiving more than just freedom; I had to keep going to see what lay ahead.

After becoming willing, an attitude of humility prepared the way for the release as facilitated by God. Humility is an often-misunderstood word. Many think it's related to humiliation, but it's not. Humility means a modest way of looking at oneself, something missing from the typical egocentric way of considering one's importance. As I moved into freedom from pride and self-importance, I also came into alignment with the truth that there was a better way of living through our higher power.

Step seven meant humbly asking for these defects to be taken away. I had to lay them at God's feet. Then it would be my responsibility to cooperate and not take them back. Humility was the first aspect; the second was realizing that I was nothing by myself, but, through union with God, greater things were possible. By becoming open to the mysteries that lay ahead and the removal of the fear and pride that interfered with God's purpose for me, I was empowered beyond what my finite self was capable of alone.

With my list made in step four, I prepared for the healing that took place as I admitted my role in the wrongs that had taken place with others. No longer being guided by my self-reliant nature, learning instead to rely upon divine guidance meant that I no longer had to plan. I only needed to remain willing. When God saw fit, he would place an opportunity in front of me. It would be my job to accept those opportunities.

Another fierce resentment I held involved a circus man, Johnny, who had rejected me in my greatest time of need. I chewed on that resentment for years. But as Dwight had pointed out, it was my behavior that placed me in that position in the first place. The bitterness for Johnny's behavior showed up in my fourth step and logically meant that at some time in the future the time would come for me to make amends as part of the ninth step process.

Wouldn't you know it? The circus was coming to Jackson. Of course, I had to go see the show and that very afternoon I came face to face with Johnny, the subject of my resentment. I knew what I had to do. Bracing myself, I approached him.

"Hey, Johnny," I said, humbling myself.

He looked at me guardedly.

"I am now a sober member of AA," I began. "Years ago,

when I wrecked my truck, I was mad at you for running me off the show. But I see now that I was wrong for the resentment I held toward you. I would like to do whatever I can to make it right."

"Wow," he responded, relaxing his tensed muscles. "I, too, have sobered up, Dave. Now that I am off the sauce, I realize there were many things I did that I am not proud of." He shook his head in disbelief at our chance encounter bringing about this mutual healing opportunity. "Thank you for reaching out with your willingness. You are an inspiration to me to do a better job, and I truly wish you all the best."

That experience taught me two things. First, that I could not trust the memory of the episode stored away in my mind as being the one sole truth. And second, the outcome of making amends would not always resemble what I predicted. I had no business running my life except to use my energy to remain open and willing to the path God laid out before me.

Step ten suggested that I continue to take a personal inventory. This was different from the deep dive of the fourth step in that we were on the lookout for subtle hints of regression into our old ways of thinking and acting, something that we must remain vigilant about for the rest of our lives.

I learned to pause at the end of each day to review all that took place. This kept integrity and the pursuit of doing my very best uppermost. Now I would make amends whenever necessary. My newfound humility made a nice segue for maintaining contact with my higher power—something which I knew little about, but would soon be enlightened.

"Oh, Dave, that's wonderful!" Mary exclaimed, delighted to

hear about my sobriety and the progress I was making.

Extending gratitude to those responsible for playing such a big part in encouraging me to seek sobriety was also apropos at this stage of my recovery. Mary had been a big part of my journey as we drank together, explored a fleeting attempt at sobriety, and fell victim to it once more. In her own sobriety, she was the one who'd made that final push for me to seek the help of AA. If it hadn't been for her, I might never have reached the place I was in now.

As I shared the impact of the huge moments of self-discovery and growth, Mary appreciated my willingness to acknowledge my part in our relational turbulence, leading to the healing of our joint past. I will forever cherish our healing conversation that day and the promise we made to remain friends and a support system for each other no matter what.

Chapter 12

Finding My Rhythm

*"In an age of acceleration,
nothing can be more exhilarating than going slow."*
—Pico Iyer

Evanescent Love

Two months into my role as sign man in Jackson, I received a welcome surprise—the indoor Nordmark Brothers Circus was coming to perform a couple shows in the theater downtown, just two blocks from Kelly Imports. On the morning of their arrival, I went to see who was in the show, pleasantly surprised to find my friend, Joanne Wilson, with her baby elephant. Our conversation picked up right where we'd left off the last time I'd seen her.

For the first time since the compulsion to drink had been lifted, I had an audience with someone wise to the ways of the road. From this relatedness, affection grew.

While in my presence, Joanne thought maybe I'd be able to help with her issue with the cube van the elephant rode in, especially since I now called this area my home.

"Hey, Dave," she asked, "do you know a mechanic? I think I have a drive shaft issue."

"Let me make a few phone calls," I offered.

I contacted Kelly to see if he could help out, and soon we had Joanne's elephant truck in one of his service bays.

Working underneath her truck was a humorous challenge for the mechanic. Because the baby elephant kept swaying inside, the truck rocked back and forth while he worked. The situation intensified when the little elephant had to relieve herself. The mechanic maneuvered underneath to find the right place to avoid the deluge as the underside of the truck dripped the rest of the time it was in the shop. We were the only ones laughing.

Inspired with the unique situation of having an elephant at the garage, I recognized the opportunity for an attention-grabbing photograph. When Joanne's truck was fixed, I told her my idea and she was immediately on board. She unloaded the elephant while I assembled the crew for a photograph. I included the Snap-on diagnostic machine for a nice effect and even had Rick climb up on top of the elephant. With the guys surrounding Joanne and the elephant, I captured evidence of the most unique job that shop had ever experienced, framing an enlargement of it with the Kelly Imports logo across the top and the slogan "We work on most imports" across the bottom.

It was almost showtime back at the theater. While I interacted with my friend, I discovered she was no longer married. My overactive imagination really started to percolate. Seeing Joanne's radiant smile and being reunited with the reality of her charm and ability as an all-around circus girl, an internal desire that had lain dormant for all these years was sparked once more.

The thought of love had occurred to me many times while in the circus, but due to the life of going up and down the road, love always eluded me. This part of normal life was made difficult by the touring lifestyle of the circus. But with Joanne, my instinctual desire combined with relating in our common circus background caused me to entertain a romantic notion.

When the circus was over in Jackson, Joanne and I hugged farewell. After she went to the next town, I decided to test the waters by arranging to have a bouquet of roses delivered backstage at her next show. She called to thank me afterward, seemingly appreciative and flattered.

"It was fun witnessing the roses arousing envy and curiosity from the rest of the troupe!" she said, laughing.

As her joviality bubbled back down, we had a hard talk.

"Look, Dave," she began, "I like you, but I don't know if this is going to work."

She didn't need to say any more; I already understood. Romance was difficult as a circus performer. Now it was especially difficult. I was planted in a town while my romantic interest was still a touring circus star. I was grateful for reuniting with my special friend, but a real chance at romance wasn't in the cards for us. I would see Joanne occasionally over the years, but for now, all we could do was stay in touch, dream about tomorrow, and attend to our different lives.

Letterfly Sign Works

It has been said that a business with no sign is a sign of no business. Among the painting projects that kept me busy around town was one I entered with gusto—a shop sign for myself. My intention was to showcase all my talents into one special piece - a four-by-six panel with a depiction of a marble frame, dimensional scrollwork with a theatrical curtain background, and a centrally featured image of a merry-go-round horse. This accumulation of all my recently learned painting specialties was accompanied by both prism-edged and incised letters that stated the name Letterfly Signworks.

Each day, I was pumped to add the next step to this complicated design. Once the depiction of marble satisfied my critical eye, I had to wait until it was dry. Good thing, because there were paying projects waiting to be worked on. The next day, I transferred my scroll pattern and begin to make the effects that would resemble a fanciful shape playfully interacting with the rest of the motif. I exaggerated the perspective of my horse to make it look as if it were jumping out of the scene, creating an interactive vibe that truly caught the eye.

With the last of the glimmering effects on each of the many components, I could finally stand back and admire the finished piece proudly mounted to the face of the Kelly Imports building.

My new sign did its job, catching the attention of Herman Gumpertz, the local fair manager. The next thing I knew, I was on the fairgrounds freshening up all the pavilion signs as I helped him get ready for the fair. I included my merry-go-round horse, acquired from Butch Webb's lack of payment, in the homespun display section of one of the exhibit buildings.

Herman also thought having a large spectacular painting underway during the fair would add to the attractions for the patrons to enjoy. We put our heads together and designed something big to go on the end of the grandstand. And I mean big—this design would extend fifty feet up. Every day of the fair, I ascended scaffolding and began my task of painting the large depiction that stated "Jackson County Fair" completely surrounded by flowers. The weather proved cooperative for such a task, although the temperature reached into the nineties. I was in the direct sun all day with the exception of when I walked downtown to the noon meeting.

"You look tired," Larry observed at one such meeting three days into the project. "Are you taking care of yourself while you take care of everyone's requests?"

Huh… I had never directed the focus of my attention on myself. My mind was always consumed with the project at hand—percolating ideas, composition planning, layout delineating, and painting. Larry was a good friend, introducing me to the idea of paying attention to my body and taking notice of what it was telling me. As I zeroed in on this new responsibility of self-care, I became proactive with my health, monitored my body and mental condition, and provided myself with rest and nutrition as needed.

Gail

My painting mentor, Ken, enjoyed my ambitions in town and invited me to attend a civic group luncheon at the nearby Elks Club. He had the idea that I would make a good companion for his stepdaughter Jana's sister. Gail was recently single, and Ken made sure she would be attending the luncheon, too.

On that special day, I found my way into a large group of people, sitting across from a beautiful tall, dark-haired and somewhat reserved lady. I recognized her physical similarities to her sister. Gail's lovely almond-shaped face was framed with long straight hair that cascaded past her shoulders. She radiated an ambiance that aroused my curiosity.

As she warmed up to my presence, Gail began to reveal a pseudo=exotic air of mystique. Through our conversation, I discovered she enjoyed many creative connections with the community, including civic theater. She was currently directing a play with rehearsals occurring on most evenings.

As I accumulated more information about this wonderful creative soul, I began to appreciate Ken's plan for me to meet her. When lunch wound down, I asked if I could call on her at the store where she worked. She perked up, seeming to glow.

"Yes," she said, smiling. "I would like that."

Soon after, I met Gail downtown and she introduced me to her world. Just three blocks from where I worked, the company she worked for was not unlike an entire city—the department store was a whole entity unto itself. Inside Jacobson's, a whole culture existed with makeup experts, fashionistas, clerks, art directors, marketing experts, and the support staff who augmented the large company infrastructure.

The complicated layering of egos and personal agendas in the chain of command provided me a glimpse into corporate insanity. I was grateful to be on the outside looking in; at least none of it impacted me. On the other hand, Gail enjoyed the hierarchy protocol and interesting social blend.

Gail's job at Jacobson's was to decorate each display window with an apropos setting, chic accompaniments, and the latest fashions. She showed me one window in particular. Her latest arrangement of the new fall fashions included a faux brick wall with a chalk graffiti heart that included our initials, GJ+DK. My heart skipped a beat.

I began to meet Gail for breakfast at Jacobson's regularly after that, and we also attended church together every Sunday morning. The Unity Church met in the Women's Club building, the one-time home of an affluent family. The large house was still filled with fine furniture, paintings, and interesting appointments as an ode to its former inhabitants.

The small group that met there each Sunday enjoyed a spiritual analogy that was a perfect fit for my budding spirituality. With a foundation in the gospel, the Unity Church also addressed contemporary concepts in a practical and positive way. Because of my exposure to a variety of spiritual concepts at Shiloh, I had questions that the AA community did not have answers for. I could discover them here.

As Gail's and my relationship continued to unfold through our conjoined activities, I learned more about her involvement with the theater and her collection of vintage clothing utilized during her dramatic contributions. One evening, I attended a play she directed called Pizza Man. While I watched the production, and even afterward while mixing with the actors and crew, I became aware how Gail's talents, observations, insights, and encouragements were easily transferred to others in her presence. This reflected her regard for lifting others to greatness, and I found myself wanting to be around her more and more.

When autumn approached, I began to think about my living arrangements. Staying in the horse trailer would not be adequate during the cold Michigan winter. While contemplating this dilemma, a solution presented itself.

"Will you please housesit this weekend while I am out of town?" Gail asked.

Her house, a tall brick home with four apartments, sat on Washington Avenue in nearby Jackson. With no pets or plants needing attention in her absence, I didn't understand why anyone was needed in her home during the weekend away, but I agreed anyway. Besides, it would be nice to be in an actual home setting while I figured out my living situation for the rest of the winter.

When Gail returned, I was there waiting for her. We seamlessly entered into coupledom, and true love took off like a rocket. I was grateful when Gail invited me to move in not long after. Though it was an odd feeling to have a home—I had not lived in a house since I'd hit the road as a teen—this would solve the problem of my living situation.

As I moved my meager belongings into Gail's tidy home, she explained the wall color remained from when her grandmother lived there. She had another color in mind. Together, we tackled the job of repainting the interior walls with the soothing parsley color Gail selected. Before I knew it, I was participating in all sorts of homeownership tasks such as leaf raking, snow shoveling, interior repairs, and, of course, painting.

Her home also had a dug-in basement with a small garage on the face and a large terrace with front steps that led up to the front door. Gail encouraged me to utilize the basement for my projects. I was thrilled. With a boiler that heated the home, the basement stayed warm even in the winter months and was the perfect place to make sawdust and apply paint. Sign carving, other building projects, and paintwork were soon all handled in that space while our relationship thrived.

But with my eye always on the future, I began to think about the upcoming summer. Inspired by my past opportunities at the fairgrounds, I rekindled the idea of resuming my T-shirt enterprise and started to build the components of a new and improved T-shirt painting booth, a project Gail was mystified with.

Having met me after I'd planted some roots, she couldn't figure out why I still felt the need to travel. In her mind, I was home and I had plenty of work here without needing to travel. She didn't see that as a necessary part of my life anymore. Although I enjoyed sharing her space and having a real relationship and a home, I couldn't deny that the road still called to me. I figured I could find a balance between having a home base with some adventures mixed in. Gail tried her best to support me.

As our lives merged, we revealed more and more of ourselves to each other. I soon caught a glimpse as to why my desire to travel was a concept that created such anxiety for Gail.

"In grade school," Gail began during one of our conversations, "my teacher announced to the entire class that she'd read in the newspaper that my parents were getting a divorce."

I could see tears spring to her eyes.

"I was shocked," she continued. "Nobody had told me."

My heart beat wildly, anger rising within me on her behalf. How could her parents not confide something this important to their own kids? How could her teacher reveal such sensitive information in front her friends and classmates?

It was no wonder this incident had such a significant impact on her life and relationships. This discovery in front of her peers had a shaming and shattering consequence that set up an inability to trust others, especially men. The divorce drove a wedge between Gail and her biological father.

I was also bringing my own childhood traumas into our relationship, including the instinctive survival reaction of withdrawing whenever I sensed danger. Between my tendency toward withdrawal and her abandonment issues, we had a lot to overcome if we wanted to make this relationship work. But Gail was worth it—I had finally found true love.

Blossoming in Jackson

Elaborate sign jobs that utilized the skills developed around the carnival began to materialize all over Jackson, cementing my new home as lucrative. I had plenty of trucks to letter, business signs to make, and creative logos to design.

In those days, a four-color logo design required four individual pieces of artwork to enter the printing process, and these overlays had to be generated by hand by an artist. While making these overlays, I had to visualize how the finished art would look.

When completed, each overlay was photographed to make a photo mechanical transfer, known as a PMT, for each color plate. With careful registration, the four-color printing process began. When the finished product rolled off the presses at ABC

Reproductions, I finally got to see how my concept looked in full color.

Tom Collins was just one person who kept me busy. He was always expanding and making his business better. His latest idea was to connect the Beach Bar building with the building acquired next door to utilize as an office. Between them, he created a banquet room with a railroad train that ran on shelving around the room and behind the fireplace. He commissioned my artistic skills to give the wall surfaces behind the train track specific airbrushed scenes from local history inspired by old photos of Clarklake. This was a logical endeavor since Tom had spearheaded the local Historical Society.

As usual, this project and the contacts made while underway led to many other opportunities. In another bar downtown called the Bear's Den, I painted a comical scene with cartoon bears on an interior wall. I also helped with theatrical scenery for Gail's ambitions, and through her retail contacts at Jacobson's I was invited to create a stunning design on an old storefront downtown that was being renovated into a high-end dress shop.

For this project, my idea was to have each large window across the front of the store receive a large oval surrounded by elaborate Victorian scrollwork. This allowed the featured merchandise on display to appear to be in a picture frame of sorts. When completed, I submitted a photo of the storefront to the Signs of the Times design competition and received an award for my efforts as well as free advertising.

Soaring to New Heights

Painters Supply was a regular hangout, not only for me but for anyone who painted for a living. Situated behind the fairgrounds, this store had everything a painter could possibly need. I could get thinner really cheap. Around back were the headquarters for their commercial paint contracting company, a place to park their trucks and equipment. To complete the community feel, this whole operation was run by a family, and I soon felt a part of it.

"Hey, Dave," I heard one afternoon while looking at brushes. "Let me get my brother up here. We have a project for you."

The brothers had just finished recoating the exterior of several mega fuel tanks at a fuel depot outside of town and the job wasn't finished yet. Apparently, my timing for new supplies was perfect. Dan burst through the back and onto the retail sales floor.

Zeroing in on me, he said, "We need a Citgo logo painted on the outside of a huge fuel tank. We're talking fifty feet up. Is that something you could do?"

"You know I could," I responded, while wondering what it was I was getting myself into this time.

"We left the swing stage hanging on the job," he added. "You can use it."

I had only tackled a job this big once before at the Jackson County Fair, but I had everything the task needed at my fingertips. I'd never used a swing stage before, so Dan gave me a quick lesson.

"The swing stage has a motorized winch on either end," he explained. "The sensible thing to do would be to hire an assistant to man the other end."

Easy enough. I would recruit a man from my fellowship. The next morning, my hired help and I headed north of town where a dozen huge tanks sat next to the fuel depot. Once granted access to the compound, we made our way toward the giant tank that would receive my artistic contribution.

Dan was there already, suited up in a white canvas outfit with a breathing helmet similar to what sponge divers use. He was preparing to go inside one of the other tanks that had been emptied. He would enter through an access door near the bottom to inspect the inside, but before he departed he showed me how to operate the swing stage.

Just as he'd explained the day prior, on either end of the long work apparatus was a winch attached to the cable that went all the way to the top of the tank. By activating a toggle switch, the winch began winding up the cable and raising the device.

"When you get to the desired height, simply switch off the toggles at the same time," he said.

As Dan disappeared into the other tank, my hired hand and I loaded all of our painting supplies and climbed onto the stage. With one of us at either end, we activated the winches simultaneously and the apparatus began to rise. The ground slowly shrank from our proximity, and from our unique vantage point we saw how the terrain had been neatly altered around the fuel tank compound. We rose higher than the surrounding trees and were offered a spectacular view. Stopping at last, the steady grinding noise of the winches halted simultaneously. We found ourselves level to where the job would take place.

To best take advantage of using the help I had available, I began to lay out the large areas of the huge logo that required filling in. Once I got my assistant working on those places with a big brush, I could concentrate on the intricate parts of the logo—the lettering that accompanied the large shapes. Everything seemed to be going smoothly, and by the end of the first day, my helper had two of the major shapes filled in while I had stayed busy delineating the rest of the icon features.

By the end of the second day, although our combined efforts had produced admirable results, my assistant began to exhibit an alarming behavior that made dismissal apropos. Once back in town, I gave him his pay and let him go. Then I had to consider how to go about the remaining work to be done by myself.

Although this job was appropriate for two men, during the drive to the job site on the third day, I figured out what I would do—it wouldn't be ideal, but it would work. I arrived at the compound in the usual way, loaded my paints and supplies onto the stage, and climbed aboard. I walked the length of the stage to one end and activated the switch. That end started to rise as I made my way to the other end, my downward path becoming steeper and steeper with every step.

Reaching the lower end, I switched the other winch on and the stage began to rise, albeit at a dramatic angle. As the crooked unit slowly rose to the job height, I walked back up the steep gangway to reach the first winch. When I arrived at the concise level where the remainder of the work waited, I switched the first winch off. Without hesitating, I quickly walked down to the other end as the angle of the stage began to resume its preferred leveled stance and switched the other one off. Then I sat down.

My heart was pounding like a jungle drum and my blood was rushing with adrenaline. Because this endorphin filled my veins, I shook like a leaf. I had to wait until my nerves settled or I would not be able to articulate the fine details. After about twenty minutes, I was at last able to resume the final tasks and finish the painting.

An all-around sign man must be ready to tackle many kinds of jobs. With this particular feat complete, I could add another feather in my hat and qualify as a wall dog for accomplishing one of the biggest and highest signs of my career.

Lettering Race Cars

Homebuilt street racers, round-and-round cars, and dragsters of all types populated the Michigan suburbs where I plied my trade. The backyard garage became a gathering place for the similarly obsessed and four-wheeled projects became a focal point for the aficionados of the power, speed, sound, and thrill that accompanied their delight in freedom and independence. These wheeled machines were often altered to suit their specific needs related to racing. It made logical sense for them to want to make the outside of their rides attractive as well.

These people could appreciate the skills of a custom painter, and I was the right person to help bring their vision to reality. I usually met these prideful owners at a restaurant or near wherever I was currently working on an outdoor sign. During a break one such day, my meal was interrupted with a custom request.

"Hey, is that your painted-up van out there?"

I looked up at the young man and gave him an affirmative nod.

"I have a dragster to letter," my admirer offered. "Can you come over to paint it?"

I accepted this unique opportunity, and he gave me directions to get to the waiting metal canvas.

At the garage, I negotiated my way through piles of miscellaneous auto parts, toolboxes, stacks of lubricants, creepers, and various hoses and cables. I carefully considered the meticulously assembled four-wheeled apparatus that sat in the middle of the chaos as I listened to my customer's request. Once I visualized a plan, I created a pencil sketch of my idea.

A rough outline depicted the available space on the car. On this drawing, essential elements of the design were arranged. I utilized an artistic manner that would imply speed and domination. After approval of my design, the painting process began. All areas to receive lettering and design paint were cleaned and made ready. Paper patterns were prepared to facilitate duplicate renderings on each side of the car and the remaining elements were drawn lightly with a special pencil to complete the layout.

The tedious application of lettering enamel took place with special brushes, one stroke at a time, but with each one, the customer's satisfaction with the visual improvement to the appearance of his beloved car grew. The labored process continued until it was finally fully emblazed with color.

After paying me, the customer, whose pride was piqued, then made an effort to reward me for my troubles beyond pay.

"Hey, want to hear it run?"

Predicting an uncomfortable decibel level in the narrow confines of the garage, I frantically responded, "No, that's okay! You don't have to do that!"

My statement was lost as he reached for the ignition key.

"It's no trouble."

In one moment, the tranquil setting where the careful artwork had taken place was transformed into a loud noxious environment with an ungodly decibel level. The noise resembled a dark, hideous monster. I vividly imagined a beast with a gastronomic rumbling on an irregular cadence. In an effort to warm the fiend up and get it to hit on all licks, my host reached into the engine compartment to skillfully manipulate linkage, immediately followed by a furious fuel-consuming scream. This stimulated mental recollections of all the components that went into the engine, and my host immediately felt the need to yell all this information at the top of his lungs. I was bombarded with information about the cam specifications, the particular carburetor and crankshaft put in the engine, along with additional specs of innumerable features he apparently thought I would be interested in.

Despite the noises that built an anxiety within me, I had to admit that I, too, had a deep admiration for this beautiful car with massive quantities of horsepower. Though I didn't care for the obnoxious volume it spewed forth, I secretly felt lucky to be intimate and up close with such an incredible racecar.

The Golden Age

For centuries, the epitome of the sign maker's craft was gold-leaf lettering and ornamentation on glass. Also known as verre églomisé, from the French term meaning "gilded glass", this was a process where the reverse side of a piece of glass was gilded with gold or silver leaf using a gelatin adhesive. The result was a mirror-like, softly reflective surface that, when combined with reverse painting techniques, created a rich, shimmering, and beautifully reflective piece of artwork. Elite businesses like banks, lawyers, and upper echelon restaurants made use of this attractive and long-lasting effect that transformed a blank storefront window into a stunning artsy urban landmark. For the business and the sign maker alike, the use of gold leaf was a symbol of high status.

The explanation of why gold stuck successfully to glass remained a mystery. The technique used for centuries was to dissolve a single gelatin capsule in hot water. This mixture was flooded over clean glass, and while it was wet, the gilder used special handling techniques to lay the leaf against the wet glass.

The first part of the procedure was to completely cover the area

that would receive the sign work with many 3- to 3 3/8-inch squares of gold leaf. The window then sported a quilt-like pattern of overlapping gold squares. As the water evaporated, the gold would be sucked tightly onto the surface of the glass and a mirror-like effect occurred.

To prevent the delicate metal from wearing off, the gold was then backed up with paint in the areas where the gold would remain for the design. This part of the process involved delicate brushwork. The lettering and ornamental designs were all painted backward on the inside of the glass and acted as a protective layer over the gold. The excess gold would later be removed with another delicate process involving a mild abrasive.

My goal was to become the best all-around sign maker in Jackson, Michigan. Naturally, finding opportunities for projects like gilding on glass and accomplishing stunning projects was part of what would rocket my standing in the community. But; like most things, the road toward this elevated status was paved with entry level jobs that would prepare me for the next step.

As I sought to achieve this level of proficiency with these particular techniques of the sign maker's craft, I slowly elevated my standing in the community. Tom had been my very first client from Clarklake, and he remained of a mind to keep me employed. When he called one day and asked me to come to the Beach Bar so he could show me something, I thought, What better client to attempt my first endeavor with gold leaf on glass? As it turned out, he had the perfect project for just such a task.

"I want to create a focal-point centerpiece for over the fireplace," Tom explained as he handed me an old black-and-white picture of his dad taken back in the 1920s. "This picture will be the main event."

While I studied the photo of his dad holding a beer bottle up to the little dog in his lap, I started to have an idea.

"Best friends!" I shouted.

Tom's eyebrows went up as understanding and appreciation struck. "Best friends meet!" he amended.

"At the Beach Bar," I concluded.

From our little brainstorming session, I began to draw potential designs. I found an oval shape to display the photo that would allow for the headline across the top and the Beach Bar logo across the bottom. Since the reason for this piece was to display a photo under glass, it was the perfect opportunity to not only gild with gold but to practice some glue chipping as well. Tom's project would provide the ability to further develop my skills as a fine sign guy.

Tom had an enlargement of the photo made to the size we settled on, and I acquired two pieces of plate glass—one for experimentation in case there was a severe learning curve. Once the design was approved and my pattern was ready, I began to transfer the drawing to the layer of monument paper. I had affixed this rubber-like material, often used to sandblast names into gravestones, to the glass. When my design was transferred, I began to carefully cut away the areas of the background that would receive the glue chipping.

I was now ready to sandblast the exposed areas of the glass to create a place for the glue to adhere. Because the glue would be poured onto the surface, I had to get the plate perfectly level so the rabbit-hide glue would float into the same thickness across the entire surface, promoting consistent chipping throughout. One the glass was level, I heated up some water in a pan and added the dry glue powder. When completely dissolved, the hot glue was the consistency and color of honey. I poured the brownish liquid over the entire surface, letting it flow out until level.

As it cooled, it gelled up like thick Jell-o. When the glue attained a durable state, I began to cut along the edges of the shapes delineated by the monument paper and removed everything from the back of the glass except for the hardening glue. If all went well, as it shrank, the glue would create a beautiful chipped design to receive the gold leaf. Patience was key.

In the middle of the night, the magic began. As the glue slowly shrank, tension increased. The now-hardened mixture was firmly attached to the sandblasted surface. As the tightness extended beyond the surface strength of the glass, a popping began not unlike popping corn, except at a much slower rate. With each pop, a miniature trajectory of glass was jettisoned from the surface, showering the floor with a layer of glitter.

In the morning, I saw the results. As I stepped closer, my boots crunched on the delicate shards of glass that lay everywhere; I'd sweep it all up later. But as I studied the finished effect on the glass, I began to beam. Little delicate fernleaf shapes filled the background just as I'd hoped. I was elated, but I wasn't done.

The project required many steps with time to dry in between. The next part of the process would be to gild the areas that would have gold letters, back up all of the designs with paint, and then wet-gild the chipped areas with silver leaf to give it a highly reflective mirror-like background. With each addition to my work of art, the finished project looked better and better. I never did require that backup piece of glass, something I was rather proud of.

When I took my completed work out to the Beach Bar, Tom was pleased. Best Friends Meet still hangs in a prominent location in the Beach Bar to this day. The success of that project rocketed my ambition as a glass gilder, and with each additional project I inched my way ever closer to achieving my goal. To secure my place as an elite painter, I recognized the importance of continuing with my journey of sobriety.

Enlightenment

I pulled open the heavy aluminum-framed glass door and entered the AA clubhouse, leaving the bright sunshine behind. The original architecture of this building had settled over the years into an outcast dwelling that shared many of the features of a carnival fun house. The once-red carpet was now shiny with the dirt polish of a decade of shuffling feet.

As I moved through the faded interior, I found a rusty chrome chair with worn upholstery next to my beaming sponsor. I was glad to see Ralph, though at one time I would never have believed that would be the case.

Ralph's smile was mostly a stained ivory color with some telltale metal clips that hugged braided bicuspids. Unconcerned about his less-than-perfect dental work, Ralph smiled all the time. Heavy active eyebrows rapidly provided vivid expression to a face wrinkled with wear, his hands exploring the contours of his bald head in a nervous manner every time he interacted jocularly with one of his many friends. His voluminous and boisterous manner accompanied by constant laughing at first appeared grotesque. Yet as I grew to know him, I was drawn into the joy he expressed in his heart. Ralph was at peace with himself and strongly dedicated to uplifting others. He greeted everyone with a laugh as they entered our midst, radiating energy, love, and acceptance. It wasn't long before I asked him to be my sponsor.

As I took my seat next to him, Ralph gently patted me on the shoulder.

"How'd it go?" he asked.

My eyebrows formed a quizzical stance as I frantically searched my recent memory for whatever it was my sponsor was referring to. How'd what go?

Ralph laughed and then asked me again, "How'd it go?"

With an impish grin and a relentless stare, Ralph awaited my response, but my mind was a centrifuge still reeling from the day's activities. The demands of my clients, rigors of the process, and the creative discipline were relentless, taking up valuable real estate in my head. Even now in a peaceful haven, I remained distracted. What was Ralph asking about?

The quizzical expression still on my face caused him to dissolve into laughter. When it subsided, he clarified at last.

"How are you doing with your meditation?"

Oh. I cringed, remembering how, a few days ago in the role of my sponsor and adviser, Ralph had made a recommendation that would assist me on my spiritual path. He wanted me to meditate as suggested in the eleventh step. "Sought through prayer and meditation to improve our conscious contact with

God..." Ralph promised that meditation would open a door that would expand my relationship with my higher power. The only problem was I didn't know what that word meant, much less how to go about this mysterious procedure.

"I can't figure out how to start," I admitted.

Unlike his usual self, Ralph's demeanor shifted and he became serious as he answered kindly.

"Let me explain the manner in which I learned to meditate years ago."

He suggested I set aside a quiet time in the evening to sit with my feet flat on the floor, eyes closed, and as mentally still as possible. He went on to add encouragement and reflection on how the inclusion of regular meditation had positively affected his life. Armed with Ralph's instructions and tips, I went away from that meeting filled with enthusiasm.

I'd had every intention of accomplishing this new-to-me spiritual objective, but as I sat next to Ralph during the following meeting, I reflected on my experience. I had started just as he'd suggested, yet I couldn't remain still for long. My active mind began visualizing the next day's duties as a sign man, formulating design ideas, compiling a list of supplies, and considering the required reference materials. With so much to get ready, I jumped up out of my spot and began to jot things down, gather up the stuff on my list, and put it in a box situated next to the door. While I was at it, I thought it would also be a good idea to pay a couple of bills and write correspondence to respond to a recent query for more work. Before I knew it, the evening turned into a flurry of activity that led right up to bedtime.

Ralph laughed the whole time I recalled this shameful behavior.

"That's normal," he reassured me.

I was stunned. He recognized my dilemma and went on to alleviate my worries about the voices in my head.

"Many people struggle with all the activities on their to-do list instead of allowing themselves to remain still in meditation," he said. "But only through remaining steadfast and seated quietly will you develop the ability to quiet your mind and be still with God. The first step is to mentally move past the racket in your head."

I went away from that meeting with a newfound determination to continue on my quest. I had adopted the policy of being self-sufficient as a child. Through discovering the ease and ability to do just about anything I desired, skills typically came easily to me. This additional exercise in mental discipline, I was sure, would be just one more skill to add to my repertoire.

Several attempts to do as Ralph instructed followed over the next few days. More than once, I caught myself springing up out of the chair to fetch a roll of pattern paper or a yardstick in an effort to prepare myself for the following day's duties. During each incident, Ralph's gentle encouragement echoed in my mind, and each time I returned to my seat even more determined to sit peacefully.

One evening I focused on noticing all the mental activity going on. Plenty of thoughts rationalized jumping up out of my chair and retrieving materials or organizing the next workday. But I focused on being still, simply noticing these temptations and then letting them go. I was inundated with luring thoughts, but I was determined to hold fast.

Whenever I noticed a thought pattern going on in my head, another voice would sound. *Hey, there's another pattern of thinking.* I would discard that thought and wait for the other voices to quiet down again. Eventually, with time and practice,

I made progress with ignoring my distracting thoughts and they gradually began to decline.

When I noticed the change in my mental status, another voice piped up. Hey, the chatter is beginning to subside! Then, due to my acknowledgment, the noise would begin all over again. Through constant determination, I slowly learned to let my mind quiet down and not be tempted down the pointless rabbit hole, and with each session I became better and better at allowing a void in my brain to occur and grow.

I was learning to be at peace with myself.

After each evening meeting, Ralph and I would go outside to a quiet bench. I would report the progress with my latest attempts to be still and ask other questions about what to expect. Ralph taught me the way to a healthy, happy mind and how to find things to be grateful for. In doing so, he introduced me to my higher power. Ralph always displayed interest in how I was doing, providing laughter and gentle encouragement along the way.

One evening, I arrived early to the meeting, particularly excited to report an interesting occurrence. During my attempt to meditate the night before, I had managed to quiet down all the voices. But this time, I noticed something I hadn't before.

Once the chatter quieted down, a faint ringing began. I concentrated on listening to the ringing without mentally noticing it so as to avoid the chatter that would drown it out. As my attention stayed on this new discovery, the tone became louder. In the midst of this faint sound made prominent by the elimination of all the others, I found a simple peace. I now had a familiar and desirable destination to go to each time I meditated. With each additional attempt afterward, I slowly became proficient at finding this refuge.

Ralph reflected my excitement with a glow in his eyes and boisterous laughter. He encouraged me to lengthen this exercise a few minutes each time. I was now comfortably patient with this process for ten to fifteen minutes, and I longed for more. I adhered to his advice over the coming days and weeks, continuing to practice meditation and growing stronger each time.

One session changed my experience for good. I quietly calmed everything down and became at peace with the ringing sound. As I sat and succeeded with my attention on the holy tone, an unexpected emotion began to sweep over my entire body. The sensation was quite subtle at first, but in the quiet, I noticed this feeling start to grow. Beginning in my gut and rising through my chest was an energy I had never felt before. In my well-practiced state, I sat still with it for a while and just allowed it to be.

The feeling grew and I became aware of a blend of fear and apprehension mixing with a comfortable energy that harmonized with the peace I enjoyed. The emotion gradually became more intense as I remained still and stayed with this new presence. I began to weep.

I wept tears of joy for several minutes. As I came down from the experience, there existed no questions, no need for explanation or any intellectualization about what had happened. I was filled with acceptance. It just was. That night, I had no trouble drifting off to sleep.

The next day, I told Ralph about this experience.

"Sounds like you finally met your Maker," he said, and then laughed with joy.

Ralph explained the feeling I experienced was a normal fear mixed with a few other emotions that were all a logical part of entering new territory. I had never been in the presence of God before, and to experience fearful feelings was quite normal.

Since that time, I have never again experienced the magnitude of that initial sensation. Each time I meditated going forward, I returned to a familiar place. I would sit comfortably during the evening and gaze at another perfect glowing sunset. My mind relaxed as it ignored the chatter and the guilt for not preparing or producing something. While my consciousness let go of the chatter that wanted me busy, I slipped into the familiar peace that was now a regular part of my life. I found love, gratitude, and wonder for all that God had graced me with. I became filled with a peace that surpassed all understanding.

To this day, I still think about Ralph's sincere regard for me and the gentle way he introduced meditation into my life. He's the reason I was finally able to embrace the eleventh step. To honor this loving, caring, transformed man, I gratefully start laughing whenever life throws something my way. I know now that I can connect with God whenever I need to and I can overcome even the toughest of situations.

Having had a spiritual awakening, I could now move on to the final step of AA, but my journey was far from over. The twelfth step would encompass the remainder of my life as I continually sought others to share my journey with while practicing the principles of AA.

A Life of Abundance

As I worked to understand step twelve, I also focused on gaining a deeper spirituality. Ralph began teaching me skills and loving responses to the usual bumps in the road. He encouraged me to seek and accomplish God's will. Immersed in the fellowship of AA, I strived to enter into a continual state of surrender. I had become completely open to new possibilities as provided by my higher power, and attending regular meetings placed me squarely in the solution. I had a safety network of others on this trajectory—I was no longer alone.

Life with Gail was also a blessing. She was an amazing woman, and best of all, she loved me. In support of my sobriety, Gail befriended my sponsor's wife and began joining her at Al-Anon, the fellowship for people in relationship with alcoholics. As a result, our mutual ability to love began to increase and enrich our lives as we built our relationship on the firm foundation of shared spiritual principles.

Through Gail's endorsement and the personal growth begun with my recovery fellowship, I found an increasing connection in the local community. I sought to develop this connection in all areas of my life, including my business. My skills learned on the road, combined with integrity and a commitment to excellence, helped lift the name Letterfly to prominence while serving an increasing list of clients.

My life looked very different from just a few years prior. Several dynamics in fellowship, business, community, and family had moved simultaneously to shape my present and direct my future. Everything seemed to come into perfect alignment. For the first time since hitting the road as a teen, I had a place to call home, a woman who loved me, a community in which to thrive, and a purpose.

If I just stayed out of the way and let God guide my path, abundance would undoubtedly be on the horizon.

The Beginning

After Words

"No matter how dirty your past is, your future is still spotless."
—Drake

Planting a Seed

As my presence in my new hometown expanded, I became a part of the community more and more—something that, as I look back, God provided with the knowledge it was essential for this entry phase of my recovery. Regular attendance with a variety of community groups promoted my ability to become intimate with others necessary for my growth.

But there was still one thing missing: a companion in the form of a horse. My original riding instructor, Clarence Hastings, lived nearby in a two-story home on the east side of Jackson. This allowed for frequent visits, and our camaraderie rekindled my passion for horsemanship. He knew what had happened to Sassy and we frequently talked about the criteria for my next horse.

Clarence thought it would be good for me to visit with an old friend, so we went on an excursion to see Chuck Grant. It was comforting to relay my experience with Sassy to friends who could truly understand such a loss. Finding solace in these conversations, I contacted my Saddlebred horse friends near

Fowlerville as well. Everyone was shocked to hear about my tragedy of having to put my big mare down.

I guess, subconsciously, I was planting a seed. Maybe one day I would find another wonderful Saddlebred to call my own.

No Small Miracles

Shortly after, I went to visit Clarence again. While we sat in his living room talking about the circus, horses, and the theatrical activities he had accomplished in his younger years, I noticed Clarence could hardly contain himself. Finally, my friend revealed a surprise.

"Chuck has some news for you," Clarence said, smiling knowingly. "Here, use my phone."

Confused, I dialed Chuck's number and told him Clarence had told me to call.

"David!" Chuck began. "Splendid to hear from you. Listen, I've been talking with my colleagues in the Michigan dressage world."

"Okay…" I said, wondering where this was headed.

He continued, "I found out about an opportunity that you just might be interested in."

Chuck went on to explain that Violet Hopkins needed help at her barn. Vi was best known as the pioneer for the standard for teaching dressage, a standard which would put all the instructors on the same page. Because of this desire, Vi started the USDF Instructors Clinic, hosting the event at her farm each year.

"She needs help with chores around the farm," Chuck continued, "and the arrangement comes with riding lessons and horse training. I think it'd be perfect for you!"

"Wow!" I exclaimed.

This was a tremendous opportunity, but just as quickly as my excitement built up, it dissipated. It just didn't make sense at this point in time.

"But Chuck, I don't have a horse," I pointed out. "How would I take full advantage of this learning opportunity?"

"Just think about it," he advised, pleading with me to keep an open mind.

I agreed, though I had no idea how I'd find a horse in such a pinch, much less afford to pay for one.

Fortunately, my Saddlebred horse friends in Fowlerville had also been busy behind the scenes. They'd gotten the word out about the guy who'd lost his special dancing Saddlebred he had trained and performed with in the circus. Among those who heard about my tragedy was a couple in Reading, Michigan.

This husband and wife raised and trained Saddlebred horses. Their production had been interrupted by a terrible automobile accident, in which the husband had broken his leg. He was out of commission and his horses were just sitting in the pasture. Ben had initially thought it would be temporary.

"When I get this brace off my leg," he had told his wife a few weeks into the healing process, "I'll resume training the babies."

Ben had had big plans for a particular stunning colt who showed signs of a willingness to please. But the years went by with his leg still in a brace and the colt only getting older. Finally, they started selling the horses with the exception of his two favorite mares and the colt. This colt was now a five-year-old, 16.2-hand sorrel gelding who had never had any training or hands on him at all. He was still out on pasture with his mother, and Ben hated seeing him go to waste.

Through the Saddlebred fraternity, Ben had heard about me

and what I had accomplished with my last horse. He had empathy for the tragedy that interrupted my career and recognized a mutually beneficial opportunity. Inspired with a notion, he contacted me about buying his favorite horse.

At that time, I was still getting my meager finances back in order from Sassy's care. My life had completely changed and I had to be prudent. When Ben called, I knew I didn't have the resources to pay what this horse was worth. Plus, the purchase would be just the beginning of the expenses. There would be fees for shoeing, veterinarian checkups and annual vaccines, costs for feeding, and an endless list of other items that would ravage my steady stream of income. In all the years I'd had horses, the outgoing fees had always kept me poor.

"I'm honored," I told Ben, "but I'm afraid I can't afford him."

"At least come look at him," he begged. "He's a nice horse, and I think you could give him a good home."

Deuces Wild

Even though I didn't have the funds for such a nice horse, I couldn't stop thinking about the gelding Ben had raved about. I kept imagining how having that horse would fill my heart, get me back into the horse community, and allow me to train under Vi in exchange for manual labor. So, one autumn afternoon when I had my sign painting projects done early, I decided to make the drive south to Reading. Unsure what the outcome would be, I clung to the tiniest fragments of hope.

At the end of my trek, I found the driveway to Ben's farm and eagerly pulled in. When I looked over the board fence into the pasture, I immediately spotted the tall, flashy sorrel gelding in the grass with his mother. He held one foot way out in front of him while he grazed and I could already envision him performing a bow.

When he turned to acknowledge me, I noticed a star in the middle of his forehead and bright eyes on a handsome head attached to the end of a long, elegant neck. His sloping shoulders and high withers promised a nice height of motion he was no doubt bred to produce. Studying him from the knees down, I saw his cannon bones were straight with nothing over at the knee. His hocks were well under him, plus he had sturdy-looking feet. When he stood square, he had a leg at each corner. His flowing mane had never been clipped and his long red tail dragged on the ground, just the way I liked it.

On cue, my host came out of the house walking with a cane. Ben was a sturdy man with a beaming face and an aching step, but most of all, he was glad I'd finally come to see the gelding.

"What do you think of him?" he asked, joining me at the fence.

"He looks like a fine horse," I responded, feeling the excitement building within me. "I like what I see."

Ben smiled proudly. "His registered name is Long Shot Deuces Wild, but we call him DW."

I stared at the gelding for a while before sighing. "I'd sure love to buy him, but he just doesn't fit into my life right now."

"I was going to gait him," Ben opened up, ignoring my statement, "but then this happened." He gestured toward his leg. "DW would make a nice pleasure horse for someone, but he's capable of so much more, it just seemed a pity. Then I heard about all you did with your previous horse!"

Ben paused and I smiled sadly, wishing I had the finances to purchase this gelding. I mentally crunched the numbers one more time, but I just couldn't make it work.

"I began to think about all the work that would've taken," he continued. "The commitment to teach a horse to dance—it's amazing to think about."

"Yes, Sassy was a nice horse," I agreed. My eyes welled up at her memory.

He saw the glint in my eye and rocked on his cane as though he had something to add. After a moment's hesitation, he said, "DW is a nice horse too. I think the two of you could really be something."

I didn't know how to respond to that, so I just smiled wistfully again.

"I really want you to have this horse," he said, looking me in the eye. "So much so, I want to make him a gift to help get you get back in business."

My jaw dropped as I looked Ben squarely in the face. I could hardly believe my ears as my heart began pounding wildly in my chest. This was evidence of what God had in mind for me and my future. I hadn't been forgotten. Just as AA was teaching me, all I needed to do was stay out of the way and allow God to choreograph my life. When I did that, He could use others to do His work.

I turned back to look at DW in the pasture, fully absorbing this amazing animal who had every quality I was looking for. Besides being flashy and tall, he was three-gaited and a fresh slate with no bad habits. As a five-year-old, he was at the right point in his life for what I needed—mature enough to begin the arduous process of becoming a classically trained horse. Best of all, I had the perfect opportunity to take him all the way along that path.

"Ben, I…I don't know what to say!" I said, overwhelmed with gratitude.

The door to a unique opportunity had opened. My ambitions with classic horsemanship were not over. A whole new world opened for me that day, one that I would have never been able to open on my own as a drunk. With this new horse, I now had everything needed to take advantage of the opportunity at Violet's barn, and by earning my keep, I wouldn't have to use any of my prudently spent reserves while I continued to rebuild my life.

As I leaned on the fence and looked at my new majestic colt, both Ben and I thrilled with the exchange. I couldn't wait to tell Clarence and Chuck. Even more so, I couldn't wait to call Vi and secure my spot at her farm. My future was as bright as the gleam of sunshine on my new colt's glistening coat.

DW and I had a long road ahead of us. The process of training a horse to the highest level—known as a high school horse—required specific procedures and age-old concepts that resulted in a solid foundation to achieve the epitome of this time-honored art form. There would be times when I doubted my sanity for taking on the daunting project of making a high school horse from the ground up, but just as anyone in the miracle business knows, more will be revealed as long as you don't give up five minutes before the miracle.

As our unbreakable bond began to form under the watchful eye of a perfectionist guiding me every step of the way, I never gave up on my prestigious new Saddlebred companion. The long, arduous process consumed time, required specific technique, and took hard work. But I was up for the task, and so was DW.

Together, we would go far. And that's a lengthy story for another book.

Next:

Red Sorrel
on the
Road Home

If you enjoyed reading about this segment of my interesting life, I urge you to write a brief testimonial of your impression and post it on **Amazon, GoodReads** and the **OnlineBookReview**

Your review is like gold to me.

If you did not like reading this book, please keep your mouth shut.

Thanks,

DAVE Letterfly KNODERER

About the Author

As a prolific itinerate artist, Dave "Letterfly" Knoderer qualifies as an old-school Renaissance man with a lingering penchant for performing, wandering, and creating art. First finding self-expression in the circus as a show drummer, he still says the smartest thing he ever did was join the circus. When Dave started performing with his dancing horses, he was well underway with plying his artistic skills with paint and brush to finance that passion.

As levels of finesse were accomplished with his equine dance partners, Dave was amazed to discover parallel developments with his pinstriping, airbrushing, and graphics skills. His artistic career began while apprenticing the sign painting trade in the seventies, learning design layout formulas, letterform, pinstriping, and wet-blended pictorial painting techniques. Throughout his career, the artist would paint theatrical sets, amusement park decor, fairground signage, and circus concession stands. He would also gild antique fire engines, restore vintage carousel horses, create conventional hand-lettered signage, and design award-winning storefront décor. Letterfly later broke onto the emerging RV mural scene, painting for Ma and Pa USA, and eventually earned a rep among the motorcycle aficionados with his custom graphics, pinstriping, and murals.

These days during the spring, summer, and fall, you can find Letterfly on location between the Northeast and the Midwest at an assortment of Harley-Davidson stores, hot rod shows, and similar events as he works on various projects for his dedicated fan base. During the winter months, you will find the author at his home in Florida, lovingly named ArtPark, where you can walk the lush garden pathways that connect the shop, studio, RV parking, and gallery, all situated in a quiet oak hammock haven—an ideal setting for Letterfly's creative inspiration and a unique destination for RVers and bikers alike.

Dedicated to preserving the rich culture of the circus, nuances of his accumulated artistic skills, and the lessons learned on the road of life, Dave also develops and presents entertaining and enlightening speeches as a member of Toastmasters International, something which inspired him to think about writing. While attending a creative writing class, his professor once said, "All you have to do is paint a picture." That statement caused a lightbulb to flash in Dave's mind, and so began the writing frenzy that continues to this day.

Get In Touch!

Whether you're just a curious researcher, have an artsy idea you'd like to discuss making into a reality, or simply want to say hello, I'd love to hear from you!

For more information, visit: www.Letterfly.com & www.ask-letterfly-travelog.blogspot.com

Enjoy Letterfly's blog: www.LetterflyWrites.com

Call or write: 813-505-5539 & Letterfly@aol.com

Plus you can find Dave Letterfly on Facebook: @Letterfly.Pinstriping

Other Books
by

DAVE *Letterfly* KNODERER

Speedy

Hurled through Havoc

When the road of life curves ahead, lean into it.

Why does a young man abandon everything to head out on the highway? Where will it take him? Using the road as a metaphor, the author reveals the discoveries of a life that took off like a rocket when he followed his inner urging to hit the road.

Withdrawn from a childhood with a strict and impersonal father, this intensely creative teenager opted to launch himself into the strange and exciting world of the traveling big-top circus. Developing the mindset of an entertainer, he found harmony with horses and personal expression as a sign painter. Through both passions, Dave learned rare skills in an itinerate culture that would benefit him his entire life. Yet, hitting bottom as an alcoholic brought everything to a screeching halt.

Will he find his way back into the prolific life full of performing horses, artistic creations, and adventure on the road? Follow along as the author shares how he evolved from a wandering teen into the premier producer of airbrushed murals, gold-leaf monograms, and delicate hand-painted inscriptions on both motorhomes and motorcycles.

Here's what people are saying about:

Speedy

Hurled through Havoc

Sometimes you get the gift of experiencing a true American story. This is such a gift. When's the movie?

—Larry K. Blakely

This truly authentic tale will challenge your preconceived notions about the world of the traveling show, but what makes this story shine is the way the author faced obstacles and applied his kindness, horse sense, creativity, and grit to overcome them. An inspiring and adventurous read. Highly recommended!

—Kevin Venardos, Circus Owner & Ringmaster

The circus and its thrill, excitement, and suspense are something to be experienced. What our mind can't understand we call "magic." I'm almost jealous one person gets to experience so much.

—Anonymous Online Book Club Reviewer

I absolutely LOVE this book! It's a magical mystery tour, winding through the life of this extremely talented author's lifelong journey. Definitely a must read! Letterfly never ceases to astound me!

—Anonymous Amazon Review

The strength of champions resides in their stories. Stories like this give one hope and should be read by all.

—Anonymous Amazon Review

Kinker

Circusing the Seventies

An intensely creative but frustrated teenager turned his back on his family, hit the road of the unknown, and discovered a fascinating world under the traveling big top. While thriving in this creative oasis, he discovered an affinity for animals and a fascination for the training aspects of this cultural art form. He began developing a liberty horse act of his own, learning principles of regard, encouragement, and love that promoted harmony between the trainer and his animals. But his rise to center-ring stardom included excesses that nearly cost him his life. Left behind, stranded and forgotten, there was nowhere left to turn.

Limping to where his parents had migrated from his childhood home, a surprise awaited in the form of an abundant charismatic commune. Back-to-nature hippies, discarded ministers, suffering veterans, and family rejects created a self-made family of unlikely hopefuls who joined together to bake nutritious bread, study spiritual teachings, and lift each other up to find a better way of life. Lessons begun under the big top rocketed to the next level when a mentor revealed the proactive secret to moral fulfillment, productivity, and happiness.

Armed with this new design for living his life, the artiste picked up the pieces of his show-business life and made a triumphant return to the circus. In the ring once more, he shined with a radiant vigor like never before, coming into perfect alignment with a higher purpose and discovering the gift he had been searching for had been with him the entire time.

A Teaser From

Kinker

Circusing the Seventies

The parade of show trucks meandered on picturesque roads along the northern edge of Michigan. As I drove the cookhouse bus east toward Cheboygan, I caught occasional glimpses of one of the spectacular Great Lakes.

I found the grassy lot on the edge of the little harbor town bordering Lake Huron. The big-top crew was already busy unloading while I pulled the cookhouse onto location. Willy and I went to unload the animals out on the picket line, and then we began to set up the sideshow. With nothing unusual happening that morning, the circus went up seamlessly on that picture-perfect day. In no time at all, the crew was finished and the kinkers had everything in place for two shows while the animals quietly grazed. We all had an opportunity to get some rest before the first show.

I didn't understand why the canvas boss kept an eternal watch on his surroundings. Michigan always had ideal summer weather for the circus life. Cool breezes from the lakes mixed with the heat of summer, resulting in day after day of warmth and comfort. The circus looked perfect under a cloudless sky as we soaked it all in, yet Jack Brock remained on alert.

Despite my lack of knowledge, Jack was mindful of what he had been told about the Great Lakes. Because the traveling circus was always at the mercy of the weather, a good canvas boss was proactive and diligent with what could be done at a moment's notice. Rain often killed attendance, softening the soil and making loadout and truck maneuvering difficult, not to mention wet canvas was three times heavier than when it was dry.

When I saw him still on alert the following day, I followed his gaze to the flags of the big top lazily flowing in the breeze.

"That's a good sign," he muttered.

For a moment, it appeared as if he were thinking about finally relaxing in his bunk, but some inner intuitive hunch had a grip on him. Jack glanced back up at the flags just as they dropped limp against the poles that protruded from the top of the tent. I saw his eyes narrow as he watched intently. When the flags slowly turned and began to flap in the other direction, the temperature dropped a few degrees. Jack scanned the skyline and saw an alarming sight—the horizon was growing dark.

"Elmer!" Jack hollered without a moment's hesitation. "Get the crew out here…now!"

He began to double-check the guy-lines as the crew reported for duty. "Add extra stakes and secure the jiggers," he ordered a few of them. Then to others, "Drive the pole trailer over to the long side and get all the extras tied to it and whatever else you can find. Go!"

Jack rallied his remaining crew to help him tighten the guys on the big top. Watching the ruckus unfold, I knew I'd better set down my drums and get over to the sideshow to do whatever I could.

"Willy!" I yelled.

Angry clouds boiled into a seething mass over what had just been a pristine blue sky. Willy came running from under the big top, taking notice of the unfolding storm. We scrambled to do everything we could while the sky grew blacker and blacker. I was bent over a tent stake, the rain started pouring down in sheets. As the breeze increased into a steady gale, the cold rain pelted us fiercely, not unlike getting sandblasted.

The heavy rain concealed the rest of the show, but we could hear the roar of the storm and canvas flapping like a chorus of insane fiends all around us. We held onto whatever we could as the wind grappled to take it. Instinct urged me to rush into the tent for shelter, but with poles dancing, ropes creaking, and the loose canvas flailing insanely, the inside of a tent was the last place I wanted to be.

Suddenly, a tremendous gust of wind pushed against the sidewall of the big top, causing the bottoms of the poles to lean in and disappear underneath. This created an opportunity for the wind to enter, filling the interior of the big top and toppling props, knocking over cymbals on stands, and spreading performing gear throughout the interior like scattered seed.

In a matter of seconds, the big top had transformed into a great big parachute. The billowing canvas lifted the quarter poles that began to dance dangerously off the ground, the tremendous stress against the huge fabric surface causing guy-lines to snap like guitar strings. The big top turned into an oversized sail, going up in the air with dangling poles still secured in designated places as it became an ever-changing, abstract, amorphous shape like a monster searching for prey to devour.

With nothing holding the tent to the ground, the mass billowed sideways, dragging poles across the infrastructure of the performance venue. Though I didn't see the sideshow canvas going over us, I knew it did. Our ropes had less of a load than the big top, so at least they didn't break, but our stakes had pulled up and flown over us. In an instant, all we knew was that we were standing where the tent had once been, the rain now pouring down upon our heads and saturating our clothes.

We watched as the big top settled back down in a great mess of torn canvas, tangled ropes, broken poles, and jumbled seat boards. The monstrous tent now lay dormant in a mess outside where the stake line had once been.

I now understood why Jack never took his eye off the sky. It was over in twenty minutes, but the blow-down had been an unexpected scourge of Mother Nature. The sky now returned to the pristine splendor it had been just a half hour prior and ideal summer weather returned to the circus. All the show folks stared in shock at the disaster that lay before us.

"Billy is under there," somebody yelled.

The crew scrambled over to a lump in the wet canvas and pulled on the edge to get it off. Relief washed over the crew when Billy was discovered to be unhurt.

"I knew you wouldn't leave me under there," he said, getting up from his wet respite, "because then you might miss payday."

Tales of a Traveling Airbrush

This five memoir series includes the following titles:

Speedy Hurled through Havoc
Kinker Circusing the Seventies
The Galloping Snapper
Red Sorrel on the Road Home
One-Man Show

Informative guidebooks include:

Hit the Road and Thrive
Responsible RVing

The upcoming coffee table series of picture books include:

Rolling Art: Why a Mural? Book 1
Rolling Art: Why a Mural? Book 2
Rolling Motorcycle Art

Made in the USA
Middletown, DE
19 February 2025

71465106R10226